Sundmark

"Knowledge is *the* critical success factor for *all* organizations. 'Learn or die!' must be the rallying cry for the creation of a prosperous future. *Ten Steps To A Learning Organization* is a multi-purpose guide on how to do just that — to turn every institution into a vital contributor to all its stakeholders. Peter Kline and Bernard Saunders have demystified the learning organization and translated its abstract and fuzzy notions into an extremely practical competitive strategy. Buy it and use it."

— Jim Kouzes
President, Tom Peters Group / Learning Systems
co-author of *The Leadership Challenge* and of *Credibility*

"Without question the best book ever on making the real changes needed in today's organizations. There's nothing else like it. It works."

— Graham A. Richard, Chairman
N.E. Indiana Business Assistance Corporation

"We know that organizations, like people, improve by going through an evolutionary progression as they learn, apply, adapt and learn again. *Ten Steps To A Learning Organization* offers us the first clear, practical guide to mastering and directing that crucial learning process. It will show any organization or group how to assess itself as a learning organization, and the steps it can take to maximize the potential of all its participants."

— Chuck Roe, Vice President of Quality Systems
Philips Electronics Display Components

"*Ten Steps To A Learning Organization* is a much needed attempt to put flesh and bone on one of the most exciting concepts of the decade."

— Ron Zemke
co-author of *Service America! Doing Business in the New Economy*

"Lightyears ahead of any training program I've ever seen or worked with. It deals with every measurable key point where leaders and trainers have to be effective in order to really change an organization. And unlike the "canned" programs that many corporations have wasted literally millions of dollars on, the Ten Steps are clear, commonsense, easy to follow, and can quickly be "owned" by the company. Senges' *Fifth Discipline* gave us the theory, *Ten Steps To A Learning Organization* gives us the tools to implement it."

— Tom Norfleet, Group Leader
Training & Employment, Subaru-Isuzu Automotive, Inc.

D0018798

TEN
STEPS
TO A
LEARNING
ORGANIZATION

SECOND EDITION

Peter Kline & Bernard Saunders

GREAT OCEAN PUBLISHERS
ARLINGTON, VIRGINIA

Book and cover design by M.M. Esterman
Cover painting by Periklis Pagratis

Permission to quote from the following sources is gratefully acknowledged:
Doubleday/Currency: *The Fifth Discipline* by Peter Senge; Linda Honold, Empower-
ment Systems; Harry Hoff, Principal, Susan Lindgren School; Houghton Mifflin Co.:
Grit, Guts, and Genius by John Hillkirk and Gary Jacobson; Omni Publications Inter-
national Ltd.: "Running the Numbers: The Ruminations of John Allen Paulos", (*Omni
Magazine*); Macmillan Publishing Co.: *Apprentice to Genius: the Making of a Scien-
tific Dynasty* by Robert Kanigel; McGraw-Hill, Inc.: *Quality is Free* by Philip B.
Crosby, *The Learning Edge* by Calhoun W. Wick and Lu Stanton Leon, and "How
Much Good Will Training Do?" (*Business Week Magazine*); Pantheon Books: *Genius,
The Life and Science of Richard Feynman* by James Gleick; Tom Peters Group: "On
Excellence," (syndicated column), and *Liberation Management* (published by Alfred
A. Knopf); Avice Saint: Continuous Learning Within Japanese Organizations; Barry
Sheehy, Achieve International; Simon & Schuster, Inc., and Sterling Lord Literistic,
Inc.: *Complexity* by M. Mitchell Waldrop.

Copyright © 1998, 1993 by Peter Kline and Bernard Saunders
Artwork copyright © 1993 by Periklis Pagratis and Great Ocean Publishers

All rights reserved. No part of this book may be used or reproduced in any
manner whatsoever without written permission from the publishers.

For information contact:

Great Ocean Publishers, Inc.
1823 North Lincoln Street
Arlington, Virginia 22207-3746

Second Edition

Library of Congress Cataloging in Publication Data
Kline, Peter, 1936-
 Ten steps to a learning organization / Peter Kline & Bernard Saunders — 2nd ed.
 ISBN 0-915556-32-4 (alk. paper)
 Includes Bibliographical refernces.
 1. Organizational change. 2. Organizational learning. 3. Organizational
effectiveness. I. Saunders, Bernard, 1942- . II. Title.
HD58.8.K58   1998   658.4'063—dc21   97-49213

Printed in the United States of America

CONTENTS

To Syril and Connie
our wives and mentors

ACKNOWLEDGMENTS

This collaborative excursion could not have been so enriching, and indeed would not have been possible at all, without the dedicated willingness of many friends and colleagues, none of whom should be held responsible for its final form. Time and again, for about two years, people were invited to review, suggest and debate the merits of our thinking and passions. No one ever said no. Though we did not adopt all suggestions, we deeply appreciated all of them. Others influenced us over the years in ways that left a permanent mark in these pages. For these commitments and efforts we are forever grateful and renewed.

And so, thanks to: Rosie Barry, Shona Bellew, Bob Blake, Robert Cournoyer, Mary Ann Donahue, Hope Esparolini, Dot Feldman, Bill Gjetson, Charles B. Gompertz, Deane Gradous, Bob Heberger, Ron Heidke, Tom Huberty, Harvey Jackins, Mark Kinnich, Peter Koestenbaum, Nancy Kline, Thomas Jefferson Kline, Myron Lowe, Carol Lucas, David Meier, Paul R. Messier, Lewis R. Mobley, Thomas A. Norfleet, Jerri Olsen, Karen Osterling, Becky Reid, A. B. Reynolds, Graham Richard, Bruce Richardson, Chuck Roe, Paul Scheele, Barry Sheehy, Audrey Siemens, Robin Smith, John Solberg, Tony Stockwell, Larry Van Etten, Keith Von Seggren, Frank Vullo, Robert Ward, Ed White, Doug Whitfield, and Barbara Whitmore.

At the same time, it is not fair that some people deserving thanks have to be left out, but we trust that they will understand and be forgiving.

We are grateful to the following groups and organizations for providing learning oppotunities to test some of the key concepts in the books: Participants in the Masters in Learning Technologies Program, St. Thomas University, St. Paul, MN; the class of Dr. Charles Warfield at Western Michigan University, Kalamazoo, MI; Minnesota Chapter of the National Society for Performance and Instruction; Minnesota Chapter of the American Society for Training and Development.

Mayor James Perron of the City of Elkhart, Indiana, and Celia Leaird, Elkhart County Director, Division of Family and Children, had the vision to apply these concepts in a city government setting, under the name Aurora Project.

Merrill Leffler devoted great care and skill to the manuscript in its later stages. Emily Taylor performed a similar service in preparing the book for the press. Bruce Whitehead helped shape the Learning Organization Matrix into its final form.

Our tireless editors, Mark and Margaret Esterman, have left a permanent shape and sheen on this book it would have sorely missed otherwise.

INTRODUCTION TO THE SECOND EDITION

Since this book was published five years ago, we have had the opportunity to assist many different organizations, both profit and not-for-profit, in implementing its principles. We have also discussed its insights with many different kinds of groups during our public presentations. We have seen our book translated into four other languages, and have heard about its usefulness in countries where, though translations were unavailable, people were willing to study it in English.

This widespread and growing interest has reaffirmed our conviction that the Learning Organization is a viable and vital means for developing a culture of high performance learners. Such transformed people become much better adapted to get results that affect the bottom line and the quality of life in their organizations. In other words, we're not talking about another fad, or failed program.

Many users of this book have worked with us in implementing its ideas. We have witnessed some astonishing results from this process. Others have chosen to read the book and use it as a guide to their own restructuring. On occasion we have been privy to the success of such efforts, which have sometimes been quite impressive.

This new edition has given us the opportunity to add some of the insights that in the intervening years we have gleaned from working with many different kinds of groups and seeing the application of these principles in many different settings — in corporations, schools, government agencies, not-for-profits and even in individual classrooms. While the basic structure of the book remains unchanged, we have added some insights and activities that we believe may increase its usefulness, including a new chapter on organizational learning which follows this introduction.

THE ASSESSMENT TOOL

We would like to call the reader's attention to one particular change: One of the most popular features of the book in its first edition has been the *Learning Organization Assessment* presented in Step 1. In response to many comments and requests, we have expanded, refined and improved this Assessment as a stand-alone instrument. The version of the Assessment included in the book was not intended to be a complete instrument; the new Assessment provides the user with a much better view of the respondent's attitudes and practices in relation to each of the Ten Steps. It is also a one step, self-scoring instrument that is easier to answer and to evaluate. This instrument is available from the publisher of the book, as is a *Facilitator's Guide to the Learning Organization Assessment.*

AN IMPROVED, MORE HUMANISTIC BUSINESS CLIMATE

Meanwhile, we're aware as we issue this second edition that the business climate is far more receptive to our approach than it was when the first edition appeared. Business leaders world wide recognize the need for sharper definition of company goals so they can achieve competitive advantage. The best way to achieve this is through the kind of culture change that will provide for more intelligent and effective management systems, so the book has a chance of making a greater impact than ever before. And the best way to do that is to help all members of the organization discover that the way they learn best is not necessarily the way they learned in school, but something personal and unique to each one of them. For indeed, to have a Learning Organization, you must begin by having an organization of learners, and then show them how to function in such a way that the organization as a whole can learn.

Many are now aware that the Information Age is behind us and the Age of Relationships has come into being as perhaps the final stage in a series of steps that have evolved the old autocratic organizations of half a century ago into modern, finely tuned agencies of human service and change. After all, human beings are the ultimate recipients of business and the ultimate point of it. No business or other agency that does not respect and honor them can really, in the long run, remain successful. Those which do embrace the human dimension, soon discover that most of their profitability is in what is variously called human capital, learning capital or intellectual capital. It is here, in the brains of the people who work for a company, and the way they collectively use those brains to build systems which work to the advantage of all, that we can find the true and essential focal point of business.

Best-selling author and consultant Jim Collins has spoken of mechanisms that can be used to produce important changes in a culture.[1] In doing so he has refined W. Edwards Deming's observation that when things go wrong, it isn't the people who are at fault, it's the systems. Mechanisms are tools for achieving change, and they subtly generate or invoke new systems within the existing ones. They entail getting people involved in activities or concerns that themselves provide systematic change.

Creating a Learning Organization is best accomplished by adopting a series of mechanisms that stimulate that change. Many of these are to be found in this book, for the activities we have suggested can function as mechanisms that generate new kinds of systems, leading to culture change producing more effectiveness and efficiency in the organization. Most mechanisms of this sort work because they challenge people to form more effective relationships with each other.

So the transformation of relationships is what, in business settings, we increasingly must deal with. That is one of the reasons the human values emphasized in this book are proving to have such practical value in so many different situations. It is now more widely recognized than ever before that a company's greatest asset is its people, provided they are able to work well together and proceed on the path of continuous improvement. It's also recognized that cooperative teamwork beats out competitive territorialism every time, and that to the extent that work can enhance the lives of the workers, the workers will give more of themselves to the work.

The authors have deeply appreciated hearing from people who have had experiences with the Ten Steps processes and mechanisms and have been willing to share with us what they have been doing to create Learning Organizations. We welcome further reactions and ideas, which may well lead to insights that could improve a future edition of this book.

WHERE IT ALL BEGAN

In October, 1985, two executives of a major U. S. corporation invited the authors to design and deliver a training program on quality management. They came to us because of our experience in applying innovative approaches to learning and education in a wide variety of settings, and requested that we use Integrative Learning as the vehicle of instruction.

Integrative Learning appeared to be particularly appropriate for this purpose, because it aims to realize the enormous potential for learning inherent in all people at any age, and to transform the environment in which it occurs in ways that are most supportive to successful learning. Descended from teaching methodologies like Accelerated Learning, Neuro-Linguistic Programming, Systems Thinking, Cooperative Learning and Suggestopedia, it had been tested in public schools since 1982, with results that grew increasingly powerful. It proved extremely effective both with high risk students in inner city schools, and with academically talented students in suburban schools. By 1985 it had been implemented at every grade level and used in the teaching of every subject.

THE PROFITABILITY OF CHANGING THE WAY WE LEARN

Meanwhile, corporations had begun applying a similar technology with outstanding results. Corporate trainer David Meier used Accelerated Learning techniques to save Bell Atlantic Company enormous amounts of time and money on essential customer-service-representative training for its employees. The savings were impressive. But so was the phenomenal upgrade in employee performance documented by Meier and trainer Mary Jane Gill. Newly-trained employees were described by their supervisors as improved in the areas of professional confidence, problem-solving ability, ability to work without supervision, accuracy, speed, ability to give complete information, personal accountability, people skills, and use of reference material.[2]

We believed that equally good results could be achieved in corporate quality programs. As our training program proceeded it became evident that we were right. All the participants concurred that the Integrative Learning format was giving them far more value than they had expected from a course on quality. They were excited by how easily and thoroughly the course concepts were internalized, how naturally and effortlessly they were applied in the situations where they were needed, and how durable the learning proved to be. Many participants went on to say that soon Integrative Learning would sweep the field of corporate training everywhere.

Unfortunately, though, we had made the mistake of entering a major corporation at too low a level on the ladder of power politics. Recognition for what had been — and could be — accomplished was confined to a relatively small part of the company. Eight months after we began the program, it had been caught in a crossfire of bureaucratic in-fighting and was summarily dropped.

In the first edition of this book the story ended there. However, shortly after the book was published, one of us happened to run across a member of that group in the street one day.

"We recognized ourselves in your book," she said. "We knew you meant us. You might like to know, though, that we're still doing everything you taught us. We kept it alive, even without any support from the top."

It would have been nice to know that at the time, as three years were to pass before either of us had another chance to show what Integrative Learning could do to improve efficiency in the workplace.

TRAINING THE LEARNING LEADERS AT KODAK

In 1989, Peter Kline, together with some of his associates in the National Academy of Integrative Learning, including Laurence Martel, Larry Van Etten and Syril Kline, were hired by Ron Heidke, Director of Manufacturing at Kodak Park in Rochester, New York. Their mission was to train a group of approximately twenty-five managers to develop and deliver a Manufacturing Resource Planning (MRP II) course, using Integrative Learning as the primary method of instruction. The new group was called the Learning Leaders.

This project, which we describe at some length in the pages of this book, was a stunning success. Dr. Heidke summarized the process:

As we were trying to improve our competitive position in

the world, it became apparent to me that changing the culture and increasing the capability of the workforce was absolutely essential to our future competitive position. As we looked forward to the things we needed to do, we recognized that education, educating the workforce, was a major hurdle we had to overcome.... We were facing a massive educational challenge and saw this as an opportunity to test whether or not Integrative Learning could be effective. So we put together a team which was trained to use these learning capabilities to improve the learning process. And we began to teach our workforce what MRP II is all about. We've been successful.

Any tool, any process which can accelerate the rate of learning and accelerate the rate at which you can improve your operations will be vital to success. That's why Integrative Learning is so significant — it offers that opportunity to managers throughout the world. For them to understand the power and capability of Integrative Learning, they have to approach it from the vantage point of cycle time, cost reduction and enhanced capability of the workforce. That's where it's proved its value.

Doug Whitfield, team leader of the program, estimated that it had saved Kodak at least ten million dollars and possibly a great deal more than that during its first year and a half of operation. In addition, Heidke and other Kodak managers were also struck by the visible transformation in atmosphere and morale that occurred in the workforce — which they could also relate to the bottom line and to the company's success in the future.

It's interesting [Heidke notes] that all of those fun things we learn to do at home with our families don't easily translate to the workplace. The workplace is someplace where you're supposed to concentrate, things are rigid. There's discipline, you have to follow procedures, you're not allowed to be creative, you have to follow the rules. Well, that kind of workplace is not competitive. The workplace of the future is one where people can feel the same way they do at home, where they can enjoy working with people, where they can share things, be creative. They can have a sense of teamwork and accomplishment, openness. That's the winning combination.

Meanwhile, in Minneapolis, Bernie Saunders was hired by a large corporation to design and deliver a company-wide information system. Together with his associates, whom he had trained in Integrative Learning, Saunders delivered this course to approximately 250 of the company's employees. Again the results achieved or exceeded expectations.

THE NEED FOR ACROSS-THE-BOARD CHANGE

These successes could be attributed at least partly to the fact that Integrative Learning not only greatly increases the efficiency of company training and development, but also leads to a spontaneous culture change in organizations that adopt it as a training program.

Nevertheless, we found there were limits to the culture changes that occurred. We were able to spark high hopes in the trainees that a far more benign, enjoyable and productive work place was possible. In many cases, however, these hopes withered as old patterns of management and group behavior reasserted themselves, damaging the trust and expectations many of our trainees had built up.

The resulting deterioration in the quality of performance, though minimal in its effect on the quality of the training delivered by the group, nevertheless concerned us. We recognized that something more was needed to foster and protect the culture that seemed to arise spontaneously when Integrative Learning was used in training and development programs.

At about that time we both read Peter Senge's influential and widely admired book, *The Fifth Discipline*,[3] which developed the notion of a Learning Organization. This was exactly the direction we felt that Integrative Learning must take if it was to consolidate and increase the gains it was making in the corporate training field. We also noted that many of those who had read Senge's book seemed to want more specific information about how to build a Learning Organization.

WHAT WAS MISSING

Integrative Learning, we knew, provided an essential tool that any organization could use. But, as we had come to believe, more was required. What was still missing was a clearly delineated process for building a Learning Organization: to develop and sustain an environment favorable to learning at every level, to reawaken and stimulate the power and joy of learning in all the members of the organization, regardless of their position and background, and to harness the new learning that was generated in order to produce maximum benefit for the organization.

At the suggestion of consultant Peter Koestenbaum, we decided that a Ten Step Process could be developed for building a Learning Organization. We began to envisage a process from the initial phases of assessment to the mastery of systems thinking — the fifth discipline that Senge advocates, and that has been so powerfully championed by W. Edwards Deming.

EVERYONE HAS TO BE INVOLVED

In recent years, the widespread failure of many Quality programs throughout the country has become a matter of increasing concern. According to many analysts, at least fifty percent of all these programs were so unsuccessful that they should never have been undertaken at all. Only about twenty percent fully achieved the goals for which they had been designed.

When the concepts of quality were well understood and applied with the full commitment of management from the very top of the organization, the results were outstanding. Such model quality organizations are living proof that the race is indeed worth running. But what has been lacking in too many cases is the internal understanding and commitment that must be present in the organization in order to make quality a part of the entire culture. This, we felt, Integrative Learning could provide if it were properly structured into the organization.

In his book *Megatrends*,[4] John Naisbitt provides a clue to why this too often missing ingredient is so absolutely crucial. He notes that as the level of technology becomes increasingly complex, the need for the sensitive treatment of human beings is increased. He refers to this phenomenon as "high tech — high touch." Naisbitt's insights run counter to earlier fears that the rise of technology would mean a bleak future for individual freedom and creativity, and predictions that with ever-increasing automation most human beings would become mere cogs manipulated by a power elite.

History has proved otherwise. At the same time the Soviet Union has come to an end, the industrial nations have found that automation requires employees far better educated than ever before. Furthermore, many organizations find themselves dependent on the wise decision-making of a high percentage of their workers, since operations are far too complex to be understood by a small group of managers. Thus human freedom and responsibility is actually increased by technology. This development points to the need for a significant new style of management.

WHY SCIENTIFIC MANAGEMENT WORKED AND WHY IT DOESN'T

Scientific Management, as developed by Frederick Taylor, served the production lines of the first half of the twentieth century. But the old school of thought has become increasingly outmoded as workers cease to be passive extensions of production line machinery and are required to become thinkers and problem solvers, whose creative ability is a major factor in their usefulness to their company. Managers can no longer rely on military styles of management and instead must move in the direction of becoming teachers, coaches and facilitators. A new era of human freedom, responsibility and intelligence in the workplace has arrived.

The stage is clearly set for the Learning Organization. The old style of management, with its pyramid of power ascending to a single, all-powerful CEO, is yielding to the new dynamics of shared power, teamwork, flattened organizations, and peer review. Reflecting on this transition, we became aware of the need for a new corporate psychology to ensure the success of organizational change.

If you're running a sweat shop or an old-style production line, it may not be good manners, but it is good business to push people around and make them conform. However, as high tech industries develop, such attitudes get in the way and greatly diminish the effectiveness of business.

What's needed now is a system for teaching the entire organization to function with respect for the creativity and uniqueness of all its members, a system that gives them new tools for thinking and communication, while exciting them with the drama of taking on the challenges their organization must face.

That is what the Ten Step process is designed to do. It establishes a program not merely of management, but of cultural change. We recognize, for example, that it makes no sense to develop a corporate vision when the vast majority of the people in an organization have no concept of what a corporate vision might be. The capacity for shared vision can be created, however, as people learn to relate to each other in new ways that are both more intelligent and more humane.

GETTING STARTED

We suggest that organizations heed the sequence of the Ten Steps as we've outlined them in this book. It will become clear as you read the chapters in sequence that many people in your organization already grasp some, perhaps even most of the principles in the Ten Steps. There are no arcane or insider secrets here; in fact the process wouldn't work as effectively if there were. But throughout the typical organization there is a wide and very uneven spread of comprehension and mastery of the principles and practices we advocate. Some individuals may still be unable to think positively about their jobs (a problem we discuss in Steps One and Two), while others are experienced and effective systems thinkers (Step Nine).

However, we want to emphasize that this book is not about the evolution of individuals, but about the evolution of the organization as a whole. We suggest that you begin with Step One and make certain that everyone in your organization has achieved the goals of that step before you make an official organizational demand for Step Two. We thus suggest proceeding in an orderly way, signing off on each step as you go. You'll want to adopt some means, which your organization must devise specifically to fit its unique character and needs, that will help you determine at what point the entire organization has internalized each step.

Nonetheless, you may choose not to take this route, at least at first, and therefore we have filled the book with the kinds of activities, exercises and philosophy that can still be useful in a more general application, even if the Ten Step Process is not followed sequentially. There is no reason, for example, why you couldn't introduce an exercise described in Step Seven into a training program you plan to lead the day after you finish reading this book. Use of the exercises out of the order in which they are presented here will not cause problems, except in instances where we have clearly indicated the need for some background or preparation for a particular exercise.

EMERGENCE OF THE LEARNING ORGANIZATION

We expect that the initial response of many readers of this book will be to think about it as applied to themselves, and to try some of the exercises either on themselves or in their training programs. (It's usually a good idea, by the way, to try something on yourself before you introduce it as a group exercise.)

Eventually, we think, readers will come to the conclusion that the Ten Step Process should unfold in the sequence in which we've presented it, so that every member of the organization has become fully involved in each step. In this manner learning begins at the level of the individual, proceeds through the level of the team, and is internalized, codified and stored at the level of processes and systems so well established that everyone who comes in contact with them is able to participate in them in a consistent manner. This is the surest path to the emergence of a true Learning Organization, which is an organization that learns on its own, quite apart from the many individual learnings that will also take place within it.

Our experience with these processes has been largely through our use of many of them in the Integrative Learning classes themselves. However, this book is not specifically about Integrative Learning, and those who wish an explanation of that concept should read *The Everyday Genius* by Peter Kline.[5] The present book is our answer to the many problems we have seen arise in corporations and other organizations as a result of pursuing changes in what we believe to be the wrong order.

MAKING WORK BRAIN-COMPATIBLE

We believe the loss of revenue due to inefficiency in U. S. business and industry is enormous. Much of this inefficiency is due to inadequate training programs, combined with corporate cultures that breed discontent and resentment.

The most efficient workers are often also the happiest. While that is not invariably true, it is true that no job and no career need be fundamentally unrewarding. Work that is unrewarding is usually organized in a way that we might call "brain-antagonistic". That is, it does not fit well with the way the human brain is designed to operate. The same work can often be transformed into a different structure that makes it "brain-compatible." When we learn to think in these terms, we can see that the human mind is capable of restructuring organizational behavior so everyone has a chance to flourish, both professionally and personally. We believe that while this may take some doing, it is never impossible.

What we envision is organizations whose design takes into account the needs of the people that make them up. Just as physical structures can be designed ergonomically so the human body can be comfortable with them, the Learning Organization is envisioned as an organization whose structure is fully compatible with human psychology — one which invites joyous affirmation of everything an organization must do to achieve its community-enriching goals.

SIXTEEN PRINCIPLES THAT PROMOTE LEARNING

What does a "brain-compatible" workplace, a Learning Organization, look like? That's a question that we've frequently been asked, and which we asked ourselves as we thought through the conditions necessary for creating and sustaining one. We have gradually evolved a set of principles which we feel underlie everything we're saying in this book. These principles, once they are accepted at the upper levels of an organization, necessarily extend to the inner belief systems of employees and become implicit in the organizational culture and structure — so much so that they eventually require no further discussion.

We mention them here not because we expect readers to automatically endorse them or to see their relevance to the changes which they might wish to make in their own organizations. On the contrary, they may at this point seem to some readers neither relevant nor desirable. Nevertheless, as the Ten Step process unfolds, we believe readers will find these principles to be logical and justifiable foundations for the kind of changes they themselves are seeking. For the moment they constitute a kind of preview and guide to the changes in attitude and behavior that characterize an emergent Learning Organization.

1. **Prime the mind of individuals at every level to be self-directed.** Learned helplessness has too often been the result of formal education. Because of its need for results that hold up under the harsh daylight of reality, an organization, particularly a manufacturing firm, can benefit greatly from reversing this trend. As people learn to help themselves and others in their own learning, continuous improvement for the organization is guaranteed.

2. **View mistakes as stepping stones to continuous learning, and essential to further business growth.** Some of the world's greatest discoveries have been the result of mistakes. A healthy

level of mistake making is essential to an organization's success, because it means new possibilities are being created. Those who make the mistakes learn to take responsibility for them so they are not repeated.

3. **There must be willingness to rework organizational systems and structures of all types.** This is the growth process, for growth is impossible without continuous redesign, as old habits are discarded and new possibilities investigated. All systems and structures were evolved to meet practical needs. As the needs change, so must the structures.

4. **Because learning is an emotional process, the corporate culture is a supportive place to be.** As each employee is able to experience continuous growth in self-esteem, morale rises and commitment to the organization deepens.

5. **Celebrate the learning process for its own sake, not just its end product.** As employees rediscover the gifted learners within themselves, the thrill, surprise, recognition and celebration of continuous discovery and learning are reborn. Learning itself, not just its product, is important because we can never predict what new practical benefits may result from frequent exercise of the learning process.

6. **Celebrate all learners equally.** Domineering and punishing hierarchies make everyone uncomfortable. It is not true that everyone has developed equal talent, knows the same amount or learns at the same rate; but every learning experience is unique and valuable, so all are worthy of equal appreciation.

7. **Accomplish as much transfer of knowledge and power from person to person as possible.** Whenever two people get together they can share information, and thus teach each other. In a fully developed learning culture, this will happen almost constantly. People who surround themselves with mentors they have selected make monumental strides in their learning, so the culture that encourages this will build more effective members.

8. **Encourage and teach learners to structure their own learning, rather than structuring it for them.** When the information is available and can be approached flexibly in a variety of ways, anyone can learn. Every learning experience should encompass at least two components: learning the subject/skill, and learning to learn. Those learning experiences which approach the basic ambiguity of human existence will generally have the most to offer.

9. **Teach the process of self-evaluation.** As we perceive ourselves more realistically, we become better able to guide our own

learning and thus continuously improve our work. Learning to evaluate ourselves is a route to personal freedom and empowerment.

10. **Recognize and accept as a goal the complete liberation of all human intelligence everywhere.** Every step forward in the liberation of intelligence creates new opportunities for each person, for the collective wealth of the world is to be found in the combined effective functioning of the human race. Placing limitations on anyone's intelligence is no more sensible than destroying the earth.

11. **Recognize that different learning preferences are alternate tools for approaching and accomplishing learning.** The advantage of learning along with someone who learns differently from you is that you'll see new ways to activate your learning process as a result of understanding theirs better. No one's learning style is to be denigrated, all should be allowed to learn in their own most effective manner.

12. **Encourage people to discover their own learning and thinking styles and make them accessible to others.** The more we share our own styles and learn each others', the more we build a common basis of communication with all people. To an extraordinary extent basic mental health results from understanding and control of your own learning processes. Optimal learning is the process of self-management.

13. **Cultivate each employee's abilities in all fields of knowledge, and spread the idea that nothing is forever inaccessible to people**. There's no predicting how information or skill in one field may become relevant to or useful in another. The cross-fertilization of different areas of knowledge in your thinking can result in creative discoveries at a very high level.

14. **Recognize that in order to learn something so it is easy for you to use it, it must be logical, moral and fun.** Learning is thus a process of harmonizing and affirming the total personality and the values it has espoused, provided these are aligned with those of humanity as a whole. It is a process that enhances our basic integrity as human beings.

15. **Ideas can be developed best through dialogue and discussion.** Learning occurs in an atmosphere in which people are constantly exploring together in informal ways and regard developing their ideas with each other as a normal part of the culture. Those ideas we have tested and challenged usually end up meaning the most to us.

16. **Everything is subject to re-examination and investigation.**
There are no sacred cows, and the assumptions on which we operate should always be subjected to further reconsideration in the
light of new data. Some of our most excellent ideas may in the end
be best discarded in favor of even better ones.

TREATING CUSTOMERS RIGHT

Stanley Marcus started with the premise that "the customer is always
right," and made it the foundation of a very successful business. But what he
meant by "customer" was someone outside the store who came in to buy
something.

Lately, the meaning of the word "customer" has been greatly expanded.
Welfare workers now talk about the people they work with as customers. Divisions within a large industry that deal only with each other, and never with the
public, refer to each other as customers. There is even a trend nowadays for
management to think of the people that work for them as their customers.

If we all treat everyone we come in contact with as a customer, that means
we'll do all we can to hold their interests at heart and serve those interests.

In their book *Samurai Selling*,[6] Chuck Laughlin and Karen Sage describe
ki, the spiritual force which helped samurai warriors overpower any obstacles.
In selling, this spiritual force may be used to place yourself so fully in the customer's shoes that it's possible to see things entirely from the point of view of
the person you're trying to influence. Once you're thinking the way the customer would think, the influence and direction you provide will truly serve the
customer's needs. Thus the old antagonism towards the salesperson will disappear and a new, mutually beneficial relationship will be established.

WHAT IF —

Think about the implications of this for a moment. Suppose every human
contact were conducted in that spirit. Suppose when someone stops you on
the street to ask for directions you do everything possible to make that person
glad he or she asked you and not someone else.

Suppose every teacher were to try as hard as possible to make every student glad to be in his or her class — not because it was easy, but because it did
the best possible job of helping the student grow and learn.

Suppose every parent related to every child in such a way that the child
was continually grateful for the opportunities for real growth and development
that parent can provide.

Suppose every husband always treated his wife this way, and every wife
always reciprocated.

And suppose that on the job whenever you stop to talk with a fellow
worker you're doing everything possible to make that particular conversation

the highlight of your fellow worker's day. Suppose every manager wanted every worker to be extremely proud and happy to be in his or her particular division, every company strove with all its might to be the best company in the world to work for, and that in every interaction we learned to be as fully conscious as we can possibly be of the needs and interests of the person we are with at that moment.

Imagine what you would learn from others if you treated everyone that way, and how rich and meaningful your life would become.

Perhaps you think this sounds like a fantasy — a sort of utopian "what if everything were perfect" dream. Perhaps you dismiss this fantasy out of hand as simply impossible.

Yet, don't we take it for granted that when we buy a new car it will run properly and the brakes will not fail on the freeway? We've come to accept standards of consistently high performance in technology that go far beyond the standards we've set for each other in interpersonal relationships. We accept the notion that it's okay to blow up at each other, to find fault with each other, to engage in gratuitous criticism and rudeness, while often taking for granted the very things that are deserving of praise and appreciation. Yet it is not very difficult to change all these negative cultural habits and routinely treat each other with consistent and total respect. By doing so we would merely be setting the same standards for human relationships that we set for technological ones.

In many businesses, such standards are already accepted. If you doubt this, pay attention to the way you are regularly treated by employees of many of our largest and most successful business enterprises, and think about the evolution of business during the last fifty years.

THE MIRACLE HAS ALREADY HAPPENED

There is a popular movie shown on television every Christmas and lately remade, called Miracle on 34th Street. In it a renegade Santa Claus working for Macy's starts telling customers about what they can get at Gimbel's that would satisfy their needs if Macy's doesn't have what they want. In this impossible Christmas fantasy the movie makers imagined an ideal world in which two great competing department stores would give up their cutthroat competition enough to put the customer's needs first.

That movie is now something of an anachronism. Today, what seemed like fantasy when it was made in 1947, is very much a part of our business culture. Go into almost any store, and if you can't find what you need, ask the clerk where else you might look for it. Nine times out of ten the clerk will send you trotting off to some competitor who has what you're looking for.

Foolish idealism? No, good business. Stores everywhere now know that they gain more than they lose by always putting the customer's needs first. Of course they want to be able to serve the customer themselves, but if they can't they'll send you to someone who can, knowing in the process that they've earned your gratitude and you'll be back next time to buy something they have in stock.

ON COOPERATION INSTEAD OF COMPETITION

Alfie Kohn has long been promoting the idea that in the corporate world cooperation accomplishes a great deal more than competition.[7] Indeed it is needless and useless competition that accounts for much of the inefficiency in our present system. By concentrating on quality and giving people what they want and need, we can place the focus where it belongs — not on cutting the throats of competitors, but on serving the people we are there to serve. Those who give the best service will in the end survive those who forget that their customers are their sole reason for existence.

This kind of competition is truly humane, for it trains people to think about each other's needs and interests. As business leads the way to help us think well about each other, we transfer these lessons into our personal lives and into our community service.

So learning to enhance the quality of work-life in a company by making it a Learning Organization is not just good for business, it is good for people as well. And because of this fact we can count on a great deal more energy becoming available to make business more efficient and effective than was ever available in the days of the sweat shop and the robber barons.

TOWARDS A KINDER AND SMARTER WORLD

This book is dedicated, then, to better business — to making it possible for businesses to get their people harmoniously involved in making everything the organization must do hum along at maximum possible efficiency and effectiveness. At the same time, we're thinking of the workers themselves, for they are customers too. As the philosophy of placing the customer first pervades any organization, the workers themselves will find life more satisfying and rewarding, and they will take home from the job many techniques that will benefit their families and their friends. They will, in short, do their part to create the kinder and gentler world we all wish we could live in.

Freedom and democracy have triumphed over the nightmare of communist oppression, and the world is ready now to use capitalism to build a better way of life for everyone. The small manufacturers in the Midwest who supply the giant corporations with parts for automobiles or computers, the large franchises that sell the products and services needed all over the world, the banks and financial service organizations — even the hospitals and schools — all these are among the leaders who, perhaps more than any other segment of contemporary society, are helping to build a more prosperous and equitable world.

For business has well learned the maxim that I best serve my interests by best serving yours. Increasingly a thing of the past are slipshod products and exploitative "services". Large reputable companies — often emulating the example of smaller ones — know they must stand behind whatever they sell, to the extent of replacing it free if it doesn't give satisfaction. The spirit and ethos that is at the heart of a Learning Organization is the same as that of the astute and enlightened business person, as the social leader and the person for whom a rich and fulfilling family life is the key to happiness.

THE BOTTOM LINE IS THE BOTTOM LINE

Everything in the Ten Step process — which we now invite you to begin — is designed to enhance the bottom line profitability and success of any organization. The Learning Organization as we envision it, and as we have seen it in practice, increases profits and cuts losses to an astonishing degree. But more than that, the changes that we recommend are a response to the changes that all of us are experiencing, social and economic, local and global.

It is, we believe, more than incidental that in the process of creating and strengthening Learning Organizations we shall also be helping everyone who participates in them to lead a better life — partly because it is good business — but also because it is just plain the right thing to do.

HOW DO ORGANIZATIONS LEARN?

Organizational learning is among the most significant issues in corporations, both profit and not for profit, and in governmental institutions as well. All over the world managers and other leaders are wrestling with the questions of how to instill experiences and goals among large groups of people working together in order to insure that things happen in a learning mode.

The most obvious difference between the way organizations and individuals learn is that individuals have memories, which are essential to learning, while organizations don't. This accounts for the fact that so-called cultural improvement programs may come and go, too often with little staying power.

Therefore, if we are to have a learning organization, we need to answer the question, what characteristics that already exist in organizations might make it possible for them to learn?

The most powerful way to frame this question is to look for feedback mechanisms, for these are the most fundamental aspects of any learning process. If you're going to benefit from your experience, you have to have some idea of its impact on the world around you. That's the feedback, and that's what organizations are going to have to learn to establish as part of their systemic structure if they are to be able to learn at all.

HOW LEARNING ORGANIZATIONS AND LEARNING INDIVIDUALS ARE DIFFERENT

The main difference between a learning individual and a Learning Organization is in the information storage process. Individuals store their learning primarily in their memories, augmented by libraries, notes and other aids to memory. Organizations store it primarily in their cultures, with a secondary backup in documentation that is useful only if the culture is committed to making use of it.

Note that we say the culture, not the demand. Demand that people do things a certain way and you'll get relatively meager results. Create a culture in which it's taken for granted that they're done that way, and you'll get nearly universal results.

In simple terms, individuals learn through the activation and updating of their memories while organizations learn through change in the culture. But we can't have a learning culture until we satisfy the requirements that must be made in order for learning to occur at all.

THE REQUIREMENTS FOR LEARNING

In order for learning to be said to have occurred, whether in an individual or an organization, three conditions must have been met: input, synthesis and output.

First, new information or skills must be inputted into the matrix of ideas, information and skills already present. Second, that new information must be synthesized with what was previously there. Finally, some sort of output is essential to complete the learning cycle. In other words, new information or skills must be adapted to and must also modify what was known or understood previously, and this must lead to significant action, either physical or mental (in the reorganization of a point of view, for example). In the simplest instance, you believe something to be true and then get information that it is not true. The next step is to edit every thought process or memory associated with the change in your awareness, so it is corrected for the new conditions you have just learned about. But when the new information is both important and counter to what was previously known (the change process) the synthesis of new information into old perceptions will be very complex.

The final stage of the learning process is output, the practice of behavior which evidences your newly adjusted knowledge and thought processing. Thus a new pattern or new homeostasis is established and learning is completed.

CULTURE AS ORGANIZATIONAL MEMORY

How, then, are organizations different from individuals in the way that they learn?

The closest thing to a memory that an organization has is a culture. The culture dictates the ways in which members of that organization relate to one another. You can detect some of the characteristics of the culture of an organization almost as soon as you enter it. You may notice, for example, a common denominator among the behaviors of the people you meet. Do they look you in the eye as you walk down the hall? Do they come up and greet you, a stranger, or simply let you pass without noticing? Do they tell you how pleased they are to be part of their group, or do they quickly indicate that you are in a place you'll be lucky to escape from? Do they reflect their camaraderie inclusively or exclusively? How do they see themselves as members of the organization? Is their behavior egalitarian or hierarchical?

WHERE CULTURE CAN BE FOUND

Culture occurs in the interaction between people in any situation in which they congregate with some degree of predictability. It starts whenever two or more are gathered together on a regular basis. Every marriage, for example, has a culture, as does every partnership.

One of us remembers taking a walk one day when a car entered the intersection without stopping and rammed into another car. Almost instantly a number of strangers reacted to the situation by taking on roles. One person started directing traffic. Another went to the nearest house to phone the police. A third assisted the people in one of the cars, while a fourth assisted those in the other car. Some stood by quietly watching, perhaps ready to give assistance if it was needed. A few obviously had no intention of helping, they just wanted to gawk at the accident.

As soon as a police car appeared, this mini culture which had formed so rapidly began to shift as officials took over the responsibility for what was happening. At that point, some people, who had remained on the sidelines before, came forward to offer evidence.

This is an example of how emergencies can rather suddenly draw people together to form cultures with well defined roles. Stories which tell of events of this kind may derive most of their interest from showing the emergence of such cultures. Perhaps a plane is forced to land on a dessert island, or a group of people are snowbound together. Gradually the strangers who, prior to the emergency, kept aloof from one another, will start to form a culture. People will claim roles for themselves and build a set of relationships which will be ongoing for the duration. A leader may emerge, or a set of leaders, or, in rare instances, a culture may be established in which leadership easily passes from one person to another. This is what happens on a football team, where whoever is carrying the ball at the moment necessarily becomes the leader, while secondary leadership is shared by those leading the process of protecting the leader or ready to receive the ball.

Mechanisms which simulate these situations can be used to build new cultures out of old ones quite rapidly, thus speeding up the process of creating a Learning Organization. You'll find one of these techniques described in our discussion of Step Nine.

Sometimes a small group must be isolated from the rest of society for a long time, and in such a group the personalities will emerge and become sharply defined in relationship to each other. The relationships among the people confined together as reported in *The Diary of Anne Frank* are an example. This is analogous to what happens in an organization when a relatively small group of people have to learn to work together for long periods of time.

AVOIDANCE OF CHANGE

Both individuals and cultures have a tendency to avoid change. That's because they operate on the basis of homeostasis. After a complex set of interactions in any system, a balance is reached in which operations of all sorts happen in fairly predictable ways. This homeostasis resists change because change requires that the balances be upset and reestablished, and for that reason change is always accompanied by some degree of stress.

Hans Selye, the expert on stress in human behavior, has shown that stress occurs with any major change in a person's life, whether negative or positive. Thus it may be as stressful to win the lottery as to lose a loved one. Severe difficulties may arise for people who suddenly come into a fortune because their lives have not been organized around the condition of having available all the money they need. This means they have to find uses for their energies other than survival, and most people do not suddenly adapt well to this kind of change. Selye assigned numerical values to different kinds of stresses to show the intensity of their effect upon a person's life.[1] Stresses such as major illnesses, the death of a loved one, loss of a job, or divorce usually have profound effects because they cause so much need to adjust the way you see things. They require you to discard many of the perceptions and behaviors you have long been used to, and learn others that will take their place Such extensive relearning is a kind of grieving process. It may take a long time and be quite disruptive in its effect, until the process has been completed.

In this context it is useful to observe that experiences like grieving do not necessarily occur only in response to the loss of a person. They may also occur (perhaps under a different name) when there has been some other major change in the conditions of life, such as losing your job, or taking on some major new responsibility, such as the birth of a child, or a major change in self perception. Childbirth may produce post-partem depression as the "grieving" experience when a new person is added to the family.

Again, from Hans Selye's work, we learn that stress is a temporary imbalance which is just as much present during a healing process as in one that is injurious. In fact, when a previously injurious process is healed, the stress involved in the injury itself must, to a certain extent, be revisited. That's why it can be just as stressful to regain the use of a broken arm as it was to lose it in the first place. While the arm was in a sling, the person had to learn to operate without it. By the time the arm is ready for useful action again, a lot of balances have been established that excluded it, and it has become a stranger to its own environment.

DEALING WITH THE STRESS OF LEARNING

Not surprisingly, therefore, all significant learning (no matter how benevolently offered and experienced) brings with it some degree of stress, involved in the synthesis process and the learning of a new set of habits and behaviors required for new forms of output.

In order for large organizations to learn and change, therefore, allowance must be made for the stress which necessarily arises after new information has been inputted, and some means of maintaining the newly emerging culture must be present in order to establish it as a permanent, ongoing condition of the organization.

CYCLES IN THE CHANGE PROCESS

Understanding this process helps explain many of the phenomena that are known to accompany organizational change. For example, we have the well known cycle in the establishment of new groups or teams: form, storm, norm and perform.

The formation of the team provides a whole new set of inputs for its members, who must learn not only about each other, but whatever it is they have to do together. Synthesizing this new set of inputs is complex and leads to a lot of necessary repositioning of each of the individuals, both inside themselves and in relationship to each other. They must continuously test each other and discover the areas in which, inevitably (given their very different individual perceptions of reality) they must clash.

This is the storming phase. When it has been completed, the individuals have achieved a culture which has a certain degree of balance, or homeostasis, and they can now announce that they exist as an entity which is ready for action. That is the norming phase.

In the above sequence we see another form of our initial description of learning: input, synthesis and output. It is now form, storm/norm and perform.

COMPLETION OF THE LEARNING CYCLE: PERFORMING

In the performing phase, the group, now fully established, proceeds to carry out its business. This may last as long as the group does, which in the case of some cultures, as for example, Judaism, may continue for thousands of years. Of course, every group, once established as a performing entity, will experience transitions during which the cycle is revisited as some new learning becomes necessary to help it adjust to a new set of conditions.

If we wish to change the culture of any group, whether it's a marriage, a corporation, a whole nation, or even the world itself, we must allow time and resources for the above stated processes to take place.

ATTEMPTED CULTURE CHANGES WHICH FAIL

Because of a lack of knowledge of the conditions under which organizational learning must occur, there are many instances in which organizational learning is sought but never found. These include attempted government programs which fail, computer systems which are installed but never made to work successfully, quality programs which are given up as just another Flavor of the Month phenomenon, and so on.

Unless the culture as a whole is taken into account and a series of processes adopted which allows the three stages of learning to occur in full force, organizational learning is likely to be thwarted.

THE DIFFERENCE THAT LEARNING MAKES

We come now to the distinction between an individual and a learning individual, as well as the one between an organization and a Learning Organization.

Most people go through life experiencing learnings which come upon them more or less accidentally. They might take a good course in school, for example, or face a life challenge. However, unless there is some triggering event, they are usually not likely to learn much.

Learning individuals, in contrast, are people who habitually and systematically seek out new learnings, and have therefore organized their lives around the three stages necessarily present in any learning process.

The most important of these stages is synthesis. Without it we cannot learn. Since it happens internally, it is hard to know whether it is actually taking place or not. If we understand the process of synthesis, however, we can learn to make a habit of it.

Some conditions are far more favorable to synthesis than others. An example from chemistry is the difference between hydrogen and helium. Hydrogen can be easily synthesized into compounds with other elements. All the hydrocarbons, for example, are examples of this. Water is a synthesis of hydrogen and oxygen. And so on.

Helium, on the other hand, is an inert gas. It does not synthesize with other elements for a very simple reason. The first shell of electrons surrounding the nucleus has room for only two electrons. Hydrogen has only one and is constantly looking for another to complete its shell. When it finds an atom with a free electron, it may be able to link up with it, sharing the electron in its shell with another atom which can use an extra electron as well.

Helium, however, has a full shell. There's no room for another electron to connect up to it. That's why there are so few compounds in which helium is an element.

This is a good analogy for the difference between openness to new learning and a closed system which is impermeable to change. If you want all the members of your organization to behave like an inert gas and avoid contact with one another, then encourage them to build impermeable shells around themselves, so they're on the defensive and trying to avoid notice for fear of getting overworked or fired.

On the other hand, you can create a mechanism for change by making it appear to all your people that they're somehow incomplete. Only if they team up with others can they get anything done. For example, you can have everyone working on a production line doing one complete task isolated from other tasks. Or you can put a group of people in a room with a bunch of parts and ask them to collaborate in assembling them.

The more the work itself draws forth collaboration, the more you're likely to get people working together, and, at least in many situations, if they use proper group dynamics their synergy will beat the performance of the same number of people working alone. If the group dynamics are poor, however, their performance may be vastly inferior.

Once you've got people working together, then you need to introduce mechanisms that will get them to want to create excellent teams with high performance records. Part of what will bring this about is a genuine desire to work together that comes from individuals well matched in a team.

Encourage them to engage in activities of the type offered in this book, and you'll start to see your teams becoming stronger, more mutually supportive and more richly interactive.

LEARNING IS INSPIRED BY A SENSE OF INCOMPLETENESS

A person who is given to learning is aware of the incompleteness of their understanding. It is when we are uncertain of something important to us that we seek to understand it. If we can't learn about it any other way, we'll have to find an expert and get that person to tell us about it. Create conditions that bring about such collaborative inquiry, and you'll start to see your people teaching and learning from each other on a regular basis.

If, however, I believe I have a complete understanding of the world, new learning will seem unnecessary and I will reject it. So if your people have territories they're busy defending and a sense that they're so competent at what they do they can't possibly need to change, there's little likelihood any new learning will take place.

What determines whether I am incomplete in the sense that will define me as a learner?

THE ROLE OF GESTALTS IN LEARNING

Understanding the phenomenon of Gestalts will help to explain why some people learn and others don't. A Gestalt is a perception of something that appears to you to be complete. When you see a certain three sided figure, for example, you may Gestalt it as a triangle. This means you see it as one undivided image, even though you know it has three sides and three corners and defines a unit of space. Somehow your mind blends all the details into a single, unified perception which serves as a template for the understandings associated with that perception. Thus you can now see a triangle not simply as a geometrical form, but also as a metaphor for a certain type of relationship between three people, or a place in a city where two avenues meet at a point.

If the Gestalt is so strong that it resists change, you will then have some degree of resistance to analyzing it into its component parts — to say, for example, whether or not it is an isosceles triangle. But when you have become accustomed to viewing triangles in this analytical way, you will then include the analysis of them in your Gestalt process and they will become more dynamic for you.

OPENNESS INVITES LEARNING

Thus, the learning individual has internalized a great many dynamic or "open" Gestalts, symbols or templates that allow learning to occur at a constantly increasing rate. Such a person is full of questions and seeks answers for them. Customarily the answers sought are of a kind which lead to other questions. In this manner the learning continues and is likely to be stress free, since the process of learning has now become part of the homeostasis itself.

Even so, there are learnings which can upset the balance of the learning individual.

THE PROBLEM OF UPSETTING THE BALANCE

Certainly one of the greatest learning individuals of all time was the composer Johann Sebastian Bach, who through his own experience learned so much about music that he taught generations of great composers following him from the enormous store of knowledge he compiled. Yet even Bach had Gestalts which were impermeable to new learning.

For example, one of Bach's friends decided to write a composition that Bach could not sight-read. Since Bach was known as the greatest sight-reader of his day, this was a challenge of no small proportions. Yet the solution to the problem turned out to be quite easy. To write a piece Bach could not sight-read one had only to move the composition outside the realm of Bach's musical language as he had Gestalted it.

Bach's skill at sight-reading stemmed from his ease in perceiving musical forms, forms that served as templates which fit complex musical interactions into an immediately perceived single Gestalt. Thus, he did not read individual notes at all, but fairly large groups of notes, all forming Gestalted units.

His friend intuited what these templates must be like and simply wrote a series of notes that would not fit into any of Bach's Gestalts at crucial points in the development of the music. He left the composition he had composed on his clavichord and when Bach came over for lunch, the great composer sat down to play, as he always did, whatever was before him. As his friend listened, Bach got part way through the composition, stumbled, tried again and then gave up.

What's remarkable about this, is that a lesser musician could have played the piece quite easily.

The price we pay for excellence is often to establish a set of templates which are so solidly established that we cannot effectively interact with anything which falls outside their sphere. That's why the great revolutionaries of one age become the reactionaries of the next. Having created new ways of seeing things, they cling to them and are unwilling to admit new possibilities that go beyond what they have created.

Whenever old Gestalts have become hardened in this manner, fundamental learnings may become very difficult indeed, which accounts for the fact that while you can always tell a Harvard man, you can't tell him much.

EVOLUTIONARY JUMPS TAKE ADVANTAGE OF WEAKNESS IN THE OTHER GUY'S BALANCE

Evolutionary jumps occur when homeostasis is upset by the emergence of a force much stronger than those around it. It takes over the field for a while and dominates it until a new homeostasis is established. That's why a well established set of homeostatic interactions may function very well in one environment but have great difficulty adapting to a slightly different one. A business that thrives in one country, for example, may do poorly in another because of the differences between the two cultures. This difficulty of adaptation to change also explains why many organisms that ruled the world for long periods of time disappeared when the conditions that supported them changed. New, less rigidly organized creatures took their place and established new templates which enabled them to survive under the new conditions.

BALANCING SKILL AND FLEXIBILITY

What we need now is templates that combine the maximum amount of skilled behavior or perception with the maximum amount of flexibility. This means a high degree of ambiguity tolerance. If you want to know what ambiguity tolerance is, you can observe it in small children.

Any perception which cannot be resolved into a satisfying Gestalt is ambiguous. The mind will either reject it as meaningless or continue to play with it until a meaning can be Gestalted from it and closure is reached. Children, by their very nature, must tolerate ambiguity, since they daily confront so much that they cannot yet understand because of the complexity of its implications which will take years to work out into a reasonable facsimile of reality. Their main difficulty is that they have not yet developed the requisite "filing cabinets" in which to store many of their experiences so that each has a simple interpretation to explain its meaning and relationship to other elements of experience.

In fact it is our experience that even among adults the creation of new filing cabinets is essential to making significant progress in understanding that will clarify meanings in any field which have proved elusive.

For that reason, adults who can maintain a childlike view of the world frequently have attributes that we often label as "genius". Upon encountering an unresolved dilemma, they do not dismiss it, but rather continue to consider it in different contexts and from different perspectives until a Gestalt emerges which they can then share with the world.

CONDITIONS NECESSARY FOR LEARNING ORGANIZATIONS

To build a Learning Organization, we must create conditions that give permission for people to confront ambiguity and stay with it until they have turned apparently meaningless patterns into useful ones. Only in this way can we produce the innovation necessary to stay alive in a highly competitive and volatile global marketplace. We can accomplish the necessary groundwork by teaching individuals to own the beliefs or mind sets that will help them increase their ambiguity tolerance. Beyond that, we must then provide for them what neurologist Marian Diamond calls an "enriched environment"[2] — one which feeds the brain a constant diet of stimulating new experiences in all of the seven intelligences in which the brain computes information.[3]

This involves establishing a number of essential conditions within the culture, which include the following:

1) Positive expectation that dilemmas can be resolved.

2) Support for the learning process itself.

3) Willingness to delay closure long enough to arrive at significant Gestalts rather than forced and trivial ones.

4) Communication processes that bring people together to consider in a friendly and noncompetitive atmosphere many different perceptions, templates, habits of thought and possible solutions, from which the most useful may then be chosen.

5) A cultural habit that encourages exploring apparently meaningless ambiguities with the expectation that meaning can be found in them — as an expression of both a personal and organizational commitment to learning over the long haul.

6) The establishment of contexts within which meaning for new possibilities can be found as they emerge.

7) A set of modeling skills, strategies and techniques or mechanisms that allow people more easily to construct meaning out of apparent chaos.

8) A cultural understanding which is shared throughout management of the systemic interactions that will inevitably be present as complex Gestalts are formed.

9) An intuitive feeling for how complex interactions will be likely to occur.

If you examine these nine conditions, you will find that they are subsets or conditions of Steps Two through Nine of the Ten Steps to a Learning Organization.

BUILDING AN ENVIRONMENT OF OPENNESS

If you're planning to build a Learning Organization, then, you must start by creating a culture of openness of thinking and communication that uses many of the tools most effective in working with ambiguities in order to extract meaning from them. As long as the culture and way of thinking invite openness in many different forms, while at the same time providing tools that define useful directions to take, the organization will become a Learning Organization. Of course there must also be tools for closure when it is appropriate, and the capacity to decide when thought has proceeded long enough and it's time for action. In the context of doing business, too much thinking can be as deleterious as too little. In addition to remaining open to new possibility, we must avoid Hamlet's dilemma in which "enterprises of great pitch and moment...turn awry and lose the name of action."

WHAT LIMITS THE SPEED OF DEVELOPMENT

How rapidly you can build a Learning Organization is limited only by how rapidly the individuals in the organization can be taught to reexamine their own learning processes so that they become more open to new possibilities. They also have to become sensitive to provisos or belief systems accepted by the culture itself that encourage the above-mentioned nine conditions for the establishment of effective creative thinking. And they have to internalize the new systems out of which the Learning Organization will be built. If you can accomplish all this rapidly, you can create a Learning Organization rapidly. It doesn't have to be as slow as Peter Senge keeps arguing that it does. We've seen it happen in well under a year in places where the proper groundwork has been laid, and in one or two instances the necessary foundation has been laid in less than a month.

A THREE-TIERED PROCESS FOR SPEEDING UP
CULTURAL TRANSFORMATION

As we have thought about the ideal way to create the culture change that transforms organizations of all types into Learning Organizations, we have developed a three-tiered process which we believe to be ideal for getting the strongest transformation in the shortest amount of time with the most beneficial possible impact on the bottom line.

The reason so many "solutions" that have worked in one place do not work in another is that they are not fully systemic. That's true of quality circles, TQM programs, re-engineering, ISO 9000 and many others which have deteriorated into just another exercise in Flavor of the Month. Because organizations, like people, are essentially self organizing, you cannot possibly issue edicts for change and get the results you want. You have to plant ideas and mechanisms throughout every stratum of the organization and then fertilize the soil in which they have to grow. Research from many different sources has convinced us that no quality program will ever be worth its investment in a management environment which does not invite the participation of all levels of the organization in very significant ways. The thriving commerce of the future will be carried out by organizations which are democratic in the best sense of the word, without any of the slow and painful tendency to get stymied we're familiar with from so many exercises in democratic control. What we're talking about is a truly intelligent work force, harmoniously organized so everyone is thinking all the time. You can have that, but you can't have it by doing things the old way, or by forcing people to go along with you. You'll have to learn a new set of skills, some of which are counter-intuitive by the standards that the Harvard Business School may have taught you (though much of their most recent research points in the direction we're taking here). What we're talking about is the development of intellectual capital throughout the organization right down to the sanitation engineers.

THE GREAT GAME OF BUSINESS

The first and most important component in developing an all-inclusive, democratic structure is The Great Game of Business[4] an unusually successful form of open book management developed by Jack Stack, the CEO of the Springfield Remanufacturing Corporation. The Great Game of Business is a powerful new tool which we believe will spread throughout the world business community in less than a generation, simply because it is so very much more powerful than any currently existing competing management system.

To appreciate the degree of success that Stack has had, we note that the value of the company's stock has grown, in fifteen years, from ten cents to forty dollars a share. That's a growth of four hundred times, or about forty times the growth of the average share traded on the stock exchange during that same period, and it didn't happen by accident. Also during that fifteen year period, the company has had a controlled growth rate of its business at fifteen percent per year, and has spun off seventeen satellite businesses. These are impressive gains yet not unattainable for other organizations who opt to play The Game.

Of course, if we're talking about organizations like public school systems (some of which have made their own attempts to create Learning Organizations) then we're talking about student achievement as the bottom line success in playing The Game. Quantifiable results such as literacy rates, high school graduation rates, and college or career development program attendance rates can be used to measure your success. You can play the Great Game of Business with records of student achievement just as well as you can with the financial reports we'll be discussing in what follows.

REPLICATING THE SUCCESS OF THE GAME

The astonishing success of SRC can be replicated, but only if the process of replicating it is sufficiently disciplined, systemic and all-inclusive.

In order to understand how that process may occur, we must look more closely at the structure of the Learning Organization itself, and the means by which the above described culture change can best be brought about.

As a result of the widespread public attention that has been given to Jack Stack's success with SRC, many thousands of companies have made inquiries into the process. A significant number of these have attended a two day workshop offered at SRC. The number of business leaders who share their experiences and successes with the Game at a yearly "gather-in" about the Game has been growing larger every year.

But there's not much evidence yet that SRC's dramatic success has been replicated by a great many other companies, as measured in astonishing levels of improvement in the bottom line. We believe that's because so many companies that try to replicate it themselves do not fully understand the conditions that made it work at SRC.

As we see it, those conditions are two:

One, you have to have a replacement for the "burning platform" on which everyone was standing when Jack Stack and his company first tried to make the game work.

And two, you have to admit that Jack Stack himself is one of the most charismatic leaders in the entire history of business, and you'll have to replicate that element of charismatic leadership in your own organization with something at least as effective, though probably quite different.

ELEMENTS OF THE GAME

The best way to understand the Great Game of Business is to start off with its three basic elements: know the rules, keep score and have a stake in the action.

Simplistic as it may sound, this structure provides a very solid basis for developing the culture of a Learning Organization. Let's see how each of the elements contributes to that culture.

In order to know the rules, there must be rules to know. These rules must be the same for the entire organization, and they must be so much out in the open that there's never any question about them. They become, in other words, the most crucial elements of the shared culture. In order for this to work, it's essential that the rules make sense to everyone. To make clear what this means, let's look at an example of rules that don't make sense.

In many organizations it's necessary, before you do anything, to get clearance from someone above you. Sometimes this clearance has to pass through several layers of management and may take awhile. For example, if a piece of equipment breaks down, it may take three days before a key person signs a document to approve the funds needed to fix it.

Everyone who works in an organization that has rules like these knows they don't make sense. There should be a number of people anticipating repairs long before there's a breakdown, and the decision should be forthcoming immediately, so production isn't slowed.

So if you're going to have rules that everyone agrees on, you're going to have to check all of them out to the point where it's clear that they really make sense from the point of view of everyone involved.

When the rules come from an outside source like government regulation, they may not make sense, but it's possible for everyone in the organization to understand that nothing can be done about this. But when they come from inside the organization, they have to make sense, or you'll never get your organization to become a Learning Organization.

Getting all the rules to make sense to everyone may take some doing, but it's going to be a sine qua non for everything else you're planning to accomplish.

GEARING THE RULES TO THE CRITICAL NUMBER

Of course the rules must be focused on a goal — a critical number for the organization to reach. By critical number we mean the carefully and wisely chosen element of the operation that needs to be most improved in order to make the most impact on everything else in the organization. For example, if a public school system were to target 100% high school graduation by its student body, then everyone in the organization would be working for that, and it would mean that all the kindergarten teachers (and everyone else as well) would have to redesign and refine their programs.

Similarly, if a company decided that 100% improvement in customer satisfaction was its critical number, then everything in the company would be shifted in the direction of meeting that goal.

Or, if the best way to get the bottom line improved were to have a more effective relationship between sales and marketing, that would mean a different set of activities with different outcomes, but it would still affect everyone in the organization.

Just as you know you're supposed to get up in the morning, brush your teeth and get to work on time, so people in companies that play the Game know they're supposed to accomplish those jobs that will most impact the critical number. Therefore, selection of the most useful critical number is crucial to making the Game work. It's possible and even likely that after a time it will be important to shift to a different critical number because priorities have changed.

In chaos theory it has been established that self-organizing systems can develop complex systems out of relatively simple rules. The key is to select those well chosen rules that will lead to the most productive behavior. Some of the rules, incidentally, will function as mechanisms to change behavior throughout the organization. For example, if a basketball coach has a hard and fast rule that you cannot shoot for a basket until the ball has been passed among three different players first, and he enforces the rule by throwing people out of the game if they violate it, the result is a kind of team work not obtainable by any other means. That's how rules can become behavior-changing mechanisms.

In our experience, most organizations do not have many really clear cut rules that everyone can agree on. Instead, there are several sets of different rules for different groups, including the sub-cultural groups that form within the organization. If at CBS most of the important decisions are made in the men's room, at your corporation they may be made around the water cooler or in the exercise room. In other words, official meetings may have far less impact than unofficial gatherings.

But bringing the rules out into the open, actually playing by them, getting universal agreement about them, and seeing to it that they affect the culture in a measurably positive way is a key process in developing a Learning Organization.

KEEPING SCORE

Second, it's one thing to know the rules, but quite another to keep score. At this point, imagine a couple of football teams on a ball field with no rules, no scoring and no sense of strategy or direction. A great many organizations operate more or less in this manner.

But give the team not only rules to play by but a score board that lets the world know how the Game is progressing, and you'll see a lot of strategies developing to help make and keep the score as high as possible. That's what happens with the Great Game of Business.

A STAKE IN THE ACTION

Finally, it won't do to expect your workers to work twice as effectively so you can get all the profits that result from their commitment to do well — particularly if, as often happens, the result is that people work themselves out of a job. If, by some equitable system, you share the profits with them, and also guarantee that they can move on to a better job after they've eliminated the one they've got, what you'll get is a bigger pie — out of which everyone can have bigger pieces. Your profits will explode as your workers start making something extra for themselves as well as you.

In Jack Stack's version of open book management, that's what it all comes down to. The scoreboard is the company financials. Everyone in the organization can read them, and everyone sees on a daily basis how he or she is impacting them. This leads to continuous improvement in the direction of a more effective bottom line.

WHAT'S MISSING FROM THE REPLICATIONS

As other companies try to replicate the Great Game of Business, though, they often don't realize that some important ingredients are being left out of their play. It's pretty hard to see what's missing if you're a member of the culture that's missing it. That's because to a large extent your own culture is invisible to you. Starting from scratch on your own is like trying to perform brain surgery on yourself. Even if you're a brain surgeon, you shouldn't try it. A qualified colleague will do far better for you than your own fumbling with aspects of your system you're condemned to be unable to see.

In most organizations many cultures exist side by side, and they're essentially incompatible with one another. For example, if both men and women work there, and there's the slightest hint of sexism or male chauvinism anywhere, then you've got two cultures. Or, if a little unconscious racism is to be found in little pockets here and there, then you've got a culture of the majority and a culture of the minority.

One of the most common cultural divisions is the one that separates employers (or managers) from employees (or workers). Until you break down those barriers, you're not going to have a Learning Organization.

Another way you'll get separate cultures is to have cliques that stick together and are critical of other cliques. Maybe, for example, the people in sales are always running down the people in operations, or vice versa. A Learning Organization cannot require unanimity of point of view, because that would be impossible, but it must have a harmonious form of acknowledged diversity or it simply cannot exist.

We believe that in order to compensate for any elements that may be missing from the Game as you seek to establish it and play it in your organization, some additional elements must be added to it beyond those which are already widely recognized.

WHAT TO ADD

Essentially, these are three in number: Integrative Learning, Strategic Micromanagement and the adoption of measurements that go beyond the financial.

We offer a brief introduction to Integrative Learning in Chapter Six, which is about developing a strong personal learning commitment in all members of the organization. There is also a book about it, called *The Everyday Genius*, by one of the authors of this book. The key point about Integrative Learning, however, is that it is a process of restoring the kind of natural learning that all people do early in life before it is crushed out of them by socialization and our national system of education. When you have restored your people's capacity to honor their own natural learning they'll find they can learn most things from two to ten times as fast as they did before, while understanding and retaining them better.

USING THE BEST METHODS TO INCULCATE THE GAME

We have found that when Integrative Learning is used to inculcate the Great Game of Business in an organization, it will be adopted much more quickly, because the fear that many workers have of reading financial reports is overcome much more quickly than is otherwise possible. The result has been a deeper understanding of the processes to be learned, together with a more rapid development of that understanding.

STRATEGIC MICROMANAGEMENT

The second element, Strategic Micromanagement, consists of inculcating everyone in the company with a kit of strategic tools for building the essential systems that are currently missing from the organization's operations: tools for making decisions, communicating, solving problems and any number of other things that work teams need to be good at if an organization is to develop quickly and efficiently and work smart instead of just hard. Like Integrative Learning, Strategic Micromanagement is content free. That is, it can be used to help people learn anything or develop any set of skills that are needed. It is fine-tuned to the needs of the individual workplace, rather than prefabricated and offered to an organization as is. And it isn't used by management to micromanage people; it's used by people to micromanage themselves.

What Strategic Micromanagement does is take the essential rules of the organization and guide the use of them into increasingly complex forms of behavior. It's quite a bit like what a football coach does in training a team to perform brilliantly. Many of the tools of Strategic Micromanagement can be found in the book *Smart Work* by Lisa Marshall and Lucy Freeman.[5]

EXPANDING THE SCORING SYSTEM

Finally, we have the contribution of Dean Schroeder, Professor of Management at Valparaiso University, who is adding to the scoring system of the Game several additional matrices, including customer satisfaction (both internal and external), innovation and essential systems development (including communications, technical and the storage of knowledge). In other words, it's one thing to improve the bottom line, but you can get there more effectively if you're focused on the skills and behaviors that are most likely to help you do that.

This is a matter of measuring the development of your intellectual capital. In this regard, you'll find a useful companion to our book in *Intellectual Capital* by Thomas Stewart.[6] Of several books on the subject, it seems to be the most practical and readable, and it builds the relationship between human capital, structural capital and customer capital quite nicely, though it doesn't provide the scoreboard for these that you'll need to construct for yourself, or in conjunction with whoever you hire to help you implement the Great Game of Business.

By combining these elements to introduce the Great Game of Business into a company, we can with much greater rapidity create the culture change that produces a Learning Organization. Up till now the word on the streets about Learning Organizations has been that they take a long time to create — indeed, sometimes a very long time. We don't think that has to be true any longer. In groups of ten thousand or less it should be possible to effect a complete transformation in a much shorter time than most organizations have experienced, if you follow the program we have outlined above.

Meanwhile, the point of the Ten Steps continues to be that there's a sine qua non in progressing towards continuous improvement. You can't do it unless people are working well together. That's the new age of relationships coming into focus, and it's the key to your success with the bottom line.

THE MOST VALUABLE ASSET

It's pretty well agreed among most business commentators nowadays that the most valuable asset any company can have is its people. But in order to make the best use of that asset, it must develop them so they can function with continuously improving quality.

That means a company that wishes to become a Learning Organization has to get into the education business, and has to do it wisely.

In doing so, it will realize that we're not only past the industrial age, we're even past the information age. We have entered what may be the final, or at least the most important, stage of development in the evolution of modern business. That is, as we've indicated above, the Age of Relationships.

We can't be good workers if we're not good at relationships. The same goes for being good customers. In the end, business world wide is a network system of people engaged in organizations who are customers for one another. The only people who can make the marketplace viable are those who are themselves successful in business in some way. It's the only way to keep the world economic society growing and developing.

By creating Learning Organizations which know how to play the game of business to the hilt, companies are becoming more finely attuned to the human needs of their workers. What used to be a confrontational situation between management and labor is increasingly a matter of shared interests and opportunities. Workers in a Learning Organization know how to increase their own value to the organization virtually from day to day, and managers know that that effort is worth paying them for.

AN EXPANSION AND DEEPENING OF VALUES

When the program we have outlined above is followed, it will very likely turn out to be true that business values are transformed into human values; and beyond that, ecological values as well. It is clear from the experience of companies like SRC that when the interests of the workers, of management and of the stockholders are all essentially identical, then a truly benign form of organization is created. That's because a systemic view of things is shared by all in the organization. Once you see things systemically, you see why it is so important to serve your customers well, why you must contribute to your community, why you need to honor your role in the global economy and why ecological issues are your issues as much as anyone's.

Because of the great power of this kind of new perception shared by all the members of an organization, it can become very much more efficient and effective than its competitors.

This kind of approach to business will inevitably become universal because it's so much more effective and efficient that it will, in time, replace all those which are less so. This is indeed fortunate, because if we are to continue to have a viable economy, we have to learn to value each other, our communities and our planet.

ASSESS YOUR LEARNING CULTURE

S T E P   1

Since our work as training and development consultants takes us into a wide range of organizations and corporations, we pick up a lot of information about those organizations from the moment we walk through their doors.

One of us recently had an appointment with an executive in a large company who was a prospective client. As I walked down the halls, I had a sinking feeling the conversation would be a waste of time. Everywhere I looked I could see signs of discontent. It wasn't the obvious kind — it wasn't open rebellion. It was evidence, though, of a culture that bred sullenness and hostility. A noticeable symptom was that no one looked at me as I made my way through the corridors. And they didn't seem to be relating to each other, either.

Earlier, the receptionist who had announced my visit seemed more concerned with his newspaper than with me. He was an older man, slightly balding, who seemed to be marking time until his retirement.

As I passed one office, I overheard an employee saying, "You mean someone around here actually knows what they're doing?"

So by the time I entered the manager's office I already knew what would happen. I was there to discuss a new kind of training program, but I could already tell it wouldn't work. It couldn't be successful in an organization that seemed committed to defeating the best impulses of all its employees. It was clear to me that practically no one in that company wanted to be there. This company's culture could be succinctly described in the words of a participant in a workshop I'd led recently: "It stinks."

THE IMPORTANCE OF FACING THE MUSIC

As we shall see, you can't move ahead on any of the Ten Steps until the corporate decision makers are ready and willing to face the truth about what all the employees are thinking.

Facing the music — acknowledging what's working, and what's missing — is the necessary first step towards climbing out of the pit in which so many organizations now find themselves. Without that first step, it's next to impossible to build a creative and dynamic organization capable of revitalizing itself. After all, houses built in quicksand usually disappear very quickly, and an organization built on a culture of quicksand will do the same thing.

Yet very few organizations today have the qualities we would like to see in all of them. Since corporate culture is one of the most important factors affecting the bottom line — there's a measurable difference in growth rate between a good culture and a poor one, as we shall see — the only reason many companies are still in business is that all their competitors have cultures that are no better than theirs.

Lest you think we're just sounding off about this, there's considerable research which shows that no TQM or other similar program will work in an organization that does not have a culture relatively similar to the one we're positing here.[1] That's why so many quality programs have failed. Along with TQM go many Flavors of the Month, which pass in and out of fashion, almost always ineffectually. Unfortunately, some of the programs that don't survive involve highly expensive technology. A multi-million dollar computer system may be installed in a company and eventually have to be taken out, not because the system itself was no good, but because the company culture was so sick or ineffectual that the system couldn't work there.

The Springfield Remanufacturing Company has a culture that is among the best in the corporate world today. All the employees love the company and want to work there for the rest of their lives. They have ownership in the company and know exactly what to do so that their work will have a positive effect on the bottom line. Anyone in that company can rise through the ranks, and all are strongly encouraged to do so.. Seventeen former employees are now running companies they founded, in which SRC has an ownership interest. And perhaps most striking of all, the company's annual growth rate for well over a decade has been fifteen percent per annum.

The secret weapon used by SRC is called the Great Game of Business, which we've described in the previous chapter on organizational learning, and you can read all about it in the CEO, Jack Stack's, book of that name.[2] But the Great Game of Business, as a large number of companies worldwide have already discovered to their cost, will not work unless the type of culture we're describing in this book is in place. No company can play the game effectively unless it is seriously committed to, and has in place a plan to become a learning organization.

What that boils down to is that if you're going to play the Great Game of Business in your company, you can forget the whole thing unless you're willing to start by facing the music about every single thing that happens in your company from the grand plans the janitor may be secretly harboring that may lead you to new business opportunities right down to who's been stealing the paper clips.

As we have worked with the Great Game of Business in companies that have never tried it before we've discovered two things:

1) It's absolutely essential to change the culture before playing the game.

2) Any company that does this can start seeing a huge jump in its productivity and profitability in a short time.

In Step One we discuss two different ways of facing the music. The first is institutional: **know what everyone thinks**. The second is individual: once you're part of an organization that respects your opinion, **start taking responsibility for what you think and what you do**. It's a two-way street.

These two types of assessment — corporate assessment and individual assessment — go hand in hand. Alienated human beings in an alienating organization have little interest in being personally accountable in any more than a technical sense. People who know that their company cares about them will come to care more and more about their company and will want to give their best to it. They'll want to assess their own actions so they can improve their performance.

FIRST FIND OUT WHAT PEOPLE THINK IS GOING ON

The first step is finding out what people think about the culture they presently work in. This process will most likely uncover a lot of denial and fear. In some instances it might expose seething antagonisms: perhaps a labor-management conflict, or a conflict between the day shift and the night shift, or in-fighting within divisions based on a difference of values or priorities, or the aftermath of a painful merger, not yet fully resolved. In one company we discovered that a small group that worked the night shift was about seven times as efficient in its performance as any other group in the company. This was a sure, but neglected, sign that the conditions under which that group was working ought to be replicated throughout the company as a whole.

In another corporation, sixty-eight executives completed the *Learning Organization Assessment*, and discovered that their organizational commitment to continuous improvement was being undermined by their poor training of middle managers, lack of cross-functional learning, and failure to learn from their mistakes. Such "truth telling" began an internal process of developing and establishing new strategies to bridge the gap between their natural organizational strengths and limitations.

When all the cards are on the table, meaning that all have been open about how they perceive the unvarnished reality of the organization — only then can steps be taken to rectify the situation.

THE UNIVERSAL DAMAGING EFFECTS OF FEAR

If you wanted to point to a single root cause for all the confusion and lack of commitment we've found in so many companies, that cause would be fear. Pervasive and irrepressible, fear is so much a part of the atmosphere of these companies that it is hard to isolate, not to mention eliminate. But like an invisible poison in the air, fear heightens the state of tension and distraction in the employees. Looking over their shoulders, sure their plans will be disrupted, they worry that their reputations will be soiled, and their jobs put on the line. Many cannot imagine what it would be like to awaken in the morning without that little ball of fear in the pit of the stomach.

Thus the first thing management needs to know is whether the workplace is dominated by fear. Fear tends to transform people into tortoises. It says to them, "Hide in your shell as long as you can and hope nobody notices you. Just go through the motions of your work, making sure all the technical bases are covered. Don't be creative, because that could get you in trouble, and don't try to solve any problems, because that involves sticking your neck out."

FEAR CARRIES A VERY HIGH PRICE TAG

As W. Edwards Deming so often said, "The first principle is to drive out fear." When people are dominated by fear, they don't think well, their decisions are poor, and they certainly don't have a valid picture of where the company is headed — or should be headed. That's because the way our brains are wired, when we're in a state of heavy fear we are no longer able to access the higher order thinking skills our brains are capable of, so we quite literally experience a loss of effective intelligence. We "down-shift" our thinking and creativity skills in order to protect ourselves from further harmful consequences. "Dumbing down" the corporation may be a way to build a CEO's ego, but it does nothing for the bottom line.

Where there's fear of repercussions, there almost certainly has to be a crippling fear of accountability. Crippling, because accountability is precisely what's most needed in the modern workplace. For better or worse, both organizations and technologies have become so complex that only the person who's doing the job can really know what's going on and be accountable for it. And that person can't possibly do a decent job if he or she is spending a great deal of time dealing with fear.

We've been in organizations where the fear is so all-encompassing it's difficult to see how they can survive. One such company literally spent 650 million dollars one year bringing no new products to market. We met several people whose entire careers had been spent working on projects that the company failed to bring to completion.

This company pitted its various work teams and divisions against one another, determined to get the "best" by bringing to completion only half the projects that were started. They were forever reorganizing, dumping people and then hiring less qualified people to replace them, and trying to make up their minds about what they were going to do next. The only people we met who were getting anything done were living in little pockets which management didn't even know were there. One very creative manager told us, "I spend five percent of my time running my division and ninety-five percent defending its existence." In such an atmosphere, almost everything is guaranteed to fail, and yet in today's corporate world a surprising number of companies run just this way.

In general, this kind of behavior doesn't make the business magazines, because it tells the story not of what works, but rather of what doesn't work But the whole point of this chapter is that you've got to start out by discovering what's not working.

So it might be well to set a goal for the outcome of this chapter:

You can maximize the effectiveness of your company only if you maximize the effectiveness of everyone in it. You can do some of that with good training programs, but most of it you'll have to do by changing the system. And changing the system means changing the culture along the lines we've set out for you in this book.

DON'T LEAVE OUT THE HUMAN FACTOR

As they've moved towards a high tech environment, all too many companies have completely ignored the other half of a necessary balance — high touch. They're quite willing to change the equipment they're using, or the way they organize the system in a technical sense — creating better work flow patterns, and so forth. But they don't give much thought to making the company a better place for people to work in, even though people who don't like where they're working don't do a good job. So the human factor must be dealt with just as effectively as the systems, the machines, the accounts and the strategic plans. Overlooking the human factor still continues to be the costliest mistake organizations make.

One manager told us he thought the turf wars and other fear-driven behavior in his company consumed about eighty percent of its productivity. "And we're pretty good — we're one of the better companies," he said. "Some places it's bound to be true that over ninety-five percent of all the energy they've got they spend on in-fighting about trivial issues."

It's important to clear up a misconception about management right at this point. You can improve any company in the world if you find that nothing much is happening and you set up a program that frightens and brutalizes everyone. People will always work harder if they're being frightened and brutalized than if they're essentially sitting around doing nothing — or the minimum they can get away with. That's why when nothing else is happening, it works, sometimes astonishingly well. And it's easy.

The trouble is, the kind of management style that brings out the best in everyone works at least ten times better. More and more business leaders are coming to understand that their organizations will not survive and thrive under the old punishing patriarchal command and control management model.

THE TERROR OF SPEAKING OUT

At one of our recent corporate trainings, a foreman began to speak out on some issues important to him. He felt that management had treated employees badly in several crucial situations, and this was affecting the attitudes of workers. As he spoke he trembled, and beads of sweat dripped from his forehead. Clearly this anxiety didn't come from nervousness about public speaking. It came from a very deep rooted fear of reprisal for speaking out at all.

Later, when some of the managers came into our workshop and began to air their views, they immediately confirmed what had troubled him so deeply. Clearly they cared little for the people who did the work — their concern was getting the work done. That's the way of many corporations, where managers mistakenly assume that how people are treated is not related to their efficiency. The paradox is, of course, that the work gets done better, in a more timely fashion, and more efficiently if you care about the people who do it. Still, without pressure from above it would be a long time before these managers would start thinking that way.

In such cases it's devastatingly clear that few will be willing to own up to what conditions are really like. Emphatically, such failures begin with a CEO who callously disregards what it takes to improve productivity. For in a place where everyone hates the work environment, both profits and quality run downhill — gradually at first, and then in a landslide that ends in a buyout or Chapter 11.

WHEN FEAR IS JUSTIFIED

There is no denying that the fearfulness of employees in poorly functioning organizations has a sound basis in reality. When even major blue chip companies are laying off thousands of workers and the news is full of plant closings and downsizings, it doesn't take a social scientist to see that job security is at risk almost everywhere. We have a paradoxical situation in an economy where unemployment is at an all time low, but where the standard of living is falling. For too many employees there's nowhere to go but down, and that provokes a great deal of fear.

However, we found a powerful antidote to this. In one major corporation we trained a leadership group in a learning process that made it possible for them to substantially increase their work effectiveness on the job. Even though all the people in that group were in an unstable work situation and could literally expect pink slips at any moment, their fear for their job security disappeared almost completely because they knew that their value as workers was increasing, and that if they lost their jobs they could easily get better ones either in their present organization or in another one.

And that makes a point that we'll return to again and again in this book: creating a high performance learning organization is the most effective and sustainable investment an organization can possibly make. You can tell when really effective development and training is happening, because when you're using it, you'll see rapid and dramatic across-the-board changes in the performance of eighty percent of the workers who go through the training and development programs. The other twenty percent may need to consider career changes for themselves.

Jobs are most in peril in organizations that fail to grow, where the contribution, the potential, and even the responsibility of individuals in the organization is stunted. It's a vicious cycle, a downward spiral: the very same fearfulness that cripples a company's growth also prevents it from applying the remedies that might restore it to health.

When employees fear making suggestions that would improve the company because others who have tried have ended up on the street job hunting, the company itself is already in a dangerous situation. When employees sense that it's unsafe to express themselves or develop their unique talents, because they never know for sure what management will or will not tolerate from them, then management has already diminished the productivity and profitability of its work force.

INSTITUTIONS AT CROSS PURPOSES WITH THEMSELVES

The same insidious drift occurs when employees fear that the end result of their best efforts will be to work themselves out of a job. This can be, and often is, an accurate reflection of a fearfulness and lack of vision or purpose at the top of an organization. An amusing book on organizations, *The Institutional Imperative*,[3] argues that their primary purpose is to insure the continuation of their existence. This paradox is inherent in the evolution of many organizations. If the organization succeeds in solving the problem it was created to solve, it will bring about its own demise. Therefore, to avoid committing suicide, the organization must do everything possible to seem as if it were moving towards a solution, when in fact it is deliberately muddying the water in order to keep the solution at bay.

This is just as true of divisions within organizations. If you know your job will be eliminated once you've solved a problem, you're bound to exert a great deal of intellectual effort in *seeming* to solve the problem while not really doing so. It's a game some learn to play with gusto, developing great skill at the sleight of hand that suggests progress without delivering results.

The inevitable end result of this charade is of course the demise of the organization. Since organizations are made up of people, they rarely die a painless death. They're more like the cartoon characters that run straight off a cliff, and continue on for an illusory moment before they fall, screaming and protesting futilely.

The way out of this paradox is not to work less well, but to enlarge the job by redefining the work of the organization. While fearful workers may decrease their effectiveness, hoping to make the work last longer, intelligent ones will seek to make themselves more valuable to the organization, in order to increase the probability they'll be kept on after the downsizing is over. Unfortunately, when leadership is afraid of removing its blinders, it cannot be very helpful to those who seek to add value to their work, and may even imperil them for doing so.

One of the obvious corrections that management will have to make is to build trust with all its employees, and one way of doing this is to show how when they've eliminated their jobs by improving the efficiency of the system, the result is always that they end up in much better jobs as a reward for their success. It's truly amazing how many people in top management don't understand this simple cause and effect relationship. That may be because they're so attuned to technology that they think their employees are simply another form of technology, to be plugged in or discarded like computers, and it never occurs to them that corporate employees need the same kinds of things that everyone else in the world needs. Those things are generally subsumed under the category of TLC (tender loving care). Good managers should learn what all good gardeners have always known: You can't make a plant grow faster by pulling on it.

SOME PEOPLE JUST HATE CHANGE

Some people, even when the necessity for change is inescapably bearing down upon them, react like deer caught in the headlights of an oncoming car. They may know what they have to do, but they are too terrified to move. Perhaps they're afraid they won't be able to adjust to the new order, or that they will have to work harder.

Whatever the case, they are motivated to fend off real progress, while seeming all the while to promote it. Only when the organization has been transformed to the point of supporting the unique quality of their performance can they be won over to support that of others. For then change will no longer threaten as it used to. At least, this is the transformation we've seen emerge from our trainings in a great many people, including many conservatives with well-earned reputations for fighting change.

THE FEAR OF ACCOUNTABILITY

For some, fear is due not so much to the prospect of change as to the idea of accountability itself. The danger of being caught deters them from wanting to be held accountable; too many times they've already been made to feel like fools, and they don't want it to happen again.

Such fear may be present even when nothing external seems to be causing it. Guilt and shame, stemming from childhood experiences, may seriously erode a person's self-confidence, particularly in the case of those who have grown up in learning situations that overemphasized mistakes.

Many people have come to associate errors with punishment. But error, when it is part of the exploratory process (as it must occasionally be) should be accepted and valued as a learning opportunity. So the reflex to protect themselves keeps many otherwise highly competent people from examining their mistakes and learning important lessons. If accountability only invites punishment, who needs it?

Fearful people, even when told they have permission to fail, are understandably suspicious and may be reluctant to give up old habits. Habits bred from fear are very hard to break, even when one wants to break them. Just as starving people must be fed a carefully supervised diet in order to recover, so people who feel that they've always been manipulated will take a long time to trust a management that's decided to do an about-face.

THE INSIDIOUS EFFECT OF DENIAL

In the scenarios we're describing, denial is omnipresent. Management insists things are fine (except, of course, that the workers aren't any good, and you can't hire effective labor anymore). "Why can't you teach the guys on the floor to turn off the equipment when they know it's breaking down?" one CEO asked us. The answer is, you've got to care about your job before you can be persuaded to do things like that. Until then, your mind will be focused almost entirely on the time card you're punching.

And so while managers publicly deprecate their employees' efforts, workers privately complain and sometimes even express their discontent to outsiders. Until the folks at the top read the handwriting on the wall and decide it's time to develop a clear and honest picture of how employees feel and how current management is affecting them, there's almost no hope of diverting the organization's collision course with disaster.

But management usually just keeps plugging away as if nothing were wrong. It would be laughable, if it weren't pathetic, to witness the pep talks, motivational posters, and empty corporate vision and mission statements that seek to create a fantasy of excellence everyone knows is a joke. Such half measures only worsen the situation, underscoring as they do the disparity between what should be and what is.

WHAT SHALL WE DO ABOUT MANAGEMENT?

As Philip B. Crosby writes in his book, *Quality Is Free*: "When it comes to the responsibility for managing a company or a function, you have to be prepared to admit that some of the problems might be caused by the individuals responsible for that management. Otherwise corrective action will never happen."[4]

In other words, if you're in charge, assume you've made mistakes that have the effect of stifling or intimidating the people working for you — and find out what these mistakes are. This can be difficult, because a great many workers choose to take offense at things managers do without ever airing their gripes. Instead they carry around a chip on their shoulder that may last for months. In the end, it may have been only an unfortunate misunderstanding that could easily have been cleared up that was the cause of the problem.

Since in cases like this, people are afraid to tell you what you did to offend them, you might have to hire a detective. There are plenty of consultants around willing to play that role, but don't pick one that will only mollify your feelings and help you further shut your eyes to everything that's going on under your nose. Pick someone who will help your group learn the communications skills they need to tell each other how they feel about what's been happening. To get real communication going, you'll have to get rid of the hidden agendas — and even the perception that there might be hidden agendas. Sometimes that can be quite a challenge.

TAKING RESPONSIBILITY IS KEY

"Improvement itself," Crosby goes on to say, "is never the real difficulty. Once individuals recognize and agree on their position, it is never difficult to improve. The unfortunate part is that very few of us own up."[5]

Accountability is usually at the core of any success in the workplace. But in the current social climate it's not easy to be reflective about yourself and, particularly, to own up to what's happening in your bailiwick. "CYA," shorthand for "cover your anatomy," is the rule throughout much of the corporate scene. The corollary is that errors are concealed, explained away, and left to fester until the problem becomes so critical it can't any longer be swept under the rug. Meanwhile, the person who was responsible for creating such a climate is usually crafty enough to have transferred into another job and can thus afford to ignore the whole mess.

HOW LARGE GROUPS AVOID ACCOUNTABILITY

One of us was recently conducting a training for a Fortune 100 company, addressing the issue of responsibility. The consensus of the twenty-five participants, who represented a broad cross section of 42,000 employees, was that taking responsibility was pretty much a joke, and that CYA had been on the rise for a long time, until it had virtually become the norm within the company.

Habits of blame and self-justification only increase the paranoia within organizations. Together they become a negative force that can undermine the whole working environment. They subtly numb the ability of employees to work effectively and efficiently, destroying their capacity for teamwork, as well as their ability to trust.

TWO KINDS OF PEOPLE

When it comes to taking responsibility there are basically two kinds of people. The first has a remarkably convincing excuse for not doing something — an excuse that's thoroughly believable and persuades you that the thing absolutely could not have been done.

The second type of person, however, may have an equally valid, convincing, and acceptable excuse, but gets the thing done anyway — even though it was clearly quite impossible to have done it. For example, one of us once was waiting to receive a package that had been shipped through the Port of New York. The trouble was that the package was somewhere among a pile of such packages about ten feet high and two miles long that had been stranded there by a dock strike. But the manager on duty knew how much the package was needed, and therefore, against all conceivable odds, succeeded in finding it. As for getting the package past the picket line, suffice it to say, where there's a will, there's a way.

It is this kind of problem-solving-no-matter-what orientation that any self-respecting corporation would like to have as part of its culture.

ORGANIZATIONAL ACCOUNTABILITY

In order to acquire such exceptional loyalty, however, an organization, far from manifesting wanton disregard for both human and business values, must exhibit a sense of accountability throughout its entire structure. This organizational accountability is much more than just public relations. You can verify the consistency of its performance any time you want, by noticing how anyone connected with the organization behaves. You can see it when the Federal Express person comes to call, or when you place your order at McDonald's. You always know exactly what kind of quality you're going to get.

The second kind of accountability, at the organizational level, is of course impossible without the first kind, on the individual level. Organizational accountability is the more powerful, however, since it is a systematic way of bringing everyone up to the same high standards. Such an organization often actually ennobles the people who work for it. They respond, in turn, with a tremendous sense of loyalty to the team of which they are a part.

JUST HOW GOOD IS YOUR WORD?

A reputation for accountability doesn't come ready made. You acquire it painstakingly over time as you learn to make a precise equation between word and deed, and to keep all the records you need to verify that if you say something will happen, it actually happens. Too many people think they can say whatever sounds good now, and worry about the consequences later. But true accountability takes commitment. It is the result of a long series of experiences in which you learn to accept reality and come to understand clearly what role you play in its creation.

Accountability of this sort is often not possible without some record-keeping, because you don't really notice what you're doing otherwise. One of us had the experience of being asked by a doctor to keep track of everything eaten for a week. I carried around a little notebook and whenever I took a handful of potato chips I noted the fact. At the end of the week I had formed a completely different picture of my eating habits than the one I'd had before. I started to think long and hard about what I might want to do to change them.

It's interesting that the doctor never asked to see my accounting, nor did I offer it. The experience of record keeping was, by itself, enough to get across what he'd been trying to tell me.

Organizations are filled with loopholes and bottlenecks that people have stopped noticing. Keeping track of what really goes on will often reveal that good intentions are simply not enough. In order to get the job done properly, you have to notice every aspect of the process.

Noticing what's really happening in a process may sometimes require you to step out of the shoes of Scotland Yard and pick up Holmes' magnifying glass. A friend was asked by the National Zoo in Washington to determine why whenever they brought in a captive three-toed sloth it died. He began by studying the diet of the animal. The sloth was being fed exactly what it ate in the wild, the leaves of a tree in which it slumbered so ubiquitously. Our friend finally discovered, however, that the dietary experts were ignoring the fact that this particular type of tree was usually overrun with ants, and that the ants were the source of protein in the sloth's diet. In the minds of the dietitians, the ants had simply been something that wasn't supposed to be there.

Corporations, like animals, live on diets whose make-up may not always be obvious. Sometimes the things that aren't supposed to be there are the very things that make all the difference. We've noticed, for example, that hotels have caught on to the fact that people love to steal the soaps and take them home to their loved ones. So there's been a major cut-back on the amenities you can find in hotel rooms. What's being cut from the budget is the little bit of advertising that occurs when someone who was never at the hotel makes use of the soap back home. Sometimes a budget cut can turn out to be very costly, but unfortunately the accountants may have failed to see the big picture.

THE IMPULSE TO DUCK RESPONSIBILITY

All too often, accountability is viewed as something that applies to others rather than oneself. And yet it's amazing how free you feel when you know you can make yourself personally accountable for what you do — or, even better, that you're part of an organization which can guarantee its accountability.

Still, most people would prefer not to ask, "What am I doing to limit the success of this organization?" They'd rather pretend the whole thing is the fault of some individual in control, the whole group, or the system itself. Nor do most of us like to face the possibility that we might benefit from doing things differently.

Therefore, the behavior we observe in others can be sorted into three broad categories: responsibility, blaming others, and justifying one's own position

Responsibility requires facing the implications of your behavior head on; the other two paths are attempts to get the "monkey" off your back by not owning up.

Responsibility suggests you're taking an active lead in making things work the way they should. Its cousin, accountability, is your willingness to say exactly what happened and what can be done about it. Both must permeate the organization so much that they become the personal concern of all participants, not just a select few.

A note of caution here, however, prompted by our experience with a CEO client who'd suddenly found a way to avoid a six month delay in getting a project started. The turn-around was exhilarating, but we're wondering whether this isn't just an example of the addictive pull of crisis management: let the problem develop first until it becomes agonizing. Then become the knight on the white horse who gallops in to the rescue at the last minute. There's little glory, unfortunately, in building a system that works to prevent such problems, except, of course, the glory of pushing the bottom line up abnormally high abnormally fast.

THE REWARDS OF ACCOUNTABILITY

When a person or system learns to act at all times on the basis of accountability, what can we expect?

Self-validation and recognition (the clear understanding that one's own performance is valuable and valued) — This includes the "self" of the individual as well as of the whole system. It's an opportunity to tell yourself and the groups you work with what you've accomplished. Self-validation is a celebration of accomplishments, in which the story of your achievement plays a central role. Thus, accountability sets the stage for reward and recognition.

With the establishment of a learning culture in which people react to situations positively, the habit of accounting for your own actions not only makes it possible to know what's needed for improvement, but also helps you get recognition for what you've achieved. It's like keeping track of the money you've got in the bank, especially when your balance is continuously growing at a favorable rate. All this, by empowering the system you're part of, adds further to your self-esteem.

An increase in everyone's power — Clarity is power. Accountability makes it possible to be clear about what's happening in the work situation. If everyone is clear, there will be no more of the kinds of surprises and rude awakenings that breed an atmosphere of helplessness. No longer will you have to live with that nagging fear of discovery of what you've been struggling so long to hide. If you know you're not supposed to use the office phone to make long distance calls to your significant other, and you respect that, you won't have to worry about having your career ruined by being cited on an ethics charge.

An increase in personal integrity — Personal integrity can be a problem in any organization, and everyone knows that it can't be legislated. But the culture of the organization — the degree to which individual responsibility is respected — can go a long way toward encouraging or discouraging personal integrity. A culture that recognizes and rewards personal accountability and responsibility is much more likely to promote integrity than one that inspires fear and evasiveness.

Such clarity is vital for the continued adjustments that have to be made to keep a project on the track of continuous improvement. Accountability helps keep the project on its toes, away from the traps of excessive comfort and complacency. When you're not keeping all the defects a secret, but are routinely facing and correcting them, you know you're progressing towards a conclusion that has complete integrity — a full solution to the problem you're paid to solve. Such clarity is a key ingredient in protecting projects from early retirement.

When the habit of accountability is clearly encouraged, and people are committed to it, the energy of mutual cooperation among workers will be self-renewing. The result will be a self-motivating synergy that generates its own positive force. Of course, this won't happen until fear and threat have been expunged from the system.

THE ROOTS OF QUALITY

What's at stake here is **continuous improvement**, which requires continuous learning — the habitual expectation of an organization and the individuals in it that everything, no matter what, can be improved, and that the process of improvement is one of the most interesting, challenging and ennobling enterprises in which one can participate.

Unfortunately, in the U.S. at any rate, too few people have much experience in thinking this way. The trouble begins in school, where we're asked to get our work in on time and learn what we did wrong, but seldom to do it over and over again until it's just right. It's only in the "frills" of our academic experience that we're likely to encounter situations which encourage us to think in these terms.

WHERE CONTINUOUS IMPROVEMENT IS TAKEN SERIOUSLY

Continuous improvement and continuous learning are often practiced, for example, in coaching athletic teams, and music, drama and art lessons, but it is almost never practiced in the mainstream academic activity of the school. On the soccer field or in the art room you work for hours, days, weeks, months and years to improve your skill, developing a personal style and performance.

In the academic classroom, however, this attitude is likely to be foreign. Even skills like reading and writing are expected to develop under conditions that seldom involve understanding precisely how you are operating so you can revise your operations for greater effectiveness.

HOW THE ORCHESTRA AND SOCCER TEAM SUCCEED
WHERE CLASSROOMS FAIL

In "Organizational Learning: A Review of the Literature with Implications for HRD Professionals," Prof. Nancy M. Dixon clarifies this point with some interesting examples. An orchestra or sports team must depend on the performance of the entire group, not just on isolated individuals, to succeed. Furthermore, the organization shares and preserves knowledge, skills, attitudes — a culture — even though individual members may come and go. Nevertheless, as individuals become functioning participants in the group, they internalize that culture and give it life.

Prof. Dixon quotes another observer who notes that "Each individual must generate an image of the cooperative system on which his or her own performance depends .... Intelligent action depends on a continuing mutual adjustment of individual behaviors, one to another. Their organizing depends, in turn, on each person's image of the larger system. In this sense, the organization exists in its members' heads."[6]

ESTABLISHING THE POSITION FROM WHICH TO MOVE AHEAD

How then can an organization put itself on the track to greater accountability, and all the rewards that brings? You can't just appoint a team and ask them to transform the culture, as if you were asking them to repaint the walls. As we said at the beginning of this chapter, the first step is an honest and fearless self-assessment of the climate and culture within the organization. You have to get a clear picture of the current reality before it can be transformed to something else.

Robert Frost once observed that a student is someone who is somewhere and is trying to get somewhere else. An organization, too, if it is to learn, improve, and innovate, must know where it is and where it wants to go. It must know this by the kind of organically developing shared vision we'll be visiting in Step Seven, or knowing it is of no use.

THE FOLKS AT THE TOP HAVE TO DO IT

If change is to occur in the organization, individuals must change. And if the change is to be effective for anyone, everyone must change. So there is no point in even starting to transform your workplace into a Learning Organization unless the leadership volunteers to model, mentor, and guide the kind of culture change they need to create. Here's how Therese Welter describes the behavior of a CEO at the beginning of her article, "A Winning Team Begins with You":

> Roger Milliken stood on a chair in front of 300 managers at Milliken & Co. Inc.'s annual quality meeting, raised his right hand, asked them to raise theirs, and said, *"Repeat after me: I will listen. I will not shoot the messenger. I recognize that management is the problem."*[7]

Ron Heidke, then head of manufacturing at Kodak, displayed enlightened managerial behavior when he said to the Learning Leaders (the self-managed team at Kodak that we had trained in innovative educational techniques which we describe in Step Six):

> Your job is to create a business for yourselves. You must create an excellent product. You must sell it to the various divisions that need it, by persuading them of the value of what you have to offer. You must organize your business so it is profitable.
>
> I could force the divisions to take the MRPII course you are offering, but that would not be a good idea. I want the need that I know is there to pull on the excellence of the product you are creating. I know how well you can do, and I intend to support you. But I'm not going to do it for you. You are a self-managed team, and you will do it for yourselves.

And they went on to become the most successful and efficient self-managed team of their type in Kodak history, a tribute to the brilliant planning Heidke had brought to the project. So effective were they, in fact, that while most self-managed teams at Kodak took from a year to a year and a half to get up to speed, this one was up to speed and doing business well within three months.

GOOD MANAGERS ARE ALL DIFFERENT AND ALL ALIKE

So a good manager need not *make* things happen, and probably shouldn't. What a good manager should do is like what a good mother does: Be there, listen, advise, coach, teach, and believe very deeply that your people are capable of excellence. Some mothers are ham actors and some are strong silent types, but good mothers have complete integrity in the style with which they mother, and the same is true of good managers. Believe in the high quality of your people, and believe in the brilliance of the result they can achieve. Let them know you believe it. Then they will give it to you.

That's the kind of inspiration top management will have to provide if the Ten Step Process is to work. It may jump on chairs, shout from rooftops, and in numerous other ways make itself ubiquitous and obnoxious, saying in effect that it's going to back the program 100% of the way and nobody gets off the hook. Or it may very quietly, but very knowledgeably and confidently announce, as Ron Heidke did, that excellence is expected, that quality is to be a given, and that the team will get whatever support from top management it may need to turn its objectives into reality.

But anything less than total support, whatever its style may be, will only turn the Ten Step Process into the next fad, the next Flavor of the Month, another boondoggle that didn't work. Then management will scratch its head and look for something else, much as alchemists of old sought the philosopher's stone. The trouble is, there isn't time to keep trying out new approaches in the half-hearted way that guarantees failure. The world is now moving too fast for that.

GET OUT THE MATCH BOOK

So if you're going to get your organization off dead center and transform it into a Learning Organization, light a fire under the president or CEO (particularly if that person happens to be you) and insist that whatever is going to happen be modeled first from the top, and that the whole process be demonstrated with complete integrity — for mere lip service will guarantee the failure of any process, project or program.

We've watched one CEO move from being an obstreperous and rather abrasive leader who had to begin his tenure by firing a lot of people to becoming the one in the company who, during a meeting is quieter than anyone else, and pipes up only occasionally to make a suggestion to get things off dead center, or to express enthusiasm about what's going on. Everyone feels comfortable in his presence, because they know he not only expects them to do their best, he's going to give them every kind of support they might need to do it.

In sharp contrast, a friend of ours in a manufacturing corporation is forever complaining about the quality program in his division. "I'm personally committed to quality," he says. "I feel it's the most important thing we can do. But the guys who are running the program treat it like a joke. They make pronouncements and don't follow through on them. They seem to think if they say something, we'll automatically do it. But then if we don't, they just shrug it off and behave as if nothing had happened." Our friend was personally wounded by this because he cared about the program and wanted it to work.

So he deeply resented the casual attitude management took towards its responsibility.

Thus the commitment of top management to change everything for the better is necessary in order that a new kind of management performance can set the standard for change in everyone else. It's also important, of course, that management know what "better" means, because severe disagreements about this can be fatal to the culture.

Only if top management sets the example of change will everyone else be inspired to follow. In addition, the change from the top must be real and believable, or the entire organization will dismiss it as hollow and superficial. In this respect, top management must have the gift of a great football coach, a great actor, or a great sales person. It must speak convincingly from the heart and be believed. ("Why should I do it if they're not going to?" is transformed into, "If it's good enough for them it must be good enough for me.") Quality expert Chuck Roe believes the CEO must be the lead trainer in the business for this very reason. Jim Kouzes book, *Credibility,* addresses this very issue of conflicts between what is being said and what is actually being done by today's leaders.[8]

STARTING THE ASSESSMENT

Up to this point our observations have necessarily been rather generalized and abstract. Now comes your opportunity, and our invitation, to make it more concrete and specific to your own organization. We call it the *Learning Organization Assessment.*

The *Assessment* included below is the first version of the assessment we originally developed for our clients. It proved to be one of the most popular features in the first edition of the book. Subsequently, we found that a more comprehensive assessment was needed to provide a clearer picture of the current state of an organization, in order to make the development of specific learning strategies more efficient and effective. The enhanced *Assessment* has 68 statements. It also allows users to easily cross-reference each of the statements with the Ten Steps. The results provide a matrix of which of the Ten Steps will most benefit your organization. It provides a clearer starting point, and a better map to needed change.[9] The version offered here will give readers a sampling of the questions in the *Assessment* and a taste of the process they are intended to initiate.

The thirty-six statements below could be read as at least a partial description of a Learning Organization, and the attitudes and behaviors associated with it. This *Assessment* asks you to think about the current reality of your own organization, or one of its subgroups, and to make a judgment about how well each statement describes it.

Naturally your judgments will be subjective, and you may find that the statements themselves raise questions of definition. Nevertheless, we expect it will not be difficult for anyone to complete this *Assessment*. In fact, we would be surprised if you did not find this activity both easy and interesting.

We've found when we've used this assessment that we're usually working in an organization that has already been through several assessments. We explain that ours is different because it's designed to look for what most needs to be changed in the culture in order to make the culture more effective — a necessary first step prior to any other changes. When one CEO, on learning that we were in the middle of analyzing the results of this assessment, looked us in the eye and said, "Why are you wasting time with this?" we immediately pointed out to him that we couldn't possibly help his organization function better if we didn't understand the nature of its weaknesses.

We find that the assessment produces a very useful profile of an organization. The overall assessment may produces a result that's fairly flat — about the same average responses on all the questions — or it may show deep hills and valleys. If it's flat, then you need to work straight through the Ten Steps from One to Ten. But if you're seeing a very strong showing on Steps One through Three, and everything caves in on Four, then you know that most of the work has to be done on making risk taking safe.

We've found the assessment pretty reliable at showing up the kinds of problems people in the organization have been complaining about, but in the process it also diagnoses where the problems are coming from, which makes it a lot easier to do something about them. At the same time, identifying and appreciating strengths is an instructive and beneficial part of the process.

If you think the statements generate more questions than answers, that's fine. Those questions are likely to turn out to be very productive. We suggest you keep them in mind as you proceed through the Ten Steps. Or you may feel that compared to some other organization or group, yours should be more highly rated than your response implies. That's fine too. But for the moment, we are asking only for your own opinion of your present environment.

Individual Assessments are bound to differ, and these differences can be very instructive. So we will suggest ways in which the differences that emerge between individuals and among different groups within the organization, can be used to help you evaluate your enterprise as a Learning Organization, and to help the organization as a whole to make better decisions about what to change and how to change it.

LEARNING ORGANIZATION ASSESSMENT

Using the response options below, write in the blank before each statement the number which best describes your answer.

Response Options:

        1 = Not at all

        2 = To a slight extent

        3 = To a moderate extent

        4 = To a great extent

        5 = To a very great extent

The current reality in my organization is that:

____ 1. People feel free to speak their minds about what they have learned. There is no fear, threat or repercussion for disagreeing or dissenting.

____ 2. Mistakes made by individuals or departments are turned into constructive learning experiences.

____ 3. There is a general feeling that it's always possible to find a better way to do something.

____ 4. Multiple viewpoints and open productive debates are encouraged and cultivated.

____ 5. Experimentation is endorsed and championed, and is a way of doing business.

____ 6. Mistakes are clearly viewed as positive growth opportunities throughout the system.

____ 7. There is willingness to break old patterns in order to experiment with different ways of organizing and managing daily work.

____ 8. Management practices are innovative, creative, and periodically risk-taking.

____ 9. The quality of work life in our organization is improving.

____ 10. There are formal and informal structures designed to encourage people to share what they learn with their peers and the rest of the organization.

____ 11. The organization is perceived as designed for problem-solving and learning.

____ 12. Learning is expected and encouraged across all levels of the organization: management, employees, supervision, union, stockholders, customers.

____ 13. People have an overview of the organization beyond their specialty and function, and adapt their working patterns to it.

____ 14. "Lessons learned" sessions are conducted so as to produce clear, specific and permanent structural and organizational changes.

_____ 15. Management practices, operations, policies and procedures that become obsolete by hindering the continued growth of people and the organization are removed and replaced with workable systems and structures.

_____ 16. Continuous improvement is expected and treated receptively.

_____ 17. There are clear and specific expectations of each employee to receive a specified number of hours of training and education annually.

_____ 18. Workers at all levels are specifically directed towards relevant and valuable training and learning opportunities — inside and outside the organization.

_____ 19. Cross-functional learning opportunities are expected and organized on a regular basis, so that people understand the functions of others whose jobs are different, but of related importance.

_____ 20. Middle managers are seen as having the primary role in keeping the learning process running smoothly throughout the organization.

_____ 21. The unexpected is viewed as an opportunity for learning.

_____ 22. People look forward to improving their own competencies as well as those of the whole organization.

_____ 23. The systems, structures, policies and procedures of the organization are designed to be adaptive, flexible, and responsive to internal and external stimuli.

_____ 24. Presently, even if the environment of the organization is complicated, chaotic, and active, nevertheless it is not on overload.

_____ 25. There is a healthy, manageable level of stress that assists in promoting learning.

_____ 26. Continuous improvement is practiced as well as preached.

_____ 27. The difference between training/education and learning is clearly understood. (Training and education can be so conducted that no learning takes place.)

_____ 28. People are encouraged and provided the resources to become self-directed learners.

_____ 29. There is a formal, on-going education program to prepare middle managers in their new roles as teachers, coaches and leaders.

_____ 30. Recognition of your own learning style and those of co-workers is used to improve communication and over-all organizational learning.

_____ 31. Management is sensitive to learning and development differences in their employees, realizing that people learn and improve their situations in many different ways.

_____ 32. There is sufficient time scheduled into people's professional calendars to step back from day-to-day operations and reflect on what is happening in the organization.

_____ 33. There is direction and resource allocation planned to bring about meaningful and lasting learning.

___ 34. Teams are recognized and rewarded for their innovative and paradigm breaking solutions to problems.

___ 35. Managers have considerable skills for gathering information and developing their abilities to cope with demanding and changing management situations.

___ 36. Managers enable their staffs to become self-developers, and learn how to improve their performance.

EVALUATING THE RESULTS

The results of this *Assessment* can be compiled, analyzed, and used in several ways. The quickest is a simple results average, dividing the sum of all the ratings by 36, the number of statements. This average indicates, on a scale of 1-5, the degree to which the respondent believes his or her organization possesses the characteristics of a Learning Organization.

However, it is our experience — and the premise of this book — that a Learning Organization has certain mutually interdependent attributes which can be identified, and can be developed step by step. With that in mind, we have constructed a *Matrix* (see below) which suggests how the issues raised in the *Assessment* are related to the Ten Step process leading to the emergence and success of a Learning Organization.

USING THE MATRIX

We have not attempted to make the *Matrix* a precise instrument.[10] That would not be possible in such a short space, and with so much room for individual variations in responding to the *Assessment*. Instead the *Matrix* is designed, first, to give an overview of — and stimulate discussion about — many of the major issues which must be addressed by any group on its way to becoming a Learning Organization. Second, it shows which of the Ten Steps applies to the issues raised by each statement (and where, in this book, the reader can find material relevant to those issues). Again, this should not be interpreted in a cut and dried manner, because the Steps are all interdependent, and cannot be fully implemented in isolation from each other. Third, the results suggest where the organization (as currently viewed by individuals or groups within or outside it) is currently weak or strong, and which of the Ten Steps may be particularly useful to it. Applied again at a later date, the *Matrix* can serve as a yardstick for measuring changes over time.

With these qualifications in mind, the reader can take the *Matrix* as a preview and a pointer to some of the highlights of the Ten Step process. Filling it out is a simple matter: enter in the white boxes to the left of each of the 36 items from the *Assessment* the rating for that item (as scored by an individual, a sub-group, or the organization as a whole). The same score is to be entered in each white box to the left of that item. For instance, if the response was "3" on the first item, a "3" would be entered in the columns under Steps 1, 3, and 4. The respondent's assessment of the organization's rating for each of the Ten Steps is found by totaling the sum of the numbers in each vertical column and dividing it by the number of white boxes in that column.

LEARNING FROM THE DIFFERENCES

As we said earlier, it is to be expected that the culture of the organization will be assessed differently by different groups and members of the organization. That is actually one of the most important benefits of the *Assessment*. The differences in perception can be as significant as the perceptions themselves, for they offer sharp insights into what is really going on in the organization — insights that can be the foundation for new growth and strength. And of course it goes almost without saying that you're not going to get any reliable information about these issues unless the answers to the questions are submitted anonymously and it's impossible to tell who said what.

Suppose, for example, the *Assessment* shows that top executives believe people are free to speak their minds, and other employees believe that in doing so they are putting themselves at risk (item 1). Without being melodramatic about it, it's not hard to see how such a difference of opinion could drastically undermine morale and productivity. This disagreement presents the organization as a whole with a valuable opportunity to clarify its policies and its priorities, and to make sure they are understood and shared from top to bottom.

So a crucial part of the *Assessment* is to insure that these disagreements be recognized, in order that their implications can be explored for the benefit of the organization. This is in fact a vital part of the learning that will transform it into a Learning Organization. The Assessment can answer essential questions, and raise some new ones:

What is the spread of attitudes throughout all members of the organization on each issue in the questionnaire?

How does that spread shift as we move from top management to middle management to white collar workers to blue collar workers to customers and to vendors? Also, how does it differ among the various divisions and functions in the organization? You're likely to find, for example, that the culture in some of your divisions or departments is very different indeed from that in others.

Where are the points of greatest difference between these groups, and what can we learn from these differences?

PUBLISHING THE RESULTS

When the results of the *Assessment* have been obtained, they can then be published so that this information is clearly stated and widely understood. In addition, a summary report may be published that captures the essence of the cultural information revealed, and all members of the organization can then be assessed again to determine the degree of their accord with the summary report.

We've found it a good practice not only to publish the report, but to have outside consultants present it to the entire organization or division in such a way that questions and comments are invited after each section is read. This not only clarifies possible misunderstandings, but makes everyone in the organization feel more actively a part of the assessment process.

A REPORT ON THE DESIRED LEARNING CULTURE

The results of the Assessment can be used to powerful effect even before consensus is reached on all issues arising from it. For example, if there's a widespread belief that the current culture does not sufficiently support risk-taking, then a report could be published dealing with this issue head on, committing the new learning culture to make risk-taking easier at every level of the enterprise. You'll find that such a report may be greeted with a good deal of skepticism. Some people don't want to believe that change is possible, because they don't want to hope that things will get better and then be disappointed when they don't. So you could have some problems winning the necessary trust to reduce the amount of risk in the environment. You'll have to be humble about that, and patient, as you do the things that will eventually bring about the change. Sometimes changes occur only after you've become certain that they won't. Unless, that is, you already have a culture that's very far along and doing well.

Focusing on areas of agreement, while suspending for the time too much discussion of disagreement, may help to bring people together towards common goals. The report need not spell out a plan to reach the goal. When President Kennedy said we'd land on the moon within the decade, he didn't presume to know how we'd do it. If the goal is definitely clear, and shared by the whole organization, the means can be developed later.

It is also not necessary or even feasible to agree on a complete set of goals before setting out to realize some goals that are widely endorsed. It is possible to make many effective changes in an organization without having established the final vision that everyone is expected to share. Nearly all organizations are seeking to develop many general qualities, such as better communication and teamwork, that do not require a fully developed vision to be perceived as beneficial.

However, what is critical to the development of a Learning Organization at this stage is focusing not on the cures, but on the diagnosis. When there is wide agreement and clarity about the assessment, the organization is ready to proceed to Step Two.

LEARNING ORGANIZATION

STEPS:

	1	2	3	4	5	6	7	8	9	10
	Assessment	Promote Positive	Safe Thinking	Risk Taking	People as Resources	Learning Power	Map the Vision	Model the Vision	Systems Thinking	Get Show On The Road

Enter Assessment Rating for Each Item	ASSESSMENT ITEMS
	1. People speak their minds
	2. Learn from mistakes
	3. People see better ways
	4. Different views encouraged
	5. Experimentation encouraged
	6. Mistakes are opportunities
	7. Willing to try new ways
	8. Management takes risks
	9. Work life improving
	10. Learn from each other
	11. Structured for learning
	12. Learn across all levels
	13. Awareness beyond speciality
	14. "Lessons learned" sessions
	15. Obsolete practices replaced
	16. Improvement expected
	17. Employees training expected
	18. All get relevant training

The **Learning Organization Assessment Matrix** can be filled in after the **Learning Organization Assessment** on pages 38-40 has been completed. Enter in the white boxes to the left of each of the 36 items the rating for that item (as scored by an individual, a sub-group, or the organization as a whole). The same score is to be entered in each white box to the left of that item. For

ASSESSMENT MATRIX

1	2	3	4	5	6	7	8	9	10	ASSESSMENT ITEMS
										19. Cross-functional learning
										20. Middle managers' key role
										21. Learn from unexpected
										22. Eagerness to improve
										23. Systems are flexible
										24. Not overloading
										25. Stress is manageable
										26. Improvement not just talk
										27. Training may not = learning
										28. Learners self-directed
										29. Middle managers prepared
										30. Learning styles recognized
										31. Learning differences respected
										32. Time for reflection
										33. Resource for learning
										34. Teams rewarded
										35. Managers cope with change
										36. Staff enabled to improve
										Total Overall Score
(10)	(11)	(15)	(13)	(14)	(19)	(6)	(9)	(9)	(7)	**Divide Score by These Numbers**
										Results Average

The heading spanning columns 1–10 reads: *Enter Assessment Rating for Each Item*

instance, if the response was "3" on the first item, a "3" would be entered in the columns under Steps 3 and 4. The respondent's assessment of the organization's overall rating for each of the Ten Steps is found by totalling the sum of the numbers in each vertical column and dividing it by the number of white boxes in that column.

PROMOTE THE POSITIVE

S T E P   2

Having completed the assessment called for in Step One, you should have a clearer picture of where your organization stands. You may also have a clearer picture of how you would like it to be. What remains to be clarified is how to get there from where you are now.

To begin making the changes that will create a Learning Organization, you don't have to import any new technologies or wave some mysterious magic wand. The next step is changing the attitudes and behaviors of people in your organization so they learn to think positively. Without denying reality, they need to switch from describing the glass as half empty to seeing it as half full. At the same time, their behavior towards each other and towards the outside world probably needs to become more positive and supportive.

If that sounds like an impossibly elusive and utopian task, consider the following story:

MAKING CHANGE

One of us had a student who became intrigued by her reading about culture change through modeling — how individual actions change the behavior and culture of a group. She was working at McDonald's at the time, and decided to see whether she could affect the culture there without telling anyone what she was doing.

She wanted to add one action to her job performance that, by shifting people's perceptions of what was happening, could thereby affect the whole system. She made a brilliant choice.

Whenever she gave change to a customer, she cupped the customer's hand in her own left hand, while depositing the change with her right hand. This was a very gentle, quickly completed touch, a human contact that made people feel good. Forgive us for observing that she thereby became a multi-dimensional change manager.

After a while the customers, who had begun to notice an indefinable warmth in dealing with her, began to line up in front of her register even when no one was waiting at the other registers. The other clerks naturally wanted to know what she was doing to provoke this response, so she quickly demonstrated for them her way of giving change. After that all the other clerks also returned change to their customers in this new way.

The restaurant was transformed. The burgers and fries still had the same ingredients, the pace was just as quick. Maybe the food only seemed to taste better. But the atmosphere was certainly improved, interactions among the employees becoming more warm and caring. You could almost see flowers blooming all over the place. Business seemed to be improving, too.

Then a new manager was transferred to that store. It didn't take him long to sense the difference. Experienced as he was with the details of McDonald's procedures, he still could not figure out what made this McDonald's so unlike the one he had just left. The cause was too slight and subtle for him to notice. But the change was clear and dramatic.

WHAT'S THE MESSAGE?

While we could draw several morals from this simple story, we want to emphasize a couple of points that are particularly relevant to the process of creating a Learning Organization. The first has to do with the kind of changes that people can enjoy and are most willing to make.

Why was this small gesture so instantly appreciated by customers, and so readily copied by other employees? Because they all immediately recognized it as a powerful and positive change at the most basic, human level. The message in the gesture could not be translated into words exactly, no matter how profound or how corny the words might be. Yet it was unmistakable.

In fact, it was not a change in procedure. If it were ever to become part of a standardized routine, it would almost certainly lose its convincing warmth and spontaneity and become another empty, commercialized token, the touchy-feely equivalent of the much abused "have a nice day" or the now-vacant grin on those round yellow happy faces.

To both employee and customer, this gesture represented a change not in technique but in attitude. It transformed what had been merely the conclusion of the transaction between them (returning the customer's change), into the affirmation of a momentary, but nevertheless important relationship. A simple task was redefined into an authentic and constructive human interaction.

THE ART OF REFRAMING

Simple and apparently insignificant though it may be, what we have here is a prime example of the art, or skill, of reframing. Reframing is a way of looking at reality that allows you to see things in a new light, to sort out facts and ideas so the positive ones emerge into clarity, while the negatives, though not forgotten, are placed on the back burner.

It's as if you were to put a new frame around a gloomy old picture so you could see its rich colors and shadings, its powerful and positive statement of the beauty of the reality it depicts finally becoming clear. When you reframe something, you're not changing the situation itself — just the qualities of your thinking that surround and help to define the situation.

In Step One we asked you to concentrate on assessment because it brings into focus those areas that need to change. Now comes your opportunity to start the change process. Here you begin by reframing the negatives you found in your assessment — not by solving them, but by seeing in them possibilities for advancement. On many a shop floor, incidentally, we've persuaded people to stop talking about mistakes and talk, instead, about "improvement opportunities." For every crisis is really an opportunity, every mistake a potential learning experience. And fear, when it's healthy, is excitement that hasn't yet discovered the positives in the challenge at hand.

To reframe effectively, a positive attitude is an absolute "must". You can't even think about improving a situation when you're wringing your hands and complaining about how bad everything is. But this frame of mind is not to be confused with blind optimism that denies reality. In other words, we're not asking you to become a Pollyanna in your attitude. We're asking, instead, for a re-viewing of reality — seeing the often hidden opportunities that lie behind a situation that seems to have gone seriously awry.

So the positive thinking we're suggesting looks in two directions at once: at the current reality and the positive outcome that can be developed from it. This double orientation assures that optimism is grounded in reality.

GLOOM ABOUT THE AUDIT

We recently had a vivid experience of the usefulness and power of reframing. In a corporation we were working with, a group was despairing about the audits they had to perform in order to satisfy government regulations. They felt these audits were a waste of time, because the information that was asked for had nothing to do with their needs. All the audit did for the company was tie up staff members with filling out forms that they believed would end up in the kind of file things never come out of.

After exploring the situation together, we discovered matters weren't quite as they first seemed. To begin with, we noticed that the organization was having other kinds of problems, stemming from lack of communication.

"What if you were to regard the audit as a way of collecting information that could be used by the whole company to keep track of what's going on?" we asked.

At first no one thought this would be useful. However, as they continued to explore the matter, these managers began to see things in a different light. Perhaps an audit team could be created to collect all the required information. At the same time it could collect closely related information that would be valuable to everyone in the company.

An audit is a tool for developing an objective, quantifiable picture of the real conditions in the organization, so whatever is amiss can be corrected. Thus an audit team could serve a central coordinating function within the company, helping it keep its various divisions and activities on track, providing a continuous supply of feedback to everyone who might need it. An audit team could function much the way the nervous system does, carrying information between centers of action, while keeping the whole operation properly coordinated. It could, in short, become the "brain" of the organization.

MAKING THE SILK PURSE

As we continued exploring these possibilities, people began to perk up. They began to see how an audit team could answer a crucial need. The lackluster atmosphere in the room changed rather abruptly to a creative one. Everyone was full of ideas about how the team could function. The brainstorming continued for an exhilarating hour.

One insight which quickly emerged was that the audit team should design its own operation based on what it experienced and discovered. So the work of creating the team became simpler than it had first appeared.

When we finished the session, we felt we had a breakthrough that could be of great benefit. This had come from looking in a fresh new way at a tired old problem no one wanted to be bothered with. That's just a sample of the kind of innovation reframing can accomplish when it's properly employed.

HOW LOU HOLTZ GOT HIS BOYS TO BUILD
THEIR OWN MOTIVATIONAL TALK

No one has better demonstrated this skill of transforming a gloomy and foreboding situation into one that can lead to victory than the great football coach, Lou Holtz. Here's a typical example of the way Holtz could alter the attitude of a team by helping them face negatives, reframe them, and thus create a transforming conversation which could electrify their ability to play.

While at Arkansas, [Holtz] noticed that his team lacked confidence for its upcoming battle against Oklahoma in the 1978 Orange Bowl. That wasn't surprising. Oklahoma was favored by 23 points. The media had drubbed Arkansas's chances. Holtz recalls, "The paper said we didn't have a chance in the world, and the team believed it."

Holtz called a team meeting at the Four Seasons Hotel. As the athletes walked in, they were quieter than Holtz had ever heard a team. It was time for the Holtz magic. The coach grabbed that day's newspaper and began to leaf through it. He said, "In any paper, you have a front page for those who want to read the news, comics for those who can't read, editorial page for those who can't think . . ."

He began to carefully fold the paper up into smaller and smaller squares. Then, as he continued talking, he seemed to be ripping the paper apart. ". . . and, you know, it's really amazing that you're going to roll over and die 'cause you read your obituary in the newspaper."

He warned them point-blank: "Don't let people tear you down. Don't let people cause you to lose faith and confidence in yourself and what you're doing."

Then he said, as he unfolded the paper, which was magically all pieced back together with no rips in sight, "If you believe in yourself, it's so easy to lift other people up. You know, you can win this football game if you really have a strong faith and you have a belief. If you believe someone's going to tear you up and you can't put yourself back together" — he showed them the fully reconstructed paper — "you're in real trouble."

His magic act finished, Holtz asked each athlete to stand up and say why he thought Arkansas could win the game. They got up, one by one, and pointed out they had the number-one defense and other pluses. As they talked, "you could see the whole attitude change," Holtz says. They trusted one another. They made a commitment to one another to be the best they could be. Says Holtz, "You could feel the love, trust, and commitment come together. You could tell they cared about one another when they started praising one another, and I'll tell you, it's amazing what happens when you look for something sincerely positive to say about somebody."

The next day, the Arkansas football team had an unbelievable practice. People would later tell Holtz they knew Arkansas would win just by the look on their faces when they ran out of the locker room. They destroyed Oklahoma, 31-6. But it wasn't the coach, Holtz says. "It was a prime example of trust, commitment, and love."[1]

Most motivational speakers merely tell an audience how good they are. What's striking about this story is that Holtz first set the scene by helping his players think about the chance for personal excellence. Once he'd pointed them in the right direction, he shut up and listened. He got them telling *him* why they were good. He set them up to reframe the situation for themselves, and reframe it they did — so well it took them all the way to victory against heavy odds.

This example of imbedding listening in a motivational talk in order to get the team to reframe its dilemma is a powerful illustration of one of the many ways Step Two can be brought to life through action.

You might want to take a leaf out of Holtz's book and see if you can't use questions to bring your followers, friends and colleagues to see something good in a situation that would otherwise leave them feeling down.

WHAT ABOUT YOUR TEAM?

You could argue that Lou Holtz's technique worked fine for a team that was already at championship level. What about a team that is far from successful? Holtz had a strong foundation of success and the positive bonds among his players to build on.

What happens when that positive outlook and cooperative team spirit are missing to start with? In other words, what about the more common situation in which most organizations find themselves? Building this positive outlook should be a primary task of such an organization.

What's required is the transformation of the actual culture and prevailing atmosphere of the organization to one which supports positive personal interactions at all levels. How can this be done?

WHO'S BEST, THE SUN OR THE WIND?

One of Aesop's Fables illustrates a basic principle that applies when you want to change people's behavior. The wind and the sun were arguing about which could be more persuasive. The wind bet that it could persuade a man to take off his coat faster than the sun could. To demonstrate, it blew at the man fiercely — but the harder it blew, the more tightly the poor fellow wrapped his coat around his body. The sun, in its turn, spread its gently warming rays upon the man until he relaxed and unwrapped himself, no longer needing shelter from the wind's freezing blast.

When you push and pull to get a response, you'll get only resistance, says the moral. But when instead you use warmth and kindness, then openness and cooperation will be your reward.

ESTABLISHING A CULTURE OF POSITIVE THINKING

Similarly, we respond more cooperatively when approached with a smile and a handshake than when subjected to indifference, frowns and put downs.

It's certainly easy enough to form the habit of congratulating others on what they've done well instead of chastising them for the mistakes they make. This helps them build confidence, which in turn increases their ability to do well. Most people like to hear at least ten positive comments before they'll be able to respond creatively to a negative one.

People in sales departments understand this well, or they wouldn't be in business. If you don't treat your customers with warmth and respect, they'll go elsewhere. Folks on your staff, your co-workers, and the people who manage you, can't or won't go elsewhere — so it's easy to ignore the fact that they take mental vacations from you when you don't treat them well. Using the same disciplined respect and supportiveness with fellow workers we would use with customers should substantially increase the effectiveness of what we do.

The presently prevailing culture does not readily promote the positive. Sadly, much of what happens on a daily basis in organization is deficit oriented, zeroing in on what is wrong and incorrect. Many times an organization says to its employees, "Be on notice, we will catch you if we can."

To create a culture of positive thinking requires catching people doing positive and beneficial things. It means focusing on the strengths that people exhibit, developing those strengths, and learning how to manage the weaknesses or limitations.

MANIPULATING THE PREVAILING CLIMATE

Managers responsible for the implementation of new projects and products are the ones who can most effectively introduce a new, more positive prevailing climate into the daily work activity. A prevailing climate, by the way, is a group mind set, a collection of beliefs so deeply imbued in the culture that they're viewed by the majority of people as if they were reality, or some form of natural law.

We can escape the crippling effects of these beliefs by creating a new cultural reality that goes beyond the limitations of the old one. The basic premise of this reality should be that anyone is capable of anything and that any situation can be improved. It's an attitude of respect for people and what they can do, and it challenges all members of the organization to become the very best they can be. It approaches every situation with an attitude of finding the opportunities in it.

HELP IS NEEDED FROM ALL QUARTERS

A good manager can do a lot to set the stage for a positive atmosphere, but others in the organization must do their part too. Inability to relate positively to each other is a severe cultural handicap. A workforce that cannot learn this skill will inevitably function at a low level of performance if all members of the team must constantly be gearing up the emotional fortitude to resist the put downs coming their way.

INCONSISTENCY CAN BE YOUR WORST ENEMY

If you're never sure when the next salvo will be unleashed at you, you're likely to spend much of your energy preparing to duck. It's a learned behavior that is very hard to unlearn. Insult me a few times, and when I see you coming I'll steel myself for the next insult and probably think you delivered it, no matter what you do. On-again-off-again kindness doesn't work well for that reason.

In fact, it works less well than anything else. Research in behavioral psychology has shown that if you change from one stimulus to another, and consistently maintain the new stimulus, the response to the old one will disappear fairly quickly. But if you switch back and forth between two stimuli for a while, the old response will take much longer to be extinguished; it may, in fact, never quite disappear.

Inconsistency is a very successful strategy for keeping an opponent or enemy off balance. It's effective for creating a paralyzing mistrust, or fear. But if you want to create a team, you've got to be consistent. If you're on-again-off-again in the way you treat people, they'll stop trusting you, and you'll find it a long uphill road to winning their trust again.

Many managers have unwittingly created such situations with the groups they manage. The fact that this can happen and that it lowers the effectiveness of work has been one of the main forces leading to the downsizing of middle management in so many companies. Everyone wants to be treated with respect. That goes for spouses, factory workers, students in classrooms and, believe it or not, political leaders and CEO's also. Respect is always a two-way street. Many a manager has found that employees who spend a lot of time trying to undermine progress will respond very differently when they start getting the respect they feel has been lacking.

Years ago, one of us had a student who seemed right on the edge of becoming a juvenile delinquent. In a conference he looked at the teacher and said, "I don't see any reason to do the stupid assignments you're giving in this class."

The teacher responded by saying, "You're right. You really are too smart to do those assignments. Let's make up a new set of assignments for you that really challenge your fine intelligence." They proceeded to do so, and today this would-be juvenile delinquent is himself a powerful and effective educational leader.

IS THE KITCHEN A LITTLE TOO HOT?

Does this sound like a plug for weakness and coddling, like a recipe for failure in the demanding and unforgiving real world? What about Harry S. Truman's brave, often quoted maxim, "If you can't stand the heat get out of the kitchen"? Well, sure the world is a hard place. The question is, what are you trying to do in it? And what purpose is being served by turning the heat and pressure up even higher?

Thick skins are all very well, but they look better on reptiles than human beings. Criticism is appropriate where deserved, but continual sniping can only have the effect of degrading the quality of life. Respect is needed everywhere all the time, and it should flow both upwards and downwards in the power structure. So the leaders in your life are as entitled as you are to appropriate respect, and the benefit of the doubt.

THE PROBLEM WITH PUT DOWNS

We've spent so much time on this point because the put down is the all too common currency of personal exchange in our culture. Though it's often intended in fun, it is a basic reflection of lack of respect for others.

While we don't wish to appear puritanical, and we can take a good joke, we deplore the tendency to fill the air with put downs, humorous or otherwise, that is in vogue some places. But this kind of humor doesn't really make things go better. In fact, put downs may actually be a behavioral addiction, sometimes expressed sarcastically or comically in the spirit of teenage boys punching each other on the shoulder, where they know it won't hurt. Yet the habit of always responding with negative put downs, however comically well-intended they may be, makes it difficult or impossible to express genuine admiration or acknowledge excellence. It's a sign of immaturity, a kind of adolescent male machismo, and it blocks the development of a more constructive and sophisticated organizational culture.

IF YOU'RE GOING TO LOOK LIKE A FOOL, GET PAID FOR IT

It's difficult to get the proper perspective on how we should behave, because in the larger culture, nearly all jokes, cartoons and sitcoms dramatize ways we make each other look foolish and then gratuitously insult each other. Gracie Allen and Lucille Ball turned looking foolish into a fine art. Perhaps no one would mind sporting a goofy image for the kind of fame and wealth they earned. But when you're forced to do it for free, it's not the sort of thing you want to be famous for.

Popular culture — from TV sitcoms to greeting cards — doesn't help us much if we want to learn how to focus on each other's good qualities. Have you noticed how often greeting cards seem to put more creative energy into humorous put downs than compliments? Yes, there are plenty of positive ones, but too often they express sentiments that seem like clich s, while the put downs are really creative. One of us recently turned fifty years old. Several friends commented on how difficult it was to find positive birthday cards. Mostly what they found were black humor, centered around how "out of luck" a person is when they turn fifty years old. It takes just as much creativity to be cleverly positive as cleverly negative. We've all heard the saying, "You look like something the cat dragged in," which was clever when it was original. Suppose that instead someone said to you, "I see the most incredibly beautiful creature inside of you wanting to come out and play." Both of these remarks hint at the opportunity for an improved appearance, but which one would you rather hear said to you?

THE VALUE OF APPRECIATION

There's a widespread impression that if you're not being critical, you're being too easy on the folks around you. Teachers who automatically give low grades regardless of the quality of students' work suffer from the illusion that their standards are high, when in reality they're just proving their teaching is no good.

One of us once got in trouble as a teacher for giving too many high grades. I also got in trouble when the administration found out what I was teaching. "That's way to advanced for those students!" they said. The implication that demanding work is indicated by a lot of low grade point averages was thus hoist in its own petard. Managers who complain about their workers are similarly demonstrating their own ineptitude.

But, if you can appreciate your followers because you have the critical perceptiveness to notice their unique excellence, that's when you'll see good performance from almost everyone. For research on human behavior consistently shows we're more likely to do a job well if we get praise for our virtues than if we're ridiculed for our shortcomings. That's why for every ounce of criticism a pound of praise is needed just to keep the fast track to success and happiness well lubricated.

OKAY, SO IT'S MUSHY

If your addiction to put downs is strong, you may find that recovering from it forces you into a period when you feel "mushy". Saying nice things to people, instead of handing out clever insults, can make you feel like your great aunt passing out cards with hearts and flowers on them. But if you stick with it, you gradually discover ways to be just as clever, thoughtful, insightful, and generally intelligent with your compliments as you previously were with the witty insults. In fact, chances are you'll gradually discover a tone and style of speech that is really clever and interesting as you hand out kudos that sound fresh and funny. And because you know that you're not only entertaining people, but also making them feel good — about themselves, and about you as well — you'll start putting a whole lot more creative energy into that incessant joking around you like to do so much.

If it still seems too hard to be soft on other people, you might, when you feel the impulse to put someone down, try being harder on yourself first. Think of it this way: which is tougher for you, giving a sarcastic slap, or a helping, healing hand? If it's giving a hand, be tough on yourself and try saying something nice first.

When you've kicked the put down addiction and learned to be an upstanding member of the Appreciation Community, you can breathe a sigh of relief, feeling as you might after recovering from a long nagging cold or a sore muscle that prevented you from moving freely for so long that you'd almost forgotten how good you could feel.

RESPECT BEGINS WITH SELF-RESPECT

A negative attitude towards other people, like many other types of anti-social behavior, often begins with a negative attitude towards oneself. Behind the mask of cynicism that assumes no one is worthy of respect is likely to be a person who has too little respect for his or her own self. Genuine respect for others and for oneself go hand in hand.[2]

This may sound all well and good in theory, but hard to imagine in practice. What about the real world where the secretary's sloppy errors make a hash of everyone's paperwork, or a manager's offhand and supposedly friendly jokes about his subordinates are lowering morale? What happens when a reprimand is necessary?

FINDING THE PONY

There's a story about two children waking up on Christmas morning eager to get to their presents. One finds a roomful of toys but cries because none of them is what he wanted. The other is presented with a roomful of manure. Without a word, he begins to dig. When asked why he is digging, he replies, "With all this manure, there's got to be a pony in here somewhere."

When it comes to changing behavior, or when the quality of performance is slipping, we suggest you try a method of reframing we call **Finding the Pony**.

Fortunately, it is possible to criticize someone while preserving that person's honor and communicating respect. If you want to inspire a change of behavior, it helps to suggest a way for a person to move into it. Help them select a pony to ride on out of the undesirable behavior. If you're skillful enough at this kind of reprimand, you can give it to anyone, including your boss.

You think sometimes it's not possible to do that? Well, if you have enough imagination, you can find a pony under any pile of manure. In other words, you can learn to reframe anything without losing sight of the difficulties in the current situation. So even if you're confronted by unacceptable behavior , you might try responding to it in something of the following way:

"John, you're a great asset in the office, because you're so cheerful and everyone enjoys talking with you. You're great fun to work with.

"That's why I wanted to see what we could do about the fact that I'm finding more errors in the letters we're sending out than I like to see. Perhaps we could sit down and go over the process you're using to get them out. If you put the same resourceful ingenuity into the correspondence that you do into making everyone feel good around here, I know I'm going to end up with one of the best secretaries that ever was. And I'll bet if we go over this situation together, we're going to find some ways to make your job easier and more pleasant — and that should make everyone happy."

That's how we go about finding the pony. You'll note there's no pussy-footing about the typing errors. Yet how can John feel bad or get defensive when he's being so highly praised for other things he does? And what's more likely to motivate him to be a better secretary — this kind of encouragement or more negative remarks?

Well and good if John is your secretary. But what if he's your boss? Here's one way:

"John, one of the things I like best about working here is being on your team. You're a charismatic leader, and I greatly respect you. You have a deep understanding not only of how this business has to function, but also how it fits into the community at large. And I know this opinion is shared by many others, because I hear it frequently from people that know you or know about your work.

"That's why I thought you might like some feedback that would help you be respected even more, and might help our division function a little better. I've noticed that sometimes, with the best intentions in the world, you make a joke that's funny to you but rankles with some of the folks who work for you. For example, I remember one time when you joked that you wished you did-n't have to pay any of us so the company could make more money. That was funny to you, but a lot of the guys really resented it. It was as if you didn't care about us, only about making money. I think you didn't mean that, and I've said to a lot of them that you were just joking with us. But I thought you might like to know the difference between the leadership you demonstrate most of the time and how you come across sometimes when you probably think you're just joking around."

Here again, the basic attitude is one of respect and admiration. If you were the boss, would you mind hearing these things about yourself? And wouldn't you also want it pointed out to you if you were unwittingly doing something that alienated people?

With such approaches to criticism, we can rebuild a negative culture effectively. So it's time to ask yourself how much positive energy is routine-ly exhibited in your organization. Are you more likely to hear remarks like: "I knew I should have stayed in bed today," than comments like these: "It's good to be here working with you guys," or "I'm so excited about this project I can hardly wait to get to work in the morning"?

So once again the challenge is to lift the darkness from the atmosphere. This depends not merely on the passive belief that every cloud has a silver lin-ing; it is, rather, the active search for the unnoticed and valuable benefits in any situation — even an undesirable one. With practice, the ability to seek out a positive outcome becomes a permanent mental asset.

THE MCCLOUD DILEMMA

Ogden Nash tells the story of Mr. and Mrs. McCloud. *He* was an ace reframer, finding something good in everything. *She* was a member of the opposing party:

> Mrs. McCloud, on the other hand,
> Was always complaining to beat the band."

Finally, exasperated at her husband's constant cheery note, Mrs. McCloud stuffed a tea tray down his throat.

> He remarked from the floor, where they found him reclining,
> "I'm just a McCloud with a silver lining."

Yes, there's a warning here: if you become a really excellent reframer, you might also become a threat to your friends and neighbors. Whenever they start to wring their hands and complain, you'll reassure them that things aren't so bad really, and immediately point out three or four redeeming features in the situation they came to you in good faith to complain about.

This cheerfulness can unnerve people. Nobody wants to have a good complaining session disturbed by being told things aren't so bad after all. Some people don't even feel they're alive unless they're complaining. They spend hours every day making themselves miserable, convinced the universe has been designed with them in mind: it's a precise instrument to upset and thwart, if not actively torture, them.

THE ALMIGHTY SHOULDER CHIP

That's the way they like it, because nothing makes them feel as important as having a chip on their shoulder. Some people's chips would provide enough firewood for an entire winter. So if you form the habit of reassuring people, they may accuse you of taking all the fun out of life. After all, who wants to be happy, to have everything go well, to find some redeeming feature in each new thing that happens?

> Oh, don't the days seem lank and long
> When all goes right, and nothing goes wrong —
> And isn't your life extremely flat
> When you've nothing whatever to grumble at?

Of course everyone has felt this way at one time or another. Otherwise these lines from W. S. Gilbert wouldn't ring as true and as funny as they do. But it's safe to assume that even the biggest grump would, like ourselves, rather be happy and in a good situation than go on nursing grievances forever.

POLISHING YOUR REFRAMING TECHNIQUE

The key is to practice reframing in such a way that you don't turn off the people you are trying to change. That's the beauty of the McDonald's example, or Lou Holtz's pre-game magic. When reframing is done well, it's subtle enough not to call attention to itself. Use it to highlight the positive side of a situation with a workmanlike zippiness that makes your listener say, "Of course! Why didn't I think of that?" Don't apply it mechanically, and don't make it into a technique or a cheap trick.

Use it with the confidence that you'll be able to move a situation off dead center, for it's nearly always true that when we carefully examine the positives, we can deal with the negatives more effectively. When first trying out a reframe, don't be too surprised if you get a sarcastic comeback. Successful reframing requires conviction and ease, so if you seem a little nervous about what you're saying, you're inviting resistance. It's particularly important at this stage not to get self-justifying.

THE ART OF DEALING WITH PUT DOWNS

To avoid defensiveness, adopt the attitude taught in some of the martial arts. Rather than resist the negative force coming at you, assist it to pass by, leaving you unruffled. If someone says, "Boy are *you* a terrible disappointment," you don't defend yourself; you say something like, "I could probably do better if you'd be good enough to give me some hints that will help me know more about what you want."

Use the energy of your opponent to win, instead of putting up your own resistance, which is easily overpowered by a more powerful opponent. In karate, the stronger your opponent's force, the greater chance you have of winning. For example, as your opponent attempts to hit you in the nose, gently step aside and nudge the oncoming fist, helping it to follow through on its motion with even greater force. You can even wave good-bye as your opponent rushes past you and careens against the wall. Eventually people will see that trying to hit someone who merely deflects assaults is not very satisfying, and most people don't like to end up flat on their face.

GROUP REFRAMING ACTIVITIES

It's valuable to train teams to listen to new ideas positively and, when they need to be improved, reframe them in a more effective direction. Sometimes this can be accomplished simply by allowing people more time to reflect and to be heard in group meetings. If the culture is one of pessimism and complaint, a committee can be formed to assess and suggest improvements in the tone of company interactions, and to evaluate how well employees give positive feedback to each other.

There are a variety of group activities that can be used to promote more positive attitudes. Some of them may at first glance seem rather soft and out of place in your organization. This is a common and understandable reaction, but it should not deter you from trying them. It has been our experience over and over again that when people tell us such activities would never work in their group, they mean that they would be willing to try them, but think others would not. Ninety-nine percent of the time, when the activity begins, everyone joins in willingly.

Of course an outside trainer or facilitator can sometimes ease the awkwardness of trying something unfamiliar. But once you try these activities you'll see that they don't require any expert instruction. On the contrary, you'll probably enjoy them more as you evolve your own group's techniques. So we recommend that even if you think the other guy is going to balk at these activities, go ahead and give them a try. You'll probably find out that the other guy was only hesitating out of apprehension over what you might think.

THE GOOD AND NEW

One of the best tools for teaching reframing so as to establish it permanently in your organization is an activity called the **Good and New**. Here's how it works:

Each person in the group takes a turn recounting something good that's occurred in the last twenty-four hours. This might be anything from an improvement in the weather to an elaborate success story. Of course there's no reason to limit the Good and New to on-the-job activities.

The object is to form a habit shared by the whole group — of dwelling on those events or experiences you feel best about, so you're energized by them, instead of letting the negative ones wear you down. Pose the question for yourself: what good things have happened in my life recently? The answer you get is your Good and New.

The Good and New is powerful because it is simple. If you regularly start meetings, classes, or work sessions with Goods and News, you'll notice a big jump in what your group can accomplish, while at the same time everyone's outlook will improve.

THE KOOSH AS SERGEANT-AT-ARMS

During this activity you can pass around a beanbag or "Koosh" ball as a means of keeping track of who has the floor. This helps keep order while increasing the sense of well-being in the group, for it's only fair that everyone have a chance to speak at least once so no one monopolizes the privilege. The ball is passed around until everyone has had a turn giving a Good and New, although whoever doesn't want to participate is allowed to "pass" and not say anything.

By the way, once you use the Koosh for this activity, you'll probably continue to use it throughout the meeting, and you'll be surprised at how this simple prop facilitates communication. You'll particularly notice its value when a couple of people monopolize the meeting with an argument and then someone says, "I want my turn to have the Koosh." Soon the filibustering is exposed for what it is and the meeting gets back on track.

THREE NICE THINGS

Sometimes a member of the group may not be able to think of a Good and New, which creates an occasion to bring out another reframing activity called **Three Nice Things**. The object is for members of the group to tell the person who has no Good and New three things they appreciate about him or her. These can be as simple as liking what the person is wearing, or they can delve more deeply into the person's character and contributions to the group. It's an opportunity to appreciate things that may never have been mentioned before.

As this technique is adopted by the culture, people who are feeling a little down may stop in the middle of a conversation and say, "I need to hear three nice things right now." This may seem awkward when you first try it, but with a little practice you'll be surprised to find how easily this process can give you the pickup you need to renew your energy for the day's activities.

ABUSING THE GOOD AND NEW

In one corporation the Good and New was quickly adopted by the team, but was used all too rigidly. Its effect was, in general, good, but the rigidity applied to it tended to undermine the spirit it was intended to create.

For example, the team would gather each morning to do their Goods and News, but if a member missed this gathering to finish an important task of benefit to everyone, that person might be criticized for missing the gathering, instead of praised for using the time to accomplish something important.

The result was a buildup of resentment in a context intended to achieve the opposite. It's possible, of course, for people deliberately to avoid the Good and New, thinking it trivial or embarrassing. If that happens, don't worry. They'll come around eventually.

In one organization we worked with, some people deliberately came late to the meetings to avoid having to give a Good and New. For them it was hokey, and suggested a mushiness and touchy-feely quality they didn't like. But all these people later greatly appreciated the culture change that resulted from the Good and New exercise, and eventually participated in that just as enthusiastically as if they'd thought of it themselves. So there's no need to make everyone do everything the same way, particularly when you're first trying out a new process. The point is honor and respect in the workplace, and this ritual is one powerful way to move in that direction.

The fact that it's not necessary to require everyone to participate, especially at first, demonstrates how true it is that if only some of the group become more positive, everyone will benefit. Eventually, positive behavior will be adopted by consensus, particularly as the group will understand that it doesn't make sense to go on to Step Three until everyone has accepted the wisdom of Step Two. Meanwhile, confronting people who are choosing to hold back only delays the desired outcome, making them nervous and inviting retaliation.

This is a good place to mention a phenomenon that really surprised us when we first noticed it. It takes a while to establish a new culture in any organization. That's because organizational learning cannot happen terribly quickly. Over time more and more people will jump on board the new culture, but you tend to have hold outs for quite a while after the first ones have joined up.

When the culture has been well established, however, what you'll notice is that new people coming in will learn the new culture very quickly, perhaps in a few hours or even minutes. Not only will they accept the culture as if they'd been there since it was first established, they will tend to become strong advocates of it.

That's because it's relatively easy to learn a new way of behaving if everyone around you is behaving that way. So you're not going to have to worry about putting newcomers to your organization through the same long learning experience that the whole group went through. All they need is to see it modeled and they'll soon be doing it too.

Of course some people are more oblivious to what's going on around them, and for them joining in with the organizational culture may take a little longer.

THE RIPPLE EFFECT

Positive attitudes, positive interactions between people, and a positive climate within an organization are all interrelated. Changes large and small within the organization have ripple effects which reach into every corner and byway of the organization.

Consider these two stories, one of positive change in the life and treatment of one individual, the other of top down change in a huge plant. Each shows how reframing and a positive attitude simultaneously improved the life of individuals and their organizations.

THE ADVENTURES OF ROB,
WHO GAVE UP HIS BID FOR MARTYRDOM

Rob was the director of a division that handled the most arcane technology in his company. Over the years, this division had grown significantly larger and more complex, but meanwhile its procedures and practices were filed neatly in Rob's head — accessible to no one else. As a result Rob routinely worked twelve-hour days, and felt like a martyr, while things inevitably came to a standstill on those rare occasions when he was laid up with the flu or a bad back.

As Rob's work week approached seventy plus hours and complaints about backlog piled up, it became apparent that a change in procedures was mandatory. A team was formed to help Rob make the transition to new work habits, which included writing down all procedural information and training several assistants. At first, Rob was crushed. He had a great deal of ego invested in his pattern of operation, which made him indispensable to the company. He also had some doubts that anyone else could master the complex tasks he had to perform.

It became clear to the team that Rob would have difficulty writing down any of the procedures he used. In the first place, they were so well known to him that he did most of them virtually unconsciously. Secondly, if Rob were to take the time to write everything down, he would get so far behind in his work he'd never catch up.

So two or three assistants were assigned to follow him around. Their training focused on preparing a procedural manual for his department. As they watched him work, taking notes on what he did and questioning details, they received the needed training without cutting into his time. Gradually they took on more of his responsibility, thus freeing him enough so he could afford the time to explain things better, go over the manual to make sure it was correct, and in other ways further the process of transition.

After a few months the team completed the transition to a new system that was fully documented and could be used by anyone. All this they accomplished without diminishing Rob's self-worth. They expressed their unfeigned admiration for all he had done and impressed upon him that when he retired he would leave behind a legacy that would always be a tribute to his career.

And so what had threatened to develop into an impossible bottleneck was instead transformed into a smooth transition in which not only Rob, but his assistants as well, benefited from an increased sense of self-worth that accompanied the greater efficiency and effectiveness they made possible for their company.

Had the team been less respectful of Rob, he could easily have stonewalled them, making the transition practically impossible, greatly increasing the cost to the company of maintaining its technical systems, and perhaps leaving behind an almost endless legacy of confusion and red tape. Here is a case in which the ability to think positively and reframe the situation was absolutely essential to a smooth transition.

It's worth pointing out another remarkable aspect of this successful transition, which must inevitably be repeated everywhere as technology becomes more complex. It's a new kind of employee involvement. It's the building of teams who together can store and process information beyond the grasp of any single person. And this kind of employee involvement, which absolutely must occur, will be immeasurably facilitated as the positive atmosphere strengthens.

And it's this transition from an individual ownership of some part of the organization's operation to the involvement of teams that's an important part of the transition process into the learning organization. When an individual develops something like a process or a technology, he or she may or may not make all of its secrets available to others who might have a need to know. In Rob's case much of the necessary information was locked in his head and could have died with him, making it almost impossible for anyone else to unlock the secret codes that enabled Rob to do his job so effectively.

But in a rapidly changing work environment, such dependence on individuals who may have secret codes known only to them is fatal. In such an environment everything must be recorded in a form that makes it accessible to anyone else who has a need to know. This is simply a reflection of the developing complexity of the modern organization. The team process is essential, and it will work only as it becomes capable of communicating every aspect of what it is doing.

Obviously, though, teams cannot work if the chemistry is not right. They must be compatible with each other, and must be complementary to each other as well, an interlocking set of skills, talents and perspectives that strengthen the effectiveness of each member.

So the transition from what's in Rob's mind to what the team can understand and record is a kind of parable of the transformation from the old command and control model to the modern, democratic, *chaordic* organization: a system that organizes the endlessly shifting demands of a chaotic world into a kind of flow that makes stable organization possible.

THE GM LAKEWOOD STORY

Another example of transformation in industry is the case of the Lakewood General Motors plant in Atlanta. This plant had had a troubled history of labor and management conflict. Soon after Patricia M. Carrigan became plant manager, GM closed it down for a year and a half because of lack of car sales. It reopened in a spirit of change.

Carrigan signaled the tone of her leadership by having her office constructed on the shop floor in such a way that she was easily available to anyone who needed to communicate with her.

In May of that year (1984), Lakewood became the first plant in GM history to attain a widely accepted corporate standard for high quality in the first published audit after start-up and the first to repeat that performance just after the second shift started up.

Grievances have remained at or near zero, and discipline

incidents have declined by 82 percent since the plant has operated on two shifts. There have been no cases of protested discipline since the plant reopened.

Despite the addition of heavy daily and Saturday overtime since production resumed, absenteeism declined from 25 percent to 9 percent, saving more than $8 million.

Sickness and accident costs were cut by two-thirds. A jointly established five-year goal for reduction in sick-leave costs was attained in the first year, netting a $1.3 million credit for 1984 and lower rates for 1985.[3]

The philosophy that brought about these changes is contained in the following four principles:

- To change, take risks, accept responsibility, and be accountable for our actions.
- To respect all people, promoting unity, trust, pride, and dedication to our mission.
- To achieve a high quality of work life through involvement of all our people in an environment of openness and fairness in which everyone is treated with dignity, honesty, and respect.
- To promote good communications among all employees by operating in an open atmosphere with freedom to share ideas and speak one's mind without fear of reprisal.

These principles closely resemble the spirit and content of our first four steps. We believe the Lakewood plant was successful primarily because of their focus on the positives of unity, trust, pride, dedication, dignity, honesty and respect. In fact, these seven qualities make an excellent checklist for helping establish a positive environment, for they should be by-products of any successful change in culture or climate.

They, in turn, have other by-products, which are behaviors or modes of operation. These include responsibility, teamwork, problem-solving, creativity, listening, sharing, teaching, coaching and continuous improvement — all of which add up to the gradual transformation of knowledge into wisdom.

THE NECESSITY OF MULTICULTURALISM

It will be clear that Step Two has succeeded when every member of the organization knows that he or she will be listened to sympathetically, and believes that the organization as a whole is truly positive in whatever it undertakes.

In Step Two we're focusing on the necessity that all people be treated with dignity and respect at all times. Until this has been achieved, the Learning Organization will remain an exercise in futility. For we must have a learning culture that understands how all people add value. Not just a few.

Not just management, or some other sub-group. Everyone.

In some ways, this is one of the most difficult concepts to grasp. There has been a backlash in recent years to the notion of multiculturalism, as if the loss of the homogenizing effect of our culture on the many cultures that came together to create it is merely the introduction of chaos that makes it too difficult to get anything done.

Not that the tremendous increase of employees from different cultures isn't a big challenge for the many leaders and human resources specialists who want to create organizations that are both global and focused. One of our clients has had a 27% increase in the past two years in the number of factory workers from four foreign countries. Their well established training approaches and materials are having to be reframed to address the background differences all these people are bringing to the company.

There is another way to view multiculturalism, though, which we shall explore more fully in Step Five. It sees diversity as a resource not as a problem, recognizes the differences among people and seeks to bring about a synergistic interaction between them, so that the best of all the different cultures are brought together in a way that reflects the motto of our nation: *e pluribus unum* — "from many, one." The organic interaction among many different cultures which remain viable in themselves can produce a much richer and more competent culture in which all participate and to which all contribute, and which no one is expected to conform to in all respects. Such a supraculture expects of everyone certain behaviors, like respect, that make it possible for all to interact.

In the end, multiculturalism is inescapable in the modern world, because each individual represents a unique culture. No two people speak exactly the same language, think exactly the same thoughts or have exactly the same motivations. But there's room for all of those which are not destructively oriented in the supraculture, in which the old divisive effects of prejudice have finally been broken down and replaced by an ecological ethic which shows how all of the unique beings which make up the planet can interact symbiotically, each contributing to the whole and all drawing sustenance from it.

What happens when an organization truly moves in this direction is that it is transformed from one which demands of everyone the lowest common denominator to one which ennobles all of its people, drawing them together into the highest forms of synthesis and synergy. In such an organization everyone gains from the experience — not just the opportunity to earn a living, but the much more important opportunity to grow as a person.

The best and brightest organizations have always been like this. It is time now for all organizations to become places which give to all those who make them up more than they take away from them.

In that regard, training in multiculturalism may be necessary before Step

Two can be completed. Multiculturalism begins when we each appreciate the legacy of our own culture and the influence it has on our life and work. With that background of appreciation, we then afford the same degree of respect to cultures different from our own.

Respecting other cultures, beginning at the level of individual experience, doesn't mean we have to share them, but it does mean giving up the tired old bugaboo "When in Rome, do as the Romans do." In a multicultural society, who are the Romans anyway? Each culture will operate best according to its own lights, and if its values do not contradict those of the organization (an unlikely situation), they should be respected.

Cultural awareness is often lacking among those in dominant cultures. In a world that generally favors white males, the only people who don't know exactly what it takes to succeed are — white males. They're the only ones who haven't consciously had to learn the rules, so they usually don't even know they're there. A white male doesn't know, for example, unless someone convinces him it's true, that if he were a woman he'd have to work twice as hard to succeed as he does being a man, or that if he were African-American or Hispanic he'd have to work even harder, particularly if he happened to be a woman as well. In any event, a white male can learn to appreciate these realities only in the abstract. He cannot experience them directly.

People of non-dominant cultures are often sensitive to words and gestures that the dominant culture ignores. As a result, hurt feelings and resentment can be wide-spread and deep because of trespasses that may seem trivial to those who do not have to bear the brunt of them. In general, minorities want to be treated as absolute equals without any hint of distancing.

SPEAKING OUT FOR GREATER UNDERSTANDING

A powerful exercise that can help here is the **Speak Out**. When a member of a group that has been ill-treated (usually unconsciously) speaks out to inform everyone of what the ill treatment has felt like, a powerful learning experience is possible for all.

The Speak Out begins when a person who has suffered ill treatment feels safe enough to tell the group about it. This will not occur in a group in which some people are known to be bigoted and are supported in their attitude by the prevailing climate. But it may occur as the sense of safety and positive attitude in the group begins to build. Then the offended person, speaking for an offended group, will voice, often emotionally, what it's been like to suffer certain kinds of treatment that have been hurtful. Those listening may feel deeply what is being said, but they do not interrupt or comment in any way.

It's appropriate at the end of a Speak Out to express support for the feelings of the person who has spoken, but not to challenge any of the issues raised. The purpose of the Speak Out is to inform others about feelings, and when that information has been received, it can be thought about until what's been learned is used to improve the situation.

DON'T MIX MULTICULTURAL AND POLITICAL ISSUES

It's important to take the precaution that multicultural issues are never confused with political ones. We can all choose our political affiliations, our positions on such issues as merit pay, labor unions, stock options and other matters that are open to public debate and legitimate difference of opinion. None of us, however, choose to be a member of a certain race or sex, or to be handicapped or otherwise in some fundamental sense different from others. There's also increasingly strong evidence that our sexual preference is not chosen, but is biologically determined.

In addition, none of us should be made to feel defensive about our cultural and economic heritage. Being born into a minority ethnic or religious group or a working class family can never be allowed to become a badge of inferiority or dishonor. That's just fundamental human rights.

Groups that can use Speak Outs successfully to help increase their multicultural awareness are groups that are building a strong positive atmosphere and thus greatly facilitating their growth as Learning Organizations.

SUCCEEDING AT STEP TWO

To determine that Step Two has been successfully completed, we suggest the organization revisit the *Assessment* first made in Step One. When all members of the organization reflect a positive attitude which is confirmed by an anonymous evaluation form or process, then Step Two has been accomplished.

When we say "accomplished," we mean that a level of maturity has been reached from which it's appropriate to go on to Step Three. Of course, as with all the Steps, regular maintenance, revisiting and reevaluation will continue to be important. There's always the danger of reaching a high level of achievement, after which old patterns reassert themselves and cause the quality of the learning culture to deteriorate. Then the organization is in danger of relapsing into outmoded, less productive ways.

Through the practice and rehearsal of this Step, we're proposing that with proper maintenance and reinforcement, the dynamic of positive thinking can eventually be established on so deep a level of consciousness that it seems second nature. It can, in fact, become so comfortable that people will wonder how they could have operated in any other way.

When all employees have formed the habit of giving each other positive feedback, and the tone of the culture is one in which people feel supported by each other and by the group as a whole, it's time to take on the next challenge, that of making the organization a safe place for new learning experiences.

MAKE THE WORKPLACE SAFE FOR THINKING

S T E P   3

Everyone knows stories of innovative thinkers who were ignored or fired by their employers and went off to begin brilliantly successful businesses, or whole new industries. In fact, in the era of massive downsizing, that's been one of the major ways in which new, more effective businesses are arising to challenge the major corporations.

Much less famous, but unfortunately much more common, are the innumerable people who have given up pursuing their good ideas — or given up bothering to think at all on the job.

The loss to these individuals, in their careers and in the satisfaction they could have found in their work, is incalculable. The price to their employers and to society in lost creativity, stunted careers, and unproductive labor has been even greater. Until recently that was a price that American business and society were willing to pay. But in today's global economy the cost of failing to think well is too high. It is a price no one can afford to pay. And it, as much as anything, accounts for the fact that while unemployment goes down so does the standard of living for the average worker. Workers deprived, through years of lack of encouragement, of their initiative, simply aren't worth as much on the job market, now that technology is competing for the available medium skill jobs.

SOME PEOPLE WHO GOT PENALIZED FOR THINKING WELL

Not long ago one of us spent some time with a number of unemployed job seekers. In our discussion it came out that several of them no longer had jobs because they'd had the boldness — or poor judgment — to suggest improvements in the way things were done in their previous places of employment.

In several cases, changes they recommended had actually passed muster with some of the leadership. But in the end the ax fell on them because they had spoken out. Listening to their ideas and the responses they'd received was a dramatic demonstration of how business often turns its back on the idea generators that could help it the most.

"Why did your employers ignore your ideas?" I asked.

"Because they're sure we don't know anything. They don't think we're people like them, they think we're machines."

"But," I asked, "isn't it true that the person who runs the machine or works on the shop floor knows the most about what's going on there?"

Everyone, of course, agreed.

I left the discussion wondering why this intelligent and alert group of problem solvers didn't have jobs. The unfortunate reason is that too many organizations still prefer to hire warm bodies who show up on time, do what they're told and don't rock the boat, rather than seek honest and necessary improvements.

WHAT'S AHEAD IN THIS CHAPTER

In this chapter we'll look at how and why organizations routinely deprive themselves of their most essential resource: the thinking capacity of everyone in the company. This counter-productive behavior flourishes at a time when business is having to rely more heavily on the same creativity it routinely discourages. Only when this self-destructive behavior in the organization is recognized, is it possible to change it.

The news is full of stories lamenting that today's workforce, from top to bottom, is not up to today's challenges. The panacea is supposed to be "training." But training alone is not enough, for the traditional training that is offered is as damaging to the thinking process as other negative factors that discourage thinking. That's because it's almost always in the form of "do as I say not as I do" instruction that's so deadly in the public schools and even more in corporate training rooms. Standing up and lecturing with a flip chart or an overhead projector does little or nothing to teach job skills that require interaction among the workers, kinesthetic responses, and a general sense of how to deal with the more unpredictable situations that may arise in production, or how to find creative solutions to problems that no one has ever solved before.

So the real challenge is to create a climate where all will look for ways to do their job better, where the attitudes and motivations needed to power quality control, continuous improvement and all the other goals of today's corporations is built into everyone's behavior and expectations.

DON'T THEY TEACH THINKING IN SCHOOL?

We believe that our educational system should prepare people to function in the world. For that purpose, it should foster various basic skills, but even more important it should exercise and train our capacity to think independently, curiously, objectively. Unfortunately, this capacity has been so thoroughly discouraged by authoritarian forms of education and management that a whole civilization is belatedly waking up to find it in perilously short supply.

"Higher order thinking skills" are often taught in ways that discourage students for thinking at all. Again and again we find that people are essentially being told that they must learn to think the way their teacher thinks, which may be completely unlike the way that they themselves most naturally solve problems. Just one example: math teachers who insist that students must "show their work" militate against those students who approach problems intuitively, not always knowing how they got the answer. This isn't to say that showing your work isn't important, valuable and perhaps necessary, it's to say that it should be taught in such away that the capacity to think intuitively isn't wantonly destroyed.

New thinking arises and flourishes most readily in a positive and supportive atmosphere. In order to learn to think well, one must practice in an environment where there's no reason to fear the consequences of what you might discover. And that atmosphere is often sorely lacking precisely where it is most needed.

THE GREAT UNIVERSAL WALKING SCHOOL

Let's begin by recognizing that thinking, like walking, is a learned skill. We should rejoice that the way children learn to walk is the same world wide. What they do when they're ready, is just get up and walk as best they can while a circle of admiring relatives cheers them on.

The child who falls is given loving reassurance and encouraged to try again. There's no, "Oh my goodness, that child has collapsed and may never learn to walk! How will the poor creature ever get into Harvard if things keep falling apart like this?"

The result of this worldwide parental policy of being supportive whenever the New Walker falls down is that everyone learns to walk quite easily. As a result we almost never hear of any non-medical problems with walking. Strangely, we don't see Walking Awards either — diplomas hung on walls acknowledging that So and So has indeed learned to walk, and this is attested to by known and verified accomplished walkers, who have thoroughly examined the candidate for possible signs of cheating or otherwise compromising the standards according to which all Good Walking must be practiced. No, walking is taken for granted, as if there were nothing to it.

PLANS FOR A SIMILAR GREAT, UNIVERSAL THINKING SCHOOL

Thinking, like walking, is best developed through practice, and, again like walking, it is best practiced in a supportive environment. Stupidity, on the other hand, is a disabling learned behavior. Even though it should be obvious that damage to the thinking process is likely to be the result, we routinely try to teach people to think by attacking their ideas before they've had a chance to develop them as fully as they might wish.

Thinking and creativity should be normal behavior, because they are what every brain is naturally equipped to do well. Even though it's quite possible that some people are born with more of a tendency to think well than others, all can improve their thinking substantially by practicing it frequently, if not continuously, in an atmosphere that supports the thinking process itself.

Let's probe a little here. A child asks why are there stars in the sky and a parent ignores the question, or responds with something like, "Don't ask stupid questions." The obedient child stops asking about so many things and thereby learns not to inquire into matters about which everyone (except the child) supposedly knows the answer.

This habit of non-thinking is practiced throughout life; so when the boiler in the factory is giving telltale signs that it's about to blow up, the now grown adult, thoroughly schooled in never being inquisitive, looks the other way and gives the boiler no further thought until such time as possible questions have turned into irrevocable facts.

THE HIGH COST OF NOT ASKING QUESTIONS

From childhood on, the freedom to ask questions is a crucial hallmark of an environment that's safe for thinking. It should be okay to ask about anything you want, and also okay not to get an answer right away. This license ought to apply particularly in the serious corporate world where procedures, rules, management theories and other forms of accepted wisdom are often treated as sacred writ not subject to any questioning or scrutiny.

Take for example the standard method of dealing with customer complaints. We all know the squeaky wheel gets the grease. That means the customers who complain the most will get the most attention. But the customers who complain the most may be the customers who do the least for your business. That's known as the Pareto Law — you put in 80% of your effort to get 20% of your results.

So as you go on blindly paying attention to the complainers while ignoring the customers who don't complain, you're spending all your time helping those who will give you the least in return, while ignoring those who might do the most for you.

Carry this policy to extremes and all your good customers will go elsewhere, because you're not giving them the attention they deserve, while the customers you like least will become more and more typical of the people you have to deal with. The result could drive you out of business, while you drown in the complaints of people who are never satisfied.

THINKING ABOUT NON-THINKING

This is an example of the kind of non-thinking response we're likely to give in business situations if we don't ask probing and unconventional questions about what's happening and what we should do about it. But why is non-thinking so prevalent, and thinking so frequently and effectively discouraged?

One way organizations routinely stifle their most creative thinkers is by simply not listening to them. This failure to listen often takes the form of an almost knee-jerk negativity. For many of us, a negative response to a new idea is a reflex. We can think so quickly of the reasons why it won't work that we never stop to look around.

NEGATIVITY AS A REFLEX RESPONSE

One of us recently went into a client corporation to work with their teams. I visited several groups and asked them two questions: "What's working for you?" and "What's missing that would make a big difference if it were there?" Invariably the teams looked vacant when asked the first question. They were always impatient to get to the second question. When I would list on a flip chart the items they could think of that were working for them, they acted frustrated and anxious, often asking me what I meant by the question, or to give them examples. Lacking leadership models to teach them how to accept new possibilities and new ideas, they had been conditioned not to think about what worked well for them.

When it came to answering the question about the things that weren't working, they would pour forth enough ideas to fill a page or two on the flip chart with no hesitation at all.

WHY MANAGERS RESIST EMPLOYEE THINKING

The negativity of managers towards the thinking of their subordinates often comes from their own fears and hidden agendas. Peter Grazier, President of Team Building, Inc., has observed that many managers actively resist new ideas from their employees, as well as other benefits that would come with greater employee involvement. Some of the reasons for this are:

* The threat of losing their authority, which would happen if their subordinates were to do a better job than they do.
* Fear that they'll do something wrong and be punished for it.
* Ego.
* Belief that the processes needed to encourage employee involvement will take too long.
* Fear that change will be only short term and temporary.
* Fear of losing their job or being replaced.
* Inability to see what's in it for them.
* Cynicism that says "we've been through this before."
* Concern that they'll be left out of the development process.
* Fear that the effects of such a change will be very difficult and hard to measure in the early stages.

Because so many managers have hidden agendas, they are unaware that their resistance hamstrings the creativity and productivity of their subordinates. Often, when performance in the workplace deteriorates, they fall back on blaming the employee they wouldn't listen to in the first place. Having crushed the initiative out of their workforce, they wonder why their employees act brain damaged in a crisis.

THE INSIDIOUS BELL CURVE

Then again, it is unreasonable to expect people to think, when their thinking has always been dismissed from the word go. This dismissive attitude goes back to the illusion we got when we were in school that some people are smarter than others, that intelligence is a single commodity irrevocably distributed to all of us in whatever size package we received at birth. The bell curve is a valid way of measuring events in the physical world, but when applied to anything as complex as the human brain, it's unscientific, prejudicial, assumption-laden and completely inappropriate.

One of us had the following experience of the harm such thinking can do: When working with an executive to find a person who could be assigned to a special project, I recommended someone I thought had the background, creativity, and personality for the job.

"Is she on the High Talent list?" I was immediately asked.

"No she is not," I replied.

"Well, we'll just have to find someone who is," I was told.

The High Talent list included only those people who supposedly had what it takes to be successful in the corporation I was dealing with. The underlying message was that only a select few could be contributors to the success of the company.

Our experience as consultants has been, however, that when we identify those people who may be able to lead an organization forward in the most effective way possible, we often pick people that management had not considered. Yet when our advice is followed and those people are given responsibility, we usually find that their contributions are much more valuable than was predicted. It seems that most people in management use criteria for selecting leaders that is pretty far from the actual personal qualities needed to make things happen in the organization. There are a variety of reasons why this may be, but we think the main reason is probably the same one that separates the kind of wisdom learned on the job from that which is taught in graduate school.

When people in any organization are treated in an elitist way, the organization's capacity to improve its quality of learning and thinking is greatly diminished. When there's no road an individual can take that has a chance of ultimately impacting the whole organization, the result is a resigned mindlessness.

Nevertheless, for several generations our culture has used the bell curve to measure differences in performance, "proving" that some students were outstanding, others were failures, and the majority were in the not particularly distinguished average group. All it really proved was that the educational system in use wasn't properly designed to serve the needs of the people in it — whether students, teachers, administrators or the public. As several studies have demonstrated, the relationship between success in school and success in life is purely coincidental and statistically nonexistent.

ELIMINATE THE BELL CURVE FROM YOUR THINKING ABOUT PEOPLE

The bell curve was applied from lack of knowledge of, or respect for, individual differences in learning, thinking and problem solving. Today, organizations can only be misled by such antiquated performance notions. If they want to succeed, they must use the knowledge and observations with which neuroscientists, psychologists and educators are enriching our understanding of how people learn, behave and think.

We'll explain more about these new insights into learning differences in Step Six, but for now we want to emphasize the need to recognize that no two people think or solve problems the same way. This more accurate assessment of human intelligence should help us to acknowledge and reward the unique value of each individual's potential contributions. Addressing the issues of learning diversity is crucial for any organization that wants to use the learning power of all its employees.

WANTED: REWARD

Management can lead the way by rewarding thinking and creativity wherever these are to be found. In one corporation, we offered the recommendation that a suggestion box be put up. We were literally laughed at. "We have one now," I heard from all parts of the room at once. "Management collects whatever we put in there and dumps it in the trash," said one person. "We never see any results, so what difference does it make?" said another. "They don't care what we think."

Later we heard a different story from someone willing to speak to us in private about a job she had once had. "You have to watch them like a hawk," she said. "We always put our ideas in the suggestion box, but then we insisted the boss read them while we were watching. After that we kept after the managers until they finally put what we had said into practice. Eventually we'd see it, and it would always work." Apparently, though, this behavior was enough to cost her the job that enabled her to force her managers to think.

ON GETTING OUT OF THE WAY

Linda Honold, formerly of Johnsonville Foods, has some wise observations about thinking in an organization:

> To encourage people to begin to think for themselves at work, get out of their way. Instead of telling people what to do when they ask, learn to ask them what they think should be done. It's truly amazing what can happen when you allow people to answer their own questions.
>
> I can illustrate that point with a true story. A young man (formerly a supervisor) at Johnsonville Foods was the well-liked coach for the second-shift sausage-stuffing department. Whenever any problems occurred on the line, members would ask him what they should do to fix it. He always told them and then allowed them to fix it themselves. He would go home after his shift and go to bed.
>
> There was no formal coach for the third shift. Members would come in, they would read the schedule that had been set for them, they would go to work, and everything would be fine — as long as there were no problems. If a problem cropped up, members would call the second-shift coach at home and wake him out of a sound sleep to ask him what to do. Naturally, he helped them out. After he told them what to do, they would fix the problem themselves.
>
> Eventually the young man got tired of being awakened in the middle of the night. He decided to change his tactics. The next time the members called him with a problem, he first asked them what they thought they ought to do. They told him. He observed aloud that they had the answer all along and really didn't need him to give them the answer. They never called again with problems they already knew how to handle.
>
> The process of transforming your company into a learning organization is just that simple and that difficult. It's not easy for managers and executives to stop making decisions. Learning to ask questions instead of giving answers takes a concerted effort. Initiating a member-development type department can help move the process along. Once people get used to learning, decision making becomes easier for them.[1]

To create a culture which encourages people to think for themselves, management must do several crucial things besides just ask questions.

HOW ARE YOU DOING AT SUPPORTING THE THINKING OF OTHERS?

Overcoming the tendency to greet other people's new ideas with a knee-jerk negative response is a skill that must be learned. Take a crack at it now. Before reading on, set aside a few moments to list some of the times you helped a colleague develop a good idea, or at least provided support to help it grow and prosper. Even though you may have criticized some features of a proposal in the process of shaping and refining it, you qualify if the overall effect of your contribution was to give it life.

Now make a second list: this one of the ideas you helped kill. Never mind that some ideas really are terrible. Think back over the times when you pounced on a fledgling thought, helping seal its fate, guaranteeing it could never have its day in the sun.

Don't feel too guilty if this list is the longer of the two. We're all compelled to reject new ideas from time to time. There may be occasions when we do an ill-judged inventor a favor by reducing the time he or she spends trying to rescue a hopeless project. Still, right now take a look at yourself both as nurturer and squelcher. Later you'll have a chance to look at how you've been nurtured — and, sadly enough, also how you've been squelched.

REVISITING YOUR OWN CREATIVE BLOCKS

When you've finished the lists we suggested above and have time for another exercise, recall the good ideas you've given birth to when you've had an assist from an associate who cared enough to help you get them going.

Now dig a little deeper. Recall some of the unfortunate times when your cherished ideas were torpedoed by people you'd hoped would support them.

Rejection can spur some people on to greater persistence and effort. But most of us are persuaded by rejection to shut up shop in the creativity department. It may be that as you mentally go back in time to recall these events — complete with the discouragement associated with them — you can revisit the originality that once inspired you and bring it back to life again.

A LEARNING ENVIRONMENT DEPENDS ON SAFETY

Safety is a basic human need. It is indispensable at every stage of the growth and development of an individual or an organization. A Learning Organization provides continual permission and incentive for everyone in the organization to think well and benefit from the thinking of others.

People dedicated to the challenge of creating a Learning Organization seek to provide a working environment that does not focus solely upon money, power, control, status, or superiority. Instead, it develops the capacity to be involved with a pair, a group, a team, or an organization, and to engage in networks that extend beyond the local group. Such associations enable a person to be constructive, and to feel honored, respected and recognized.

Participating in productive and meaningful relationships with others, in which both giving and receiving are valued, generates safety. Only in such a work environment does the whole person become integrated enough to achieve full potential. A Learning Organization thus enables positive and unrestricted growth to flourish.

Feeling safe also fosters the ability to discover and experiment, and to experience learning "mistakes" without guilt or shame. Feeling safe leads to knowing how to enjoy the possibilities of creative action, both individual and collective.

In a successful Learning Organization safety is fostered by asking: What helps? What hurts? What matters? What doesn't matter?

Note that "safe" does not imply freedom from challenge or accountability. These are often necessary to provide the excitement needed for the best kind of learning. Safety implies support for the learning process itself — an atmosphere in which one can depend on being respected for productive thinking all the time.

MAKING IT SAFE

What can managers do to create a safe environment as a background for developing the Learning Organization, and specifically for making it safe to think creatively?

Everyone will benefit from thinking through an answer to the question, What does *thinking safely* mean to me? In practical terms, the question could be — What are the specific actions or changes that would prove it's actually safe for me to think here?

The *Assessment* in Step One should be an excellent source of information on current attitudes towards thinking in the organization. If necessary, that can be supplemented with anonymous questionnaires, which is one of the best ways to get a lot of useful information about how to improve your organization.

KNOWING YOUR JOB IS SAFE

Innovative thinking can put people out of work as mercilessly as non-thinking and failing to adapt to new challenges. People need to know that new ideas will not endanger their jobs by making them superfluous. Management must develop a strategy for increasing each individual's employability. The goal should be to assist employees to develop work skills that will make them more valuable to their present company and to anyone who hires them.

Any company that knows what's good for it will also prove to its managers they'll always have a job there. Then it will be easy to encourage them to set up strategies for eliminating their jobs as managers. The job of management should be turned over to the workers. Trust the synergy of the team and the organization. Well-organized collective action gets you there the fastest.

As we pointed out earlier, this policy cannot possibly be effective unless managers are specifically rewarded for eliminating their jobs with better jobs and higher pay. If I'm asked to eliminate my job with only the prospect that I'll have to find another, you can bet I'll suddenly get as inefficient as I possibly can.

THE VALUE OF IGNORANCE AND ERROR

The organization needs to encourage everyone to ask for help. When managers say, "I don't know," they're also saying, "I'm a human being, too, and maybe I can learn something from you." This builds cooperation and teamwork, for everyone loves to give help, while the willingness to ask for it is a powerful sign of strength in any success-oriented person. The culture will be strong when all are willing to be open and candid about recognizing what they don't know.

Management can set the stage by admitting its own mistakes and making amends when necessary. Confidence is built within the organization whenever a new structure is developed as a result of learning from someone's mistake. Thus it makes sense to appreciate and celebrate mistakes that have been recognized and corrected. Do so on a monthly or quarterly basis. Such milestones of celebration might be supplemented with an ongoing journal chronicling the lessons learned by the team.

THE THREE REQUIREMENTS

There are three requirements for creating a safe learning environment. The first is an agreed-upon **structure**, supported with ground rules specifying how the team, committee or organization is going to behave. The framework thus created is like the rules, together with the playing field, in a football game. It helps focus the action, and clarifies the boundaries of the team's activities. The rules should be open to amendment, though, because some of them may not have the desired effect. If the team considers alternative sets of rules, it will eventually find the ones that provide the most effective structure in which to work.

We'll have more to say about this in Step Nine, because the way in which rules are created can dictate the success of the system, particularly of a chaordic system — which must respond flexibly and constructively to frequently chaotic real world conditions. In other words, the futuristic organization must be one which is deliberately out of control, but at the same time operates according to a set of agreed-upon rules that order activities enough so that the desired positive interactions can take place.

The second requirement is **nurturing**. In a learning environment, while members believe they can solve their own problems, they nurture and support each other in doing so. Nurturing involves helping others to succeed, not pre-empting their job. So, rather than doing other people's thinking for them, nurturing supports them in finding creative, often unpredictable, methods of resolving things for themselves. The tendency for many people is to rescue, or be the caretakers, for others. Nurturing is about guiding others to solve their own problems, not coming up with the "right" solutions for them.

From a manager's point of view this combination of structure and nurturing means, negotiate specific tasks, projects and outcomes and then let the designated people do them. Get out of the way and stop micromanaging, because too much oversight says to people, "we think you are incompetent." It's been found that in laying out instructions for a task or a job, **minimum critical specification** will get the most creative results. In other words, tell people only what they need to know in order to produce the results you're after. Let them figure the details out for themselves.

Teams that make their own operational discoveries are far more dynamic and powerful than those whose members are forever trying to remember manuals or sets of regulations given them by someone else. This is one of the reasons why the Learning Leaders at Kodak were up to speed in three months, while other self-managed teams in the same corporation usually took a year to a year and a half to get up to speed.

A non-Learning Organization is usually characterized by a leader who makes the work team's decisions for them, thus taking away their joy of discovery, the effort and excitement of exploration, and the learning experience of arriving at one's own solutions. In a Learning Organization, leaders need to be willing to take the risk to model continuous learning and improvement themselves. How can they expect anyone else to be willing to take the risk of learning something new unless they're willing to take it first?

The third requirement for a safe learning environment is for all members of the team to have their **problem-solving hats on all the time**. When curiosity is the main motive for problem solving, the team's energy is raised to its highest point. In *The Soul of a New Machine*,[2] Tracy Kidder has written of the early days of Data General Corporation when the team was self-managed and highly motivated to bring a new computer to market on time. Many members of the team worked a twenty hour day and were at high energy throughout the experience. Their work epitomized the payoff provided by a genuinely safe, yet challenging, learning environment.

At this level of group investigation, support doesn't mean rubber-stamping, and the self-esteem of the thinker is high enough to value spirited probing of new ideas. If you were testing your mettle in a sport you've mastered, you wouldn't want an opponent who wasn't able to play at your level of expertise.

Just so, genuine thinkers like to have their ideas challenged in as much detail as possible so they can keep refining them.

In the end, it's absolutely essential that **everybody** in the Learning Organization be thinking all the time, with the result that finding solutions becomes a way of life. One person uncommitted to that way of life can poison the atmosphere for everyone.

WHAT TO DO TILL THE CULTURE CHANGES

However, during the intermediate stage, while building the environment that's safe for thinking, some will still be too afraid to think, and thus may perversely act out their fear by subtly undermining "weak" ideas, while trying to prove that creativity is a sham.

They'll do this in positive language, of course, since the organization has already signed off on Step Two. But the fear, which will not go away immediately, will lead to statements like, "It's so nice that Bill has given us the opportunity to explore his new process. It should keep us from having to meet some of the deadlines we've set for ourselves, and I'm fairly sure the process itself will turn out to be relatively harmless."

Paradoxically, the best way to deal with fear reactions that strike out through subtle condemnation like this is to increase the positive support by being tolerant of intolerance without accepting its conclusions. The responses required by this challenge will stretch the organization's reframing skills to the maximum: "Bill's new idea seems over-simple, I admit, but I've been thinking about it a lot, and I suspect we'll find some payoffs in it we don't expect right now. I'm personally quite excited about that, and I have a hunch you will be too once we really get going with it. Meanwhile, keep poking at it. We need that to keep us on our toes."

SUPPORTING THE RIGHT THINGS

Since most truly creative ideas have so much trouble getting accepted, we need to improve our capacity to recognize and support their value. A large company has the resources to do that well, but all too often puts the decision to develop or discard a new project into the hands of someone who uses poor judgment in making that decision. This is because promotions in large companies may be far more influenced by territorial politics than by an intelligent drive to get the right person in the right job. A truly participative management style should correct some of the problem here. An enlightened workplace well on its way to being a full fledged Learning Organization, however, is the only really effective medicine for ailments of this kind.

Failure to respond to the full potential of creative projects could be the most costly form of mismanagement in industry today, when you consider the enormous payoffs of really successful products. Bear in mind, too, the fact that the products which misfired might well have done better with a little extra creative twist added to them at the right stage of development.

ON MISSING THE MOMENT OF OPPORTUNITY

The stakes are high. A path-breaking product that gets on the market at the right time can create a whole industry. A few months delay in getting that product out may mean a competitor's product takes over the field and the industry develops in a completely different way.

There's no guarantee the product selected by the public is actually the best one. More likely it's the one that came out at a time when enough people would adopt it so that switching to a different, though potentially better, product would be awkward. For example, once you've adapted to a particular computer program, you don't necessarily want to take the trouble to learn a competing program, even if it's quite a bit better than the one you've grown accustomed to.

So delays in reaching the market caused by lack of imagination, in-fighting in the development team, resistance by decision makers elsewhere in the company, and other unenlightened behaviors and policies, may prove costly. So costly, in fact, that a single mishap in this line could itself be the cause of bankruptcy instead of the brilliant success that might have been. Thus one can hardly imagine any more valuable resource in industry today than a team that can think creatively as well as defend and promote its ideas.

In the end, whether the organization rises to challenges it must meet depends on how the individual worker is affected by the complex pattern of political and social interactions that make up the organization's culture. That's why Step Three is so important: build a culture that's safe for thinking. Make it a top priority to protect people from ridicule, put down or lack of appropriate response when they have creative ideas, *even when the ideas still need some work.*

No one likes to be ridiculed, so you're likely to think twice before sharing your personal thought process if you think ridicule might be the result. Since truly innovative ideas often seem strange when first presented, the degree of flexibility and tolerance required from the culture will have to be extensive. It all comes down to real thought being generated at every level of the organization.

THESE ENVIRONMENTS CHANGE THEIR PARTICIPANTS

Some organizations have done well at moving toward such environments. A county we have been working with has begun the process of turning back the direction of the county to the residents. Over three thousands citizens from diverse backgrounds have been involved in a two year process of developing visions for the community's future. The ideas generated have been extensive, and ranged from common to revolutionary. However, everyone who wanted a voice, had the full attention of the county staff to do so. The openness that prevailed clearly encouraged more and more people to take the risk of getting actively involved.

The Springfield Remanufacturing Corporation, which originated the Great Game of Business, takes all this a step further. Employees there are so thoroughly involved in the business, because they know precisely how they're affecting the bottom line, that their loyalty is unshakable. The only way you can improve your impact on the bottom line is to think creatively about everything you're doing and refine it. So the personal growth that comes out of this is exciting to see. People who were at one time fairly isolated and static in their lives become community leaders because they've learned of their power from the process the company uses.

GOING AROUND AT THE MANAGEMENT MEETING

Another example is a corporation we worked with, in which one management group begins each day's meeting with a **Go-Around** that invites all participants to say whatever they want for a couple of minutes without interruption. As a result of the culture of listening thus created, the management committee has reduced by more than half the amount of time it takes them to get their business transacted each day.

A major reason for the improvement is that the hidden agendas get on the table during the Go-Around. As a result, everyone understands what is at stake for everyone else, and these issues are now easily taken into account in arriving at decisions. Trust has been built within the management group, together with ease in working together. The bonding that results from an experience like this is a powerful tool for building and sustaining teamwork.

THE THINK AND LISTEN

One way to begin creating a culture of mutual respect for thinking is to introduce the **Think and Listen** activity.

The Think and Listen can help everyone learn to think effectively, efficiently and excellently, and it's fun to use. Creativity stems from the free flow of ideas arising at random and being connected together in meaningful and exciting patterns — at first for the thinker, and later for those who can enjoy and profit from the thinker's good ideas.

Perhaps the most significant barrier to good thinking is that most people barely get a chance even to spurt and sputter at it, and seldom have an opportunity to take a thought all the way to the finish line.

That's because in order to explore your thoughts fully you have to be listened to without interruption, and most of us almost never get listened to long enough to be able to see where our thinking could lead us, particularly when we're feeling our way through it and aren't yet certain where it's going. That's partly because most people, when someone begins to grope, will try to help, supplying missing words and ideas as they seem to be needed.

Yet this is precisely what keeps the thinker from coming to terms with where an idea may be headed. Thus, thinking is too often treated like the water from a garden hose: stopped up, shut off, and blocked. It tends to be made more difficult and is often completely shut down as a result of interruptions, someone else's opinions, time limitations, and other impediments to the thought process. Nevertheless, behind the sealed lips of the silent, creatively blocked person, ideas of real power may be struggling to express themselves, like the water trapped in the hose.

Most of us are so addicted to conversation that our interruptions, contradictions and opinions tend to block the thought of the person who, in speaking to us, is trying to formulate a new idea. And it's for this reason that some folks never get to finish the delicate job of thinking, and therefore remain locked up inside themselves, because no one has ever really listened to them.

Indeed it's not hard to find a person well on in years who can honestly claim never to have been listened to for as long as five minutes without being interrupted — not in a whole lifetime!

HOW IT'S DONE

So here's a tool for breaking the interruption addiction, so anyone can become more comfortable being listened to, and thus start thinking in a new way. Here are the rules for a Think and Listen:

A. Find a partner.
B. Agree in advance on the amount of time to be used by each person, and keep track of it. (You should give each other the same amount of time, if possible within a given session. Occasionally, though, you may want to take turns separated by a few hours or days.)
C. Decide which of you will talk first, and which will listen first.
D. Establish confidentiality of whatever is said, and agree that it will never be discussed later unless the person who said it suggests doing so.
E. Trade roles when your talking time is up.
F. The listener must maintain eye contact with the talker.
G. The talker must not attack the listener.
H. The listener may not interrupt to make comments or ask questions of the talker at any time.
I. Allow for feedback after each has had equal time to talk, if both desire this.
J. If you are the talker, use the exact agreed upon time, and don't trade away what is rightfully yours, even if you believe you have said

everything you wanted to.

K. Never make "you" statements. That is, never talk about your listener. An example of a "you" statement would be, "I think this about you." The Think and Listen must, in most cases, avoid any kind of discussion of the person listening. This is because once there is such discussion, the listener can no longer be an impartial supporter of the thinking process itself.

GETTING STARTED

Once the rules are fully understood, have each member of the group pair off with one other person, and agree to an amount of time each will have to explore any subject whatsoever. Five minutes is a good length of time to start with. One partner then begins talking while the other listens without interruption or feedback for the amount of time agreed on. The listener simply listens, though positive nonverbal feedback is encouraged. The topic can be freely chosen, or agreed to in advance.

When the talker's time is up, he or she becomes the listener, while the listener becomes the talker. The rules are the same as before, and it remains important to keep track of time. Don't be alarmed by gaps or silences, or if the talker's eyes wander while speaking, since that is a normal activity when one is exploring new ideas.

After each has had a turn to talk, the pair may want to offer feedback to one another about what has been said, if both have mutually agreed to do so, and if feedback can be given respectfully and constructively.

HOW PEOPLE FEEL ABOUT IT

It is interesting to hear what people have to say about this process, once they have experienced it. Some say, "I can't believe how hard it is to talk for five minutes! I had to search for things to say!" Others say, "I wanted to interrupt and put in a few words. It was so hard to be quiet for five minutes!" These attitudes tend to crop up the first few times any group attempts a Think and Listen exercise, but once you're used to it, you'll be able to keep going more easily, whether you're the thinker or the listener.

Remember, it's fine to have periods of silence, because this gives your brain a chance to think and process information. Most of us are uncomfortable in silence, when we're with someone else, but it can be a real treat when there's enough respect to allow thoughts to be expressed as they occur.

Organizations use the Think and Listen in research and development phases, planning sessions and board meetings. It helps solve problems, promote creative thinking and improve planning sessions for long range assessment and product development.

One final note: The Think and Listen is also a useful tool for resolving a conflict or disagreement. Although you may not be successful at reaching agreement in every case, the process of exploration should help you figure out how to continue working together effectively. If you use the Think and Listen for this purpose, you may have to suspend Rule K above.

Use the rules outlined above, and remember to be clear and non-threatening when you state the facts as you see them. When this technique is used, it is surprising how often people can begin to see a point of view they once thought they could never understand. It is a tool which when used constructively can bring you new appreciation and awareness of the ideas you have, as well as those of others.

The Think and Listen is simple, yet powerful. Use it to process and understand new information, to build relationships and interactions, to create positive attitudes and increase self-esteem.

GETTING OVER FEAR NUMBER ONE

Public speaking is one of the greatest fears any of us have to face. As the practice of the Think and Listen becomes routine and safe, people who never spoke much in public will begin to feel greater ease voicing ideas and opinions.

With practice at the Think and Listen, team members will begin to listen better to each other's ideas, as well as develop more respect for their own personal thought processes.

The Think and Listen, however, may be rough going for some, so a more gradual process may be useful. It is important that we be listened to while sharing whatever it is that we care most about. One way of accomplishing this is the Good and New, described in Step Two.

With repeated use of the Good and New, employees will tend to open up and share life experiences. Then the Think and Listen will seem more natural to them, and they will find it easier to share each other's thoughts.

DIALOGUE VERSUS DISCUSSION

In *The Fifth Discipline* Peter Senge has clarified the difference between dialogue and discussion.

> In team learning, discussion is the necessary counterpart of dialogue. In a discussion, different views are presented and defended, and [...] this may provide a useful analysis of the whole situation. In dialogue, different views are presented as a means toward discovering a new view. In a discussion, decisions are made. In a dialogue, complex issues are explored. When a team must reach agreement and decisions must be taken, some discussion is needed. On the basis of a commonly agreed analysis, alternative views need to be weighed and a

preferred view selected (which may be one of the original alternatives or a new view that emerges from the discussion). When they are productive, discussions converge on a conclusion or course of action. On the other hand, dialogues are diverging; they do not seek agreement, but a richer grasp of complex issues. Both dialogue and discussion can lead to new courses of action; but actions are often the focus of discussion, whereas new actions emerge as a by-product of dialogue.[3]

This contrast is a powerful one, but it is compromised in practice by the degree to which both discussion and dialogue are complicated by unresolved hidden agendas. If either is not working in a given case, some time spent in Think and Listens should help, since the Think and Listen provides an opportunity to journey into yourself in the presence of an intelligent listener and find out what you really think about something. A Think and Listen that takes only three minutes may sometimes produce a sea change in the way you can work things through. Sometimes, however, hours in this format may be needed before people are ready to proceed towards truly rational positions.

Our experience with the Think and Listen dialogue definitely shows that once people overcome their apprehensions about it, the whole process becomes powerful and enjoyable for most people. The ability to reflect about one's own thinking, without being pre-judged or put down, is a dynamic form of reassurance.

THE PROGRESSIVE THINK AND LISTEN

A powerful variant of the process is the Progressive Think and Listen. In this activity, a group of people, say ten in number, begin by doing Think and Listens on a particular topic. After each round they share with the facilitator of the whole group what they have learned from each other about that topic. The facilitator keeps track of these new learnings on a flip chart. For the next round they take on new partners and repeat the process.

The first few debriefings will probably go quickly. People who are not used to learning from their peers and then sharing what they have learned will have little to say at first.

However, gradually the Think and Listens will become more potent as experience and insight grow. By about the sixth round, the facilitator may have to devote a much longer time to debriefing.

CREATIVE DEAD ENDS

Sometimes an idea really isn't a good one, yet its promoter won't let go of it. We're reminded of someone we once met who seemed to think the most important thing in the world was to build a foundation dedicated to a football star he happened to admire. He lost no opportunity to remind people of his vision, and often cried about it in public. It was clear that he had some unresolved personal issues about this matter, but not clear that anyone else should have to enlist in his cause.

Such dead ends of creative thinking should not be allowed to confuse the issue, but, frustrating as they are, they should be treated with enough respect so that those who have campaigns of genuine value are not discouraged by the rough treatment accorded those whose thinking is less sound.

BEWARE OF SAYING "YES" TO GET TO "NO"

One common way of handling this issue that we do not recommend is accepting an idea in a way that is really intended to let it quietly die. W. S. Gilbert once wrote that "Yes is but another and a neater form of no." This paradox was brought to life recently by a friend who said, "When someone in my organization asks me to participate in a project I want no part of, or when there's a plan of action I wish to block, I always say `yes.'"

I asked how that could be helpful.

"When they think you're on their side, they leave you alone," he replied. "Then you can just do nothing forever, and the project dies."

And so it goes in organizations where much is talked of and little gets done, where the point is to act as if you're part of a team, while in fact you're quietly building a fortress for yourself that no person or project can penetrate. No wonder nothing gets done — everyone's hidden agenda is to maintain the status quo with as little fuss as possible.

One way to avoid this dodge is for each division to develop a procedure for processing new ideas so they can get the hearing they deserve without being prematurely discarded. Based on the time and resources available, one could structure this by scheduling a series of three or four Think and Listens. If the idea survived that much attention, it could then become the subject of a short focus group involving five or six people. The focus group would then be in a position to work out the next steps to getting the idea more widely accepted. Such a gradual set of initially quiet and small steps can avoid the problem of spending too much time on possibilities that are not likely to lead anywhere.

INCREASING THE ODDS IN THE CREATIVITY SWEEPSTAKES

The odds against the triumph of creative ideas are always high. But the Learning Organization radically improves those odds by encouraging bold thinking, while providing the feedback necessary to improve it. A safe, supportive environment is the first requirement for developing the innate intelligence needed to bring an idea from its first vague form to the final success that can have a world-changing impact.

We often find it necessary to remind people that the well used Think and Listen is the single most powerful communication practice they can adopt to help improve their culture. Sometimes these reminders have to keep coming thick and fast over a period of weeks and months, because the commitment required to value one another's thinking is way too much for many people to undertake without some personal struggle.

But when this struggle is finally undertaken and the organization has committed to frequent and ubiquitous use of Think and Listens, new creative processes burgeon all over the organization.

Since it is on just such creative processes that industry is built, it is highly appropriate to develop the resources that will improve the odds. Successful completion of Step Three is a powerful road to enhancement of organizational creativity which will pave the way for the journey to a full fledged Learning Organization.

Many additional techniques beyond those we've given here may be useful to increase the effectiveness of mutual support in your organization. When the culture has changed sufficiently so everyone feels safe about sharing original, unrefined thoughts in a group process, it will then be time to take on the next step in cultural growth in the organization — risk taking.

REWARD
RISK-TAKING

S T E P   4

If you've ever done any canoeing or rafting on a river, *white water* is a term that can start your blood racing with excitement, anticipation, and fear. It describes the turbulent and potentially dangerous rapids where the water speeds up as it rushes over hazardous obstacles, following sudden, powerful currents. It can be a challenge for even the strongest, and a perilous trap for the unwary, who may not recognize the danger until it's too late to escape it.

Now imagine *permanent white water* — tumultuous, unpredictable, exciting, risky. That's the way the world feels today to many people who have to make decisions that affect their own lives and the lives of others. In a competitive and volatile global economy large corporations slide into disaster in a quarter or two, while individuals with promising careers are confronted with the specter of a pink slip. And we can't step back from it, get out of it, wait it out. We can only anticipate more of the same. We're in it, permanently.

DOING BUSINESS IN PERMANENT WHITE WATER

Peter Vail talks about the following characteristics of permanent white water:
1. Permanent white water conditions are full of surprises.
2. Complex systems tend to produce novel problems.
3. Permanent white water conditions feature events that are "messy" and ill-structured.
4. White water events are often extremely costly.
5. Permanent white water conditions raise the problem of recurrence.[1]

Under such conditions, taking meaningful, reasonable, and moderate risks is becoming a prerequisite of survival. Ignoring risks doesn't make them go away; it only increases the danger. Refuge in conformity and security no longer makes sense.

The time has come to cultivate the art of risk-taking everywhere. Without intelligent risks, success becomes impossible. And the greatest risk is in attempting to avoid all risks, for such a strategy is worse than unrealistic; it is futile.

Michael Schulhof, vice-chairman of Sony USA and president of Sony Software, believes risk-taking has now become so essential that corporate leaders should be recruited from the ranks of scientists rather than from

MBA's, for the scientists spend their professional lives learning to take risks. Schulhof was a physicist at Brookhaven Labs before he went into business. Here's what he has to say about risk-taking:

> To be truly successful in business, you have to be a creative risk-taker. I have spent about $7 billion of Sony's money to acquire companies such as Columbia Pictures and CBS Records. These were strategic acquisitions that supported our long-term vision for Sony. You have to have your own vision of the future. And you need the confidence to invest in that vision. It is not much different from the approach to scientific research. The people I admired most in science had the creativity to develop long-term visions of the future as well as the courage to stick with that vision unless research proved them wrong.[2]

While some of Schulhof's risks ended by creating problems for him, the essential point remains: in order to stay in business you must cultivate new possibilities, open up new product lines, relate to your customers in new and different ways, and relate to your employees and even your stockholders in new and different ways.

This is particularly true at a time when the window of opportunity for developing a new product may be very small. The speed of business is unprecedented as cycle times are reduced more and more. If you wait too long, or proceed too slowly, your competitors may leap way ahead of you, eliminating the market opportunity you had counted on. As we work with our clients, we find that many of them rebel when pressured to develop new products, precisely because the risk of such changes makes them feel uncomfortable. Occasionally they're right. When market research has not established that a new product will fly at the price and in the market you're counting on, the result may be a very expensive blunder. So risk taking must be intelligent and well thought out. Fools run in where angels fear to tread, it's true, but somewhere in between are the survivors, for they tread carefully in areas that open up new ground.

SCIENTIFIC RISK-TAKING

The quiet and orderly confines of a scientific research institute may not seem a likely source of guidance on risk-taking. Certainly we would expect it to be a workplace that is safe for thinking, a Learning Organization in the most literal sense. But a training ground for creative risk-takers?

The popular image of scientific research suggests a rigorously logical, methodical process, a painstaking examination of every possibility. Of course there is some truth to this. The full truth, however, is a lot more interesting. It emerges most clearly when you look at where and how highly successful and productive research actually occurs.

In *Apprentice to Genius: The Making of A Scientific Dynasty*, science writer Robert Kanigel looks closely into the dynamics of great scientific discoveries, breakthroughs which could only be made by going beyond the safe, predictable next step, past the frontier of knowledge, into the unknown. He was particularly intrigued by the string of breakthroughs in the fields of pharmacology, medicine and the neurosciences from the 1940's onward. These were truly momentous discoveries, at the highest level of what is sometimes called elite science, the Nobel Prize level where giant leaps of creative imagination are made, whole scientific disciplines are revolutionized, and new fields of inquiry are born.

WHAT MAKES THESE GREAT LEAPS POSSIBLE?

Kanigel found, as have other observers of science, that these discoveries were not made at random by lone scientists in isolated laboratories. They were made by what he calls a dynasty, including such seminal figures as Bernard "Steve" Brodie, Julius Axelrod, Sol Snyder, Candace Pert — uniquely brilliant individuals who nevertheless acknowledged their great debts to each other, and saw themselves linked, along with many others, through a generational chain of mentors and apprentices. "By this view," Kanigel writes,

> a great scientific discovery is the product not of individual genius alone but of a scientific "family," down through the generations of which something special, something pivotal, has been passed on.

But what, precisely, gets passed on?[3]

When you look at the history of these breakthroughs, it is clear that some indispensable factor beside the talents of the individual scientists is at work. That "something special, something pivotal" is what we are looking for. The crucial question for a Learning Organization is, once we have an environment that is safe for thinking, how do we encourage the kind of thinking that will make the necessary difference, the leaps of imagination, the risky and unprecedented insight that shows us the best course through the white water?

ON TAKING A FLIER

The pivotal factor is an attitude and an example set by the manager or leader, internalized by team members and subordinates, and communicated in turn by them to their fellow workers. It's an attitude towards knowing, learning, confronting problems. One scientist called it a "style of thinking."[4] It can't be codified as a set of rules or instructions. Kanigel regards it rather as a treasured and powerful legacy that has been handed on directly from one scientific "generation" to the next. He sums it up in the context of scientific work, though his conclusions are applicable to any enterprise:

> Don't bother with the routine scientific problems ....
> Leave them to others. Don't bother, either, with big, funda-
> mental problems that are simply not approachable with
> available techniques and knowledge; why beat your head
> against the wall? Half the battle is asking the right question at
> the right time — when it's neither premature to tackle it, nor
> invites too obvious an answer, when the right methodology is
> at hand, when enthusiasm is at its peak.

Bear in mind that the question must be asked in the context of what has come before. You can't wipe out the trajectory and heritage of generations of development, even if the results have been inefficient. The tendency in our culture is to throw the baby out with the bath water. You always have to fit what you offer into the context of what has come before, or it will not be able to survive. Severing connections to past work violates the natural evolution-ary process, reducing the substrate from which quantum creative leaps can emerge. Sometimes small steps, therefore, work much better than a single large step. These are the kinds of things you want to consider as you build your plan for change. But build it quickly, don't linger too long over the details.

> And then, just *do* it. Don't spend all year in the library
> getting ready to do it. Don't wait until you've gotten all the
> boring little preparatory experiments out of the way. Don't
> worry about scientific controls, except the most rudimentary.
> Just go with your hunch, your scientific intuition, and isolate
> that simple, elegant, pointed experiment that will tell you in a
> flash whether you're on the right track. Or, as Steve Brodie
> might say: Just go ahead and take a flier on it.[5]

Just go ahead and take a flier on it. Obviously this is not a matter of mere momentary impulse. A lot of study and know-how precede it. But knowledge, creativity, and preparation, though essential, are not enough. There comes a time when you have to *just do it*.

The critical point for the Learning Organization is that though the kind of fruitful risk-taking these scientists speak of cannot strictly speaking be taught, it can be stimulated by and absorbed from the example of others. It can be practiced. And in an organization that is already in the process of being trans-formed by implementing the skills of Steps Two and Three, that practice can be increasingly exhilarating, masterful, and productive.

HOW TO MAKE YOURSELF MISERABLE AVOIDING RISKS

Unfortunately, this does not sound like the profile of the typical organiza-tion, or its members. More commonly populating the corridors of businesses and bureaucracies of all sorts are people of the opposite tendency, with too little vision of possibility, accompanied by too little willingness to risk.

Those who refuse to allow themselves to take risks look for the safest approach to whatever they plan to do. They'll study *Consumer Reports* for months before buying a new car or TV. They'll take out radically overpriced insurance policies because they think they're reducing already miniscule risks. They'll fill their pantries with food every time a shortage threatens. They'll deprive themselves of most of the real pleasures of life because of a slight risk that something bad might happen — or because they're "not good for you".

The software design department of a large corporation we worked with were driving people in the organization crazy. They spent months validating and revalidating a new design, to the point where the (delay?) in implementing the new software was costing the company $10,000 per month. In the end, this strategy of avoiding risk by perfectly debugging the design may have caused considerably larger problems for the whole organization than if they had relied on the adaptability of the company and its capacity to correct software problems as they arose.

For risk avoiding folks, the means of making yourself miserable are endless, since literally nothing we do is completely risk free. More people die in their bathtubs than while flying in airplanes. And your relations, friends and neighbors are more likely to kill you than those you don't know. Life is, in fact, so dangerous that for some time now its fatality rate has hovered around 100%. Yet many seem determined to eliminate all the dangers from their lives — which only means they eliminate most of the opportunities as well. It's through risk-taking itself that we hone the skills and judgment required to become ever more seasoned risk-takers.

THE VALUE OF LEARNING FROM RISKS

Organizations need to pay serious attention to this process and adopt practices which encourage boldness and enterprise. Inevitably any organization that does not actively foster risk-taking is taking the greatest risk of all — the risk of going out of business.

The good news is that each new risk is an opportunity to learn about how to be more successful, and also about how to take intelligent risks. As we practice risk-taking, we can develop the judgment that will help us to be winners better than half the time. For a risk is **moderate** when the chances of being successful are better than even, but are still not definite. Moderate risks are the stuff of which progress and business success are made. Without them, we'd be quickly defeated by the natural process that renders the status quo obsolete.

WHAT'S A MODERATE RISK?

In the 1960's at Harvard University, psychologist David C. McClelland analyzed the components of the kind of motivation that virtually guarantees success in business: *achievement motivation*. One of the most significant of these turned out to be moderate risk-taking. From a study of his work one may conclude that if you have between 60% and 90% chance of being successful at what you're undertaking, your risk is moderate. Though the chances of failure are not great, they are nonetheless possible. Above 90% you're not taking much of a risk, and below 60% your risk is probably too great to be wise.

But what do these numbers actually mean? It's often difficult to analyze what constitutes a moderate risk until a great deal of information has been gathered, much of it only after the risk has been taken. In fact, it may well be that a truly scientific assessment of risks in a real world, real time setting will be forever impossible, as too many factors have to be considered before a rational judgment can be made.

LIVING WITH UNCERTAINTY

This leaves the judgment up to you. Most successful people know intuitively when a risk makes sense and when it doesn't. Before he built Walmart, one of the most successful retail businesses in history, Sam Walton had to go through many failures and difficult times. Yet in the scope of his whole life the risk he took was moderate, since his vision was so clear to him and included a deep understanding of what strategies would yield success in the long run.

We must accept the fact that we may never know scientifically what is and isn't a moderate risk. For that matter, we also may never be able to analyze what it means to fall in love or listen to music. That shouldn't mean, however, that we don't know anything about these phenomena — only that we are aware the judgment must be individual and intuitive. Our goal here should be to determine what we can do to increase the odds that our moderate risk-taking will become, over time, more imaginative and more fruitful.

ON AVOIDING FOOLISH RISKS

If your risk has only a 20% chance of success, you are probably being foolish. While an occasional long shot is not bad if the stakes aren't too high (or staying in your present position is the worst possible alternative) extreme risks as a way of life are ineffective, because they lead to so much unproductive effort.

Some would-be entrepreneurs approach business in the spirit of winning big at impossible odds, rather than carefully and conscientiously building a foundation that could in the end pay off handsomely. These folks fail repeatedly because they don't know how to evaluate intelligently the risks they're taking, or to design their way to the top, taking the steps that will most likely lead in the direction of the success they seek. Sometimes the risk is increased because even though they are willing to take a flier, they haven't done the preparation that would enable them to recognize where and when to make their move.

DON'T CONFUSE RISK-TAKING WITH
BEATING YOUR HEAD AGAINST THE WALL

Recently we interviewed a secretary who said she knew from hard personal experience that risk-taking was a bad thing, to be rigorously avoided. We asked why, and she said, "I trusted a friend several times and he disappointed me every time."

We pointed out that this was not an example of *moderate* risk-taking. She should have become aware pretty quickly that the conduct she kept noticing was a reliable and predictable characteristic of her friend's behavior, so it was nearly certain he would let her down every time.

Remember that risks are moderate only if the chances of success are well over fifty percent. Only if that's the case does it make sense to dive in and take a chance.

It's interesting that people often have very little idea about the actual the degree of risk they're confronting. For example, large numbers of people worry about taking airplane flights because the occasional deaths that result from airline accidents are so highly publicized. The fact that riding in a car is hundreds of times more risky than flying in an airplane doesn't seem to change their attitudes. It's a good idea to develop a sense of what is and is not really risky. As you become better at determining the actual risks involved in different personal activities, you'll start to evaluate risks more clearly in a business context as well.

The following model and process has been very helpful for individuals and teams in gaining greater clarity about assessing risk (these concepts were introduced in Step Three):

1. Take a large sheet of flipchart paper.
2. Use multiple colored magic markers.
3. Draw an up-side down triangle.
4. In the upper left write Structure
5. In the upper right write Nurturing
6. In the bottom write Problem-Solving
7. In the middle of the triangle write Risk

First, determine the change you wish to make. For example: "in the next six months we want to change our compensation and rewards system". The change is the "Risk" that you are undertaking. Be very clear with yourself, or your team members about what exactly you want to accomplish. Second, decide on the Structures (framework, boundaries) that will be necessary to accomplish the change — the Risk. Third, decide on the kind of internal and external support you will need to comfortably deal with this Risk. Fourth, decide on the problem solving elements involved with the Risk.

This kind of exercise fosters a clearer evaluation of the risk we are considering. Many times, if at all, we only evaluate the risk dynamics of a situation without the benefit of a guiding format. But without a guide or procedure, we may find ourselves going around and around an issue, and even becoming more confused.

THE NEED FOR CLARITY ABOUT RISK-TAKING

It's not uncommon for risk-taking to get lip service in the workplace. "Just go ahead and take the risk — try it" is a common line. Or, "Well, I don't know what the problem is with taking risks in this organization. I haven't heard of any employees ever getting fired for sticking their necks out that way."

But remarks like these don't guarantee that management is clear about the emotional and personal commitment that taking risks involves. If people have to guess where management stands, they're far less likely to stick their necks out than if organizational policies of supporting appropriate risks are clearly stated and known to hold sway. Management should also keep in mind that while firings may not be reprisals for risk-taking that didn't pay off, suspicion that they are may circulate anyway. Management needs to be crystal clear on all these issues.

In fact, this is probably the area in which management is least likely to be well informed about what's in the minds of employees. For some, the idea of speaking to the boss on any subject may be so great a risk that they remain silent no matter what. The boss, meanwhile, may think everything is fine and have no inkling of this fear, which may be fairly widespread. If you really want to know what the people who work for you are really thinking, you may have to become something of a Sherlock Holmes. The kinds of risks you wish people would take may be just too much for them, given the way you've been managing them.

If management is serious about making risk-taking a primary goal of the corporate culture, it's helpful to develop a strategy for making the rewards of winning reasonably high, while the penalties for losing are kept low.

BUILDING THE CULTURE THAT SUPPORTS RISK-TAKING

Bold initiatives stand a greater chance of succeeding in an environment which is hospitable to them. This seems almost too obvious to mention, except that it raises the challenge of describing such an environment.

Risk-taking for people on a team, or even in a large organization, requires that they be **protected** by their team or their management until they've had a chance to prove themselves.

They also must be ready and well-positioned to succeed. People should never embark on a project until their **capability** is assured as a result of developing or having access to all the skills required by the challenge.

Finally, they need managerial **permission** to take the anticipated risk.

Failures will sometimes occur, and they will have real consequences, but these should never be catastrophic for the individuals.

ALLOWING FOR MISTAKES

To help employees feel safe in taking the moderate risks necessary to increase the potential of building a successful Learning Organization, it's essential to develop a culture that supports risk-taking, with an almost complete absence of fear of the consequences, should failure be the outcome.

If this policy towards mistakes seems utopian and impractical, consider the alternative: unhealthy, self-defeating timidity and stagnation, plus, of course, a tendency to hide mistakes. In a climate where mistakes are not punished, missteps and miscalculations can better be examined for useful lessons. Thus the organizational policy can be designed to allow employees to make whatever mistakes may result from honest, creative and energetic attempts to move forward, while seriously encouraging them to learn enough from each mistake so a better result is possible next time.

An executive management team decided to evaluate its organizational learning dynamics. One enlightening discovery was that despite having a culture that strongly promoted continuous learning, they were failing to learn from their mistakes. In fact they were making the same mistakes over and over again. They concluded that the strong advocacy of continuous improvement they touted was merely an illusion which could not become real until they created an environment more open about mistakes. Subsequently, they developed an on-going "lessons learned" process for the whole company.

This acceptance of risk on the part of management and leadership can have a tremendously liberating effect on the entire organization. That's what happened in the heady days of the scientific dynasty we described earlier. *"Let's take a flier on it.* There was magic in the style of science embodied in that expression, a breathtaking freedom to be wrong."[6]

One of us was recently working with an employee who had put together a booth at an industrial fair. She ordered hundreds of books to be sold from the booth, but unfortunately only two of them were sold. I spoke to her about this afterwards. "Were you the one who decided to order all those books?" I said.

"Yes," she admitted, looking very sheepish and a little scared.

"Congratulations," I said. "You took a risk and stuck your neck out. That's far more important than how many books were sold."

In the months that followed the quality of this person's work skyrocketed.

When acceptance of the risk of error is built into the process of decision-making, so is the possibility of learning from mistakes that will inevitably occur. Project reports, for example, ought to have specific places in them for documenting what was learned from the errors that cropped up in the project.

This will go a long way towards helping people see error as a natural part of the learning process, rather than something to be avoided at all costs. It will also combat the tendency, often so widespread, of denying and covering up mistakes — which only makes it more likely they'll be repeated.

TAKE A MOMENT TO ASSESS

Now we ask you to stop for a moment and assess your organization's willingness to encourage risk-taking by answering the following questions:

1. What's the general attitude toward risk-taking among the employees?
2. What efforts have you seen the organization make to increase risk-taking?
3. How many instances can you think of in which it was discouraged?
4. What forces in the culture encourage risk-taking?
5. What forces discourage it?
6. What are the three best steps the organization might take to encourage more risk-taking?

THE PERSONAL SIDE OF THE EQUATION

You'll find that part of your willingness to take risks must inevitably depend on how your organization responds to risk-taking. Part of it, however, will depend on your own previous experience with risk-taking.

You'll probably notice, if you think about it, that successful risk-takers usually rise to the top. By spending the right percentage of their time, effort and energy taking risks that make sense to them, they manage to win often enough so the risks that don't pay off don't hold them back.

What about you: what kind of a risk-taker are you personally? Most people have a pretty good sense of how comfortable they are with risk-taking. However, when they consider past decisions, it often appears in hindsight that they misjudged the degree of risk involved in their choices.

The point here is not merely to take more risks; it is to become a more skillful risk-taker, taking a flier for the right reasons at the right time. These skills can be practiced, but before we consider them, let's make the picture less abstract by illustrating some of the qualities of successful risk-taking.

WAYNE GRETZKY'S SECRET FORMULA

There's always a lot of curiosity about superstars in any field. It's natural to think the difference between them and the rest of us must be some unique capability, some secret of the trade. Consider ice hockey great Wayne Gretzky, whose accomplishments are already legendary. What's his secret? "It's simple," Gretzky will say in interviews. "I always go to where the puck isn't yet."

His strategy is anticipation. Where other players will head for the puck, over the years Gretzky has taught himself to anticipate where the puck will be, and go there instead. 75% of the time he's right on. The other 25% he looks like a fool — but who cares? When he's right, he gets there first. He makes it look so simple, it seems like magic.

However, to anticipate as effectively as Wayne Gretzky does, you have to have his skill level and his clarity of purpose. You must know where you're going, and you must develop a large reservoir of knowledge that can help you to predict the next step.

Most effective risks involve sensing that something is about to happen before the actual event. For this you need to know enough about your field to understand its probabilities. As Gretzky streaks around the hockey rink, he is factoring in a tremendous amount of knowledge about the other players, about hockey strategy, about the momentary ebb and flow of the game.

You also need strong intuition, so you can act on hunches that will pay off for you most of the time. An insightful person who has an overview of the relevant data develops the skill to create mental patterns that can predict which routes to the desired goal are most likely to be productive. These mental patterns are only hunches, of course, but they're highly informed hunches — likely to pay off much of the time.

In problem-solving activities such as science these hunches are often inspired by analogies. Some process in nature or industrial production may suggest a way to reach a particular goal.

HORSING AROUND WITH ELMER'S

Inspiration can come from many, sometimes very surprising, sources. Elmer's drip-free glue container was developed through a highly unusual analogy. A member of the design group, remembering the tidy affair of equine defecation, pursued this analogy. This led to development of the cap used by Elmer's Glue, which pushes up, allows the glue to come out, then shuts down and cuts off the excess glue. Thus at least one horse contributed to the glue business without giving up its life.

Familiarity with many different ways of solving problems provides important background knowledge. For the risk-taker, learning is fundamental. It's through the flexible processing of information that hunches develop. Following up on those hunches may save thousands of hours, years or lifetimes in making a major breakthrough. But the more widely one scans the horizon for potentially useful information, the more one is likely to find the clue that triggers the hunch.

It's a reciprocal process. Playing hunches, having good instincts, any way you say it, is a very important part of problem-solving. The more fully aware of all the available and relevant data you are, the better your hunches will be.

THE IMPORTANCE OF AMBIGUITY TOLERANCE

To open your mind to intuition, though, you've got to have a fairly flexible approach to the things you think you know. Creative people seem to specialize in putting off closure when they're trying to solve problems. This means they keep an open mind longer than the average person would, and that allows them to arrive at more creative solutions.

A number of activities can help you generate new creative ideas while also improving your ability to assess potential risks intelligently. So in this Step we'll take you through nine strategies specifically geared to improving your risk-taking.

NINE KEYS TO RISK-TAKING

1. Trust your own brilliance, uniqueness and sense of purpose.
2. Create a support team.
3. Overcome any fear of making mistakes.
4. Be open-minded.
5. Develop your intuitive powers.
6. Practice the mechanics of setting goals you can reach.
7. Create images of your goals.
8. Explore the ecology of your situation.
9. Develop benchmarks and then get feedback on how well you're reaching them.

Let's explore each of these in turn:

1. Increase your trust in your own brilliance, uniqueness and sense of purpose.

Intuition can be blocked by self-imposed barriers that cause us to mistrust our judgment. We often persuade ourselves that there are limits on our ability to learn and improve our performance. Most of us possess unexplored, untapped talents. The process of making compromises with life, settling for less than we had originally hoped for, causes us to overlook our potential.

Sometimes to be successful you have to give up these limiting ideas. Perhaps the most effective way to do this is to reinterpret your limitations, seeing them as temporary. For example, when you were three years old you probably couldn't read, but instead of viewing this as a limitation, you looked forward to the time when you would be able to. What's true of us at three should also be true when we're thirty or even sixty. We'll have much more to say about recognizing your full potential in Step Six.[7]

2. Create a support team.

No matter how independent-minded we are, we're still influenced by the people around us. So naturally it's useful to surround yourself with people who are willing to cheer you on to achieve the goals you've set for yourself. This doesn't mean they have to be blind to your mistakes. On the contrary, real support helps you learn the lessons that turn mistakes into eventual successes.

Discouragement in itself is no barrier to success. In fact, motivation expert David McClelland believes that the ability to admit to and explore feelings of failure is one of the most important aspects of achievement motivation. When you feel discouraged, turn to someone who will listen to you while you explore the source of your discouragement. By exploring the feelings you have when you think you're not achieving your goals, you can learn a lot that will eventually help you achieve them. It's denying the feelings that causes trouble, because then you're more likely to pretend to yourself that things are going well when they're not.

When you feel you've made a major mistake, your associates may be able to help you analyze it so you can decide what to do next. If you've been implementing the first three of the Ten Steps in this book, you already have the tools to create a support team for yourself. Choose for your team people who are eager to help you become more successful. Of course the deal is that you'll also support them — so everyone benefits.

If you move ahead with determination and put together a strong support team for yourself, you'll soon become a more effective team player. You'll also learn how to develop your capacities and areas of commitment in life.

3. Overcome fear of making mistakes.

In Step Four the skill we're trying to develop is the one Wayne Gretzky has perfected: accurately sensing where the puck will be and heading there as early as possible. Getting rid of the fear of being wrong 25% of the time is one part of the challenge.

We believe that if you're successfully implementing Steps Two and Three, you'll already have overcome much of your fear of making mistakes. If that's still a problem for you, spend some time doing Think and Listens to find the source of the problem. Incidentally, in our work with organizations we've found that one of the most important tools for culture change is the Think and Listen. It's also the tool that we have to work hardest to persuade people to use consistently.

The goal is to approach each new challenge with confidence and a willingness to let the chips fall where they may, and the Think and Listens you do can help you build your confidence enormously. You'll probably make some mistakes, but you can always correct them and learn from the experience.

In number five below, you'll find an exercise which will reinforce your willingness to speak without fear of making mistakes. That's because giving up this fear is closely connected with developing intuition. So if you want support in increasing your confidence to speak the truth freely, read on.

4. Be open-minded.

One of the biggest barriers to progress is outworn assumptions about how things work. Our assumptions can prevent us from seeing possibilities. The ability to relax a strongly held set of beliefs seems to develop from a general sense of security within situations that are highly ambiguous. If you're comfortable with ambiguity and uncertainty, you'll be more alert to the clues you'll need to determine the best course of action.

When Alexander Graham Bell was working to invent the telephone, people tried to persuade him to spend his time instead on the obviously more fruitful task of improving the telegraph. Where would we be today if he had given up and followed the wisdom of his counselors? One of his craziest ideas, the notion that messages could be sent on light, would seem at the time of his death to be a fruitless idea. Today, however, it is the basis of fiber optics, which allows an infinite number of messages to be sent through the wires at the same time.

If you comb through the history books, numerous examples of wrong-headed but widely held assumptions spring from their pages. At one time people believed that women were too irresponsible to vote, that our nation could not function without slavery, and that not all children needed schooling. Progress on these issues occurred when risk-takers committed to social improvement took the imaginative leaps to envision a world beyond the status quo.

Today many of us assume that the risk takers of the past knew what they were doing, but that's not true today, since everything has already been thought of. It's our experience, though, that the best ideas still have to fight for their lives today, just as much as they did at any time in the past.

Such mental flights are the daily business of science fiction and fantasy writers, who must imagine unfamiliar worlds as if they were real. It might surprise you to learn that although the percentage of the general public that reads science fiction is quite low, no less than half of all professional scientists are at least occasional science fiction readers. The exercise of thinking about unfamiliar worlds, conditions and belief systems stimulates creative thinking.

It's also good for risk-takers, because if you're taking the risk to create something new, you may have to accept the consequences of being successful. Some of these consequences might shake up your life and require adjustments. So, if you can evaluate your assumptions and core beliefs comfortably, you'll be a lot better able to change those that are too rigid to allow you to proceed productively with your life.

5. Develop your intuitive powers.

A friend tells us she was selecting a nursing home for her elderly mother. She carefully inspected several places but instantly felt that one was better. At first it seemed a very subjective choice. From all objective indicators the preferred home didn't have any more to offer. Afterward, thinking about the intuitive process that led to this choice, she realized that her sixth sense was not so mysterious. Her intuition had been based on actual clues — minor observations she had made without realizing it. The way residents socialized among themselves, the facial expressions and body language of the staff, and other subtle clues, suggested an atmosphere of greater naturalness and caring. These almost subliminal indications produced no great thunderclap of insight, but nevertheless gave her a good enough sense of the place to make the choice easier. She realized that upon reflection she could verbalize the differences.

Often we notice many things we're not aware of at the time, but later they can play a decisive role in shaping our perceptions and decisions. An eye scanning the horizon together with a trust in these paraliminal or subliminal observations is a major part of the skill needed for developing intuition.

In our seminars we often play a game that helps people trust their intuitive impulses a little more. You might try it to give you the feeling of operating instinctively during a simple task. It involves circumventing your normal thinking processes and relying more on your intuition.

TAP INTO YOUR INTUITION

Hold a Koosh ball in your hand and toss it into the air. Catch it as it comes back down; but as you do so, say the word "pass" loudly and clearly, just at the instant the ball hits your hand.

This coordination between catching the ball and saying the word can be a surprisingly powerful technique for teaching you to trust your intuition. Once you're really clear on the difference between catching the ball and saying the word a billionth of a second after the ball hits your hand, versus saying it precisely as the ball touches down, you're ready to go on with this exercise.

Now take the following words in sequence and see if you can memorize them well enough so that as you toss the ball and catch it, you can say the next word in the series exactly and without hesitation every time. (This may take you about ten minutes to accomplish.)

Here is the sequence of words you're going to memorize: "assess, plan, do, verify." (These are the four stages of the quality process, and knowing them as well as you know your own name will help you think better about the subject of quality.)

When you've memorized this series of four words using the Koosh ball — so it's easy for you to catch the ball and say the next word in the series every time — you'll be better able to understand what follows.

THE NATURAL FLOW OF THINKING AND HOW WE LOSE IT

Most children have a natural flow to their thinking which comes out easily as they talk with those they're comfortable with. It does not occur to them to sort for right and wrong answers. Nor do they mind being corrected when they're wrong.

But as we grow older, most of us lose the ease of childhood and become uncomfortable when we have to give answers if there's any chance our answers might be wrong. So we form the habit of checking ourselves before we speak. The mind goes into an automatic circuit that says, "is this really right?" When there's a possibility we might not have the right answer, it's natural for most of us to feel a little fear or concern.

This mental habit results from years of believing it's important to give the right answer to any question so we won't look foolish. As a result, our thoughts don't flow nearly as well as they otherwise might, and we tend to believe we are (or might be) wrong a great deal more often than is necessary. Two consequences result from this:

* Our thinking is far less efficient.
* We're more afraid of taking reasonable, moderate risks than we otherwise would be.

It's possible to clear up this problem in a fairly short time by working with the ball in the way described above. Here's why:

The act of catching the ball causes you to focus your attention kinesthetically and takes your mind off the search for the right answer it would otherwise be occupied with. You'll either blurt out an answer — right or wrong — or you'll give no answer at all.

After you've practiced for a while, it will get easier to blurt out the correct answer. That's because you won't be censoring your thoughts the way you used to. As a result, you'll relax your thinking so answers come more easily. This ability to give a rapid response where before you were hesitating won't increase the number of mistakes you make. You'll be accurate the same percentage of the time as you were before, but you'll have a lot more to say, and you'll feel more comfortable in situations where you're likely to be on the spot.

MORE FLEXIBILITY FOR YOUR THINKING

We might say that our available consciousness occurs on at least two levels. The first is that which readily comes to mind. The second is what we might call subliminal, or below the threshold — when we know something, but can't readily bring it to mind.

As you decrease the fear of letting ideas flow through you, you can actually lower the threshold of your conscious awareness — allowing yourself to deal consciously with many things that previously were pushed outside your awareness. This will help you respond more fully to the subtle clues you've been noting but not really thinking about, like the ones our friend told us helped her make a decision about a nursing home.

Carol Burnett was asked what was the most important thing she ever learned about acting. Her response: "Learning how to get out of my own way." She had to teach herself to fully trust her intuition. Failing to do so meant not being able to perform at her highest levels of creativity. The same process needs to work for many people in order to increase their intuitive powers.

Intuition has survival value in a rapidly changing environment, but it also becomes more difficult to come by the more we're afraid for our survival, or the more the ideas we already have are locked into place and seem to be fixed descriptions of the way things always are. That's why building up our intuitive muscles with exercises like the one we've just described may be crucial in helping you face the new era of white water management.

6. Practice the mechanics of setting goals you can reach.

Here's an exercise developed by David McClelland to help you learn to distinguish moderate risks from those which are either too great or not challenging enough. McClelland found that most people, after a little practice with this exercise, were able to do a much better job of setting reasonable, realistic goals for themselves.

THE BEAN BAG EXERCISE

This game, which is ideally suited for a seminar activity, involves throwing beanbags into coffee cans. Each person selects a position that makes it possible to be successful between 60 and 80 percent of the time in hitting the target. For example, you might find that if you stand one foot from the can you have a success rate of 100%, but if you stand a hundred feet from it, your success rate drops to one percent. Somewhere in between is the level of moderate risk.

Once each player has discovered the position of moderate risk, score the game as follows: A bean bag thrown into the can from that position scores ten points. A throw from a closer position scores only two points. A throw from a distance much greater than the moderate risk position scores twenty-five points. Have the participants practice the game enough so they learn what position consistently yields them the highest score. It may be necessary, as you experiment with this game, to modify the scoring system in order to get results that consistently match those of actual life experience.

Now that everyone has learned to play the game, see who would rather win a prize by playing the game, and who would prefer to let winnings hang upon a roll of the dice. Those who still prefer dice games haven't yet discovered the joy of winning through their own efforts, rather than waiting for Lady Luck to smile upon them.

NOW APPLY IT TO REALITY

The next step is to apply what's been learned in these games to real situations in the organization. What kinds of risks need to be taken? What's an intelligent approach to taking them?

Divide the team into groups of three. Have each group list some projects your organization might undertake. When each group has made a list of projects, it may then rank them in order of potential value to the team or the organization.

When the value ranking has been completed, the group may then evaluate each activity according to its risk and potential consequences, so as to achieve a second ranking order. The goal is to determine which activities or projects have the highest potential value with the lowest potential risk.

When the small groups have completed this project, the various rankings can be brought together and reevaluated by the entire group. When the activity is completed, all will have a better idea of the risk opportunities they face, so the specific risks that would be worth taking have been identified and plans can then be made to act on them.

7. Create images of your goals.

In Step Seven we'll explore how the translation of words into images can pave the way to success in reaching your goals. For the moment, we'll content ourselves with observing that imagery plays a major role in the achievement of success. If you have a vivid, mental picture of yourself experiencing the outcome you have in mind, you're a lot more likely to reach it than if it remains a vague abstraction.

While visualizing outcomes may not be something you've done a great deal of, it's regularly used to train athletes, who learn to see themselves performing a certain way, or to see the ball going where they want it to go.

In doing so they build their visualizations not just with mental pictures, but with imagined sounds, smells, physical sensations and emotions as well.

If you want a more direct experience of what visualization can do, one which you can try out right this minute with a friend, here it is:

Extend your arm out from your body horizontal to the floor, palm upward. Ask a friend to try to bend your arm at the elbow by raising your wrist while holding down on your biceps. Your job is to resist the raising of your arm. If your friend is strong, you'll probably find the resistance doesn't work and your friend is able to bend it.

Now, go through the same process again, only this time (now that your arm has been weakened from your struggle the first time around) you're not going to try hard to resist, although you're not going to let your arm be pushed up easily either. What you're going to do is imagine that your arm is a very hard steel bar. Just concentrate on feeling the hardness of it while your friend tries to raise it.

If you're like most people, this second round won't exhaust you the way the first one did. In fact, you may feel as if you're not really exerting much effort to resist. But your friend will probably have a much harder time making your arm bend at the elbow, and may not be able to do so at all!

If this exercise worked for you, it should leave you with a strong impression of the immense power of visualization, when properly used, to make it easier and more efficient to achieve a goal.

Now let's apply what we've just learned. Suppose for example you want to develop a new kind of software that will open up a niche for you in a developing technology. Imagine yourself receiving an award for the development of the software, demonstrating to an admiring crowd what the software will do, and see the whole thing as if it were being filmed for the movies.

Such mental pictures, as we've just seen, can be extremely powerful, and may actually be realized in full detail with the passage of time. We have met and talked to many people who have done just this and who can tell us about how the realization of the imagined event corresponded in certain precise details to their imagery. We ourselves have also had many experiences with this kind of fulfillment, and can say as a result that while the connection between the image and the achieved reality is very close in many particulars, there was no way of knowing originally by what route the imagined goal would be fulfilled.

Recently one of us undertook a very challenging project, one which quickly seemed doomed to failure. However, at the very beginning I had hung a picture on my wall which represented for me what the completion of this undertaking would be like. A couple of months later I was pleading with my associates to abandon the project, which I believed to be hopeless, but they refused to do so. Today the project has turned into an incredible success, and every time I look at that picture on my wall I'm reminded of the number of times I thought of taking it down when all seemed hopeless.

To turn this exercise into a group activity, you might want to tell a story about how the group will achieve its goal. Great leaders often use this technique to inspire their followers to success. Martin Luther King's famous speech "I Have a Dream" is an example of this technique at its best.

The management team of a government agency decided to present their annual strategic plan in an easily digestible visual representation instead of their usual highly logical/analytical format They developed and circulated a short document with a cover that included a drawing for each of the six elements of the plan. It took people only a few minutes to grasp the main points of what the focus of the agency would be for the next year.

8. Explore the ecology of your situation.

The next feature of successful risk-taking we'll consider is the selection of those risks which will move the enterprise along to its next steps without taking it too far afield. In assessing risks, therefore, a great deal can be learned from considering the *possible consequences* of taking a specific action or line of reasoning.

For example, if you have a new stereo tape deck installed in your car, some risk may be involved. If the deck is defective, you might have to take time from your busy schedule to have it replaced. The deck could even burn out the electrical system in your car, which would mean an additional expense and inconvenience. But it's hard to imagine any way in which the installation of a faulty stereo tape deck could threaten your life.

But when you have a new brake system installed, serious defects could make it impossible to stop on the freeway, and could be life threatening. Obviously, therefore, the acceptable margin for error in installing brakes must be much smaller than that for installing stereo systems. In short, the degree of acceptable risk depends on the situation.

9. Benchmark and then get feedback on how you're doing.

State clearly the goals you hope to have reached five years from now. Then determine how far along the path you will be a year from now. Move back to six months, three months, one month, one week, and end by deciding what you're going to do tomorrow. For each benchmark on the path, state what resources you will need to proceed to the next benchmark.

Once you've sketched this in, do a Think and Listen with a friend to determine how well your initial ideas hold up as you talk about them with someone else. It isn't necessary that you know precisely what actions to take to reach your goals, only how far along you've come at any given point in your quest to reach them.

This form of time management is extremely helpful in moving your goals out of the area of foggy dreams into the cold, clear light of reality. If you want it to work, though, we suggest you employ it frequently. If you don't meet a friend to reassess your progress at least once a month, then make sure you do it quarterly. Monitoring your progress in this way will help keep you on track and develop a sense of accountability to the commitments you make to yourself that will help you keep your commitments to others as well.

READY FOR THE NEXT STEP?

Moderate risk-taking is a learnable skill, provided fear and threat are absent. Remember, though, that risk-taking begins with an attitude, a style of thinking which can't really take hold in an organization unless it's practiced and modeled throughout the organization, particularly at the top.

Skillful risk-taking is an invaluable asset for both individuals and groups. In a Learning Organization it is crucial for successfully navigating today's "permanent white water." In addition, it helps you learn more effectively about the world at large and your organization's potential for success.

For risk-taking is almost inevitably a process of self-discovery, and in this process members of a group or organization recognize how important the other members of the team are, and how powerful and valuable the contribution of each can be. That recognition is the subject of Step Five.

HELP PEOPLE
BECOME RESOURCES
S T E P 5 FOR EACH OTHER

One of us has two children, a twelve year old and a seven year old —
both boys.

One day the twelve year old came to me and said, "I want to build a tree
house. Can you help me find some lumber?"

We searched our property, but didn't find anything suitable. Then I said,
"They're building a new house just up the street. Maybe they have some scrap
lumber they'd be willing to let you use."

The boy became rigid. "No. If I take lumber from a construction site,
I'll get put in jail," he said.

"I didn't mean *steal* it. I meant, if there's some waste lumber, they might
give it to you."

"No, they'd never do that," he said.

I sensed we weren't talking about the real issue. The twelve year old was
too shy to ask for scrap lumber from a construction crew. At least he seemed
to be, which meant he had run into a block that wouldn't let him go on with
the project.

But our seven year old isn't afraid to ask anyone for anything. He's forever charming people at fast food places into giving him an ice cream cone or
something else they won't give to any of their other customers. They always
respond to his wishes.

So off he went to the construction site, and had soon discovered a large
pile of lumber and even some nails that weren't going to be needed. The workers said he'd be helping out if he carted some of it away.

Being seven, he didn't yet have the strength to carry a lot of lumber, but
a thirteen year old girl from next door offered to help by bringing it over in a
wheelbarrow. Soon she and her sister were transporting lumber with the two
boys.

The twelve year old, who understands the use of tools, then began to
direct the project. He found, however, that the two girls, who'd had experience
on a farm, brought an engineering background to the project which made
things work better. Soon the construction of a fairly impressive little house
was under way, designed and built by this team of four children pooling their
skills and resources.

CHILDREN SHARE RESOURCES EASILY — WHY CAN'T WE?

This story illustrates something that often happens among children spontaneously — but most of the time tends to elude adults.

One of the children, with his love of tools and knowledge of construction (some of it learned in his industrial arts class) had the savvy to build a house. But he didn't have the social skills he needed to get the raw materials. The other brought social finesse to the project. Soon it was under way, and had even acquired helpers.

Children easily learn to use each other's talents as resources, quickly building an effective team in which each makes a unique contribution. In the process they generate a flow state that helps them move effortlessly from task to task in the project.

Here the children shared their resources synergistically. Their behavior was quite different from the vertical, hierarchical division of labor evident in most organizations. Synergistic sharing promotes complex patterns of interaction that strengthen the enterprise.

This is a more natural way of doing things than is allowed by the hierarchical pyramid of management evolved over the past few centuries of industrial practice. We suggest that if you want to observe this spontaneous interactive process in action, you might sit in on a kindergarten class and watch how it's done by the very young resource-sharing experts you'll find there.

Many useful ideas for social organization, learning and team building can be learned from watching children at play. Fred Rogers (of *Mr. Rogers' Neighborhood*) explains why: "Some people talk about play as if it were a relief from serious business, but for children play is serious business. It provides a way for them to express strong feelings about important events in their lives. Play gives children a chance to cope with anxieties and to prepare for life as an adult by pretending about being grown up. Through play, children discover the world and learn more about themselves."[1]

Interesting that we adults call it learning, and children call it fun. Just maybe something got lost along the way for us adults about how all humans naturally learn.

GETTING IDEAS INTO ACTION

The tree house construction project began with someone having an idea, but feeling unable to put it into practice. As others came on the scene, a drama developed in which shared resources, knowledge and vision were used to breathe life into the idea. It's a classic resolution, reminiscent of the barn-raising practices of our pioneer ancestors, the kind of activity that has built great civilizations in the past, and even today is at the heart of most truly entrepreneurial activity.

But it seldom happens in formally structured organizations, especially those burdened with static, sometimes moribund group dynamics. An organization that can build a culture favoring scenarios like the tree house project is well on the way to becoming a Learning Organization.

THE IMPORTANCE OF SHARING OURSELVES AS CHILDREN DO

Why do children find it so much easier to learn from each other than adults do? Part of the answer is that children know they have to depend on other people's resources — and on other people as resources — whereas adults fruitlessly try to persuade themselves they are self-sufficient. We aren't, of course.

This is something we all recognize, at least intellectually. We must breathe the air around us, or die. We must eat, clothe ourselves, and get along in our communities. And so it goes. Our sense of reality increases as we observe that society is a complex web of interactive elements always dependent on specialized skills and talents to meet the needs of the community as a whole.

And yet as adults, especially in the workplace, we're almost totally unaccustomed to the spontaneous discovery of each other's talents and skills. But it is these vast and varied capabilities of its workforce (not the range of their job descriptions) which make up the greatest resource of an organization.

SEEING PEOPLE AS RESOURCES, NOT JOB DESCRIPTIONS

Many forces in modern organizations, and modern society for that matter, conspire to impose a limited view of what members of the organization may be able to contribute to its vitality and success.

However, having taken the first four steps towards becoming a Learning Organization, we are in a much better position to start seeing each other as resources. When we have strengthened the internal processes of being positive, thinking independently and taking risks, we have already gone a long way towards recognizing the values in others. These gains are further increased when all begin to share a specific understanding of the unique qualities each member brings to the team.

Accepting risk-taking as part of the culture is an important step, because for most people self-revelation — exposing one's special skills and talents to others in the group — is a risk. It means we have to be willing to be vulnerable, which we will only do if we believe we will be safe. When we do take such risks, we may discover that some of our talents were long ago put aside and forgotten. Now they can be explored and developed in the atmosphere of group support. This turns out to be a tremendously enriching experience both for the organization and the individuals who comprise it.

IF IT'S SO EASY FOR OUTSIDERS, WHY CAN'T INSIDERS DO IT?

As visiting trainers, we find it easy to see emergent talents in the participants in a course or workshop. One person is good at summing up an argument, one has a penchant for drawing. Another has a deep knowledge of music and the performing arts. Yet another has designed and built her own house. And so on.

In private conversations with participants, we often find that we're drawing them out more than anyone in their organization ever has. What a shame that strangers visiting for such a short time should be able to find out so much more about the people who work there than their fellow workers have!

For when we ask participants, who have been with us in the room all along, to describe each other as resources, they seldom mention the qualities we have observed. On the contrary, what most people seem to know best is each other's limitations, which is what most of us are conditioned to look for. Seeing other people's strengths and potential often requires getting beyond the self-fulfilling prophecy of negative perceptions.

The capacity to observe talents in others is a learned skill of great value in the workplace. Too seldom do we nurture those qualities lying just beneath the surface that with a little encouragement may flower into extraordinary gifts.

DIVERSITY AMONG PEOPLE IS AN INVALUABLE RESOURCE

We often overlook these unique qualities, but knowledge of other people's talents increases our potential contribution to the enterprise. That's because effective work is based on the ability to connect with others in order to get something done. The better you are at perceiving values in your co-workers, the more you can enhance your own effectiveness.

We recognize uniqueness in those who are famous, but the famous should alert us to the uniqueness possible for everyone. You notice it in your close friends and the members of your family, and it is what you miss when they are gone. But too often as we look at faces in the crowd, we do not discern the enormous distinctions among even the most similar of people.

True, many struggle to obscure their differences because of fear or lack of confidence in themselves. But the differences are present nonetheless, waiting to flourish. It's in those very differences that the greatest hidden wealth of any group is to be found. A Learning Organization is about learning diversity. It is about providing an environment of inclusion rather than the old organizational model which was based on a belief and practice of exclusion.

In a Learning Organization the give and take between the uniqueness of the individual and the collective mentality of the group no longer resolves downward to the lowest common denominator, but moves in the opposite direction: towards the synergy created by a community of highly functioning team members.

WHY PEOPLE DON'T SEE EACH OTHER AS RESOURCES

The excessive bureaucratic structures of many organizations hinder rather than help people see each other as resources. These rigid structures, well-intended in their day but now sadly outmoded, are a crucial impediment to productivity and growth.

At work, people stay within their job descriptions and chains of command. Valuable talents, knowledge, and experience, when not used professionally, often remain concealed and untapped. The same person who'd run out in the middle of a snow storm and help dig your car out of a ditch will remain tight-lipped at the office when everyone's stuck on a problem. Modesty? Maybe — but costly to the organization.

When we separate our work lives from our personal lives we create a work environment where we can too easily become disconnected from each other. Possibly as the result of a combination of excessive modesty, suspicion and competitiveness, we often fail to draw on a rich fund of informal skills and talents in each other.

As people develop greater insight about their co-workers, they discover previously unsuspected talents, some of which will prove of significant value to the development of business relationships, particularly when an organization must face unfamiliar challenges. Some of your associates may have strengths in self-expression, for example, that they seldom use professionally. One may be an excellent writer, another may draw or paint or be adept at making things. And some may have creative inspirations about how to market or design new products and services. A changing and growing organization will learn to develop and encourage resources like these.

This shift in the way we see each other breaks down one of the greatest barriers to an organization's efficiency: the balkanization and turf wars that waste its energy and resources.

Another tendency in organizations that robs them of the value that diversity can add is an emphasis on conformity. Actually, most cases of nonconformity are merely the product of lack of educational and social opportunity. When we can compensate for this difference in background, we can encourage individuals to explore a vast array of possible preferences in almost every sphere of life. The more we support the productive pursuit of individual differences, the more we enrich the interdependence of behaviors on which all commerce is based.

TOM PETERS ON THE "CURIOSITY WORKER"

Tom Peters, in his column "On Excellence", addresses the issue of hidden talents. Focusing on the wide range of differences among peoples' interests, Peters develops the idea of a "curiosity worker," referring to Einstein's notion that "curiosity is more important than knowledge": "Allowing — and encouraging — literally everyone to go where their curiosity takes them is important." He also refers to Peter Drucker's suggestion that a company with 1,000 people ought to have 1,000 career paths.

"The conclusion was obvious," he writes. "Wouldn't a corporation that could exploit the uniqueness of each of its 1,000 employees (or 100 or 10,000) be phenomenally powerful? Put negatively, isn't a corporation that doesn't figure out how to use the curiosities of 1,000 people headed for trouble?"[2] In a cultural framework in which hidden talents come to the fore, a great deal can be accomplished quickly, and with wonderful results.

In *Liberation Management*, he further develops this point: "Is not curiosity the principal mark of Freud's 'radiant intelligence of the child'? 'Manage' curiosity? Again, never! Develop and maintain a 'curious corporation'? Some, at least, are trying. And, arguably, few quests are more important."[3] In our work with Opportunity Enterprises, an organization which helps mentally retarded people lead more fulfilling lives than might otherwise be possible, we've pushed this notion to its limit. One of the unfortunate myths of our society is that people whose limitations keep them out of the mainstream are somehow incomplete and need to be hidden away in institutions. In reality those who work with the mentally retarded are often so moved by their experiences with these clients that they'll accept wages and working conditions they would never accept in some other career.

What makes Opportunity Enterprises so special is the way it treats each of its clients as a unique personality, even holding special awards ceremonies to recognize outstanding personalities. Meanwhile, work on the production line, or experience in a group home is something the staff grapples with to find ways to make more meaningful.

In working with them we've come to the conclusion that as we take seriously the potential of those who face the greatest limitations in trying to live full and meaningful lives, we're learning something very basic about what it is to be human. It should be the goal of any organization (which after all doesn't exist except in the collective imaginations of those who relate to it) to enhance the lives of those who interact with it in any way. We mean this in a total sense. That enlarges the notion of what business is about in a very special way.

Those who have sought to include a spiritual element in business are therefore on the right track. In doing commerce with one another, we are brought together in ways that rightfully should enrich our life experience by exploiting the deepest reaches of what each of us uniquely has to offer. If this is possible in working with the mentally retarded, it shouldn't be lacking elsewhere. Any work team, department or a company should be a place where people are eager to be and eager to return to every morning.

THE KODAK LEARNING LEADERS BECOME STAR PERFORMERS

The team of Learning Leaders we worked with at Kodak, and whom we'll describe in more detail in the next chapter, learned quickly the truth of what we've just pointed out above. They discovered experientially how to draw out of each other their many different talents and interests. This notion of "drawing out" is the essential and original meaning of education, and is part of the conceptual background necessary to understand what we are saying here.

Some of the Kodak team, being artists, provided posters for the classes the team would be teaching. Some had unusual knowledge of community resources, and knew where to get what the team needed. Some had business skills never exploited before, which proved essential to getting the team organized. Some were good at seeing a subject from an unusual angle that could add interest to a new course they were designing.

Developing the diversity of skills in a group is like mining gold. Not developing those skills depletes the sum total of human resources. A mind, remember, is a terrible thing to waste.

THE ADVANTAGES OF THE EDGE OF CHAOS

To those concerned for the efficiency and survival of the organization, this attention to individual differences may seem threatening, an invitation to chaos. However, a closer look at how complex living systems adapt and flourish should provide a clearer view of the kind of structure that organizations need. Far-reaching research on this subject recently carried out at the Santa Fe Institute may prove enlightening. But first, some background:

It's been found that for living systems the best environment in which to operate is what's been called "the edge of chaos." This mysterious and evocative phrase translates, at the microscopic level of molecular structure, into a precise and instructive concept. The edge of chaos is, in terms of chemical bonding, the point between solid and liquid. In a solid, everything's locked into place. In a liquid, everything can move so freely that no enduring structures are possible. The edge of chaos is the point where structures exist in a slowly flowing state: they're free to change continuously, but the underlying structure is never lost.

Living systems, it's thought, will evolve continuously toward that state, because it gives them the best of both worlds: an enduring structure and enough flexibility to change as appropriate. An animal has bones to give it structure, and muscles to give it flexibility. It breathes in oxygen which it circulates through the body in a stream of blood that's channeled by the structure of vessels, capillaries and veins. But as species and other complex systems develop, the structures themselves change, redesigned through genetics, blueprints or game plans. These changes also occur during the development of the individual animal from a fetus to an adult, and to some extent they continue throughout life.

ORGANIZATIONS AS LIVING ORGANISMS

Understanding the ideal environment for a living system helps us discern the most efficient organizational structures. The striking parallels between living systems and organizations are evident in the observations of Stuart Kauffman, who has done some of the most significant work in this area of science. In M. Mitchell Waldrop's book *Complexity*, which deals with the Santa Fe Institute, Kauffman talks about living systems in terms that apply directly to the very issues of corporate culture we have been discussing:

"If we're deep in the ordered regime," [Kauffman] says, "then everybody is at a peak in fitness and we're all mutually consistent — but these are lousy peaks." Everybody is trapped in the foothills, so to speak, with no way to break loose and head for the crest of the range. In terms of human organizations, it's as if the jobs are so subdivided that no one has any latitude; all they can do is learn how to perform the one job they've been hired for, and nothing else. Whatever the metaphor, however, it's clear that if each individual in the various organizations is allowed a little more freedom to march to a different drummer, then everyone will benefit. The deeply frozen system will become a little more fluid, says Kauffman, the aggregate fitness will go up, and the agents will collectively move a bit closer to the edge of chaos.

Conversely, says Kauffman, "If we're deep in the chaotic regime, then every time I change I screw you up, and vice versa. We never get to the peaks, because you keep kicking me off and I keep kicking you off, and it's like Sisyphus trying to roll the rock uphill. Therefore, my overall fitness tends to be pretty low, and so does yours." In organizational terms, it's as if the lines of command in each firm are so screwed up that nobody has the slightest idea what they're supposed to do — and half the time they are working at cross-purposes anyway."[4]

In other words, an ideal state for an organization is one in which each individual makes a unique contribution by "marching to a different drummer" but with an underlying common sense of purpose and direction. In teams, this common purpose is most readily achieved when team members respect each other's full individuality as they develop their projects together.

More recently, Dee Hock, the entrepreneur who made the Visa card system work so that it has become a world wide financial system that no one controls but everyone can use, has been given a grant from the Joyce Foundation to explore and develop the principles that govern the success of "chaordic" organizations. The word was coined by Hock as a combination of chaos and order in the sense developed at the Santa Fe Institute.

In all chaordic activities people both compete and cooperate. They compete by following a basic set of rules in a variety of different ways. They cooperate by agreeing to follow the rules. Chaordic behavior is universal in sports, but rare in other human activities. This is because it turns out to be rather complex to discover a set of rules that gets exactly the right balance between chaos and order. What's needed is a set of parameters that control an infinite variety of activities so that they all coordinate to advance some set of goals and values implicit in the rules themselves.

The universe is chaordic, and so are the capitalistic system, the telephone system, the internet, language, most of the world's cultures, and networking activities. So far the only type of business we've discovered that is truly chaordic in this sense is the kind of company that plays the Great Game of Business, as developed by Jack Stack. This is true however, we think, only if that company is also a learning organization so it doesn't stagnate at merely keeping the bottom line growing at a rate of 15 or 20% per year, but simultaneously grows the minds of all the workers.

The key to getting the most out of human interactions is to build chaordic systems that allow them to be as fully human as possible, while at the same time exploring unique individual personalities without limitation. The burst of creativity that will result when the proper chaordic systems have been developed for an emerging world culture are mind boggling, but there's some hint of what can happen if we compare the culture of fifth century Athens with that of neighboring fifth century Sparta. In a single century the Athenians laid the foundations for most of modern culture, while during the same period the Spartans kept all their citizens in a horrible kind of prison that allowed them virtually no room for creativity.

Today large corporations are the city-states of yesteryear. Some of them are horrible prisons, others are the foundation stones of opportunity for the future. The difference is in how their chaordic systems are designed, their rules for playing the game.

The key factor as far as we are concerned here, in Step Five, is that there be developed in each culture those rules, principles and cultural rituals and behaviors that bring out interactions among people which have as much range of variation as possible, while at the same time all being focused towards the mission and vision for which the organization was founded.

So it's the work you do here in Step Five that engenders the jump you could make from a company that works, where everything goes well and the bottom line is well served to one that is a new kind of opportunity for human experience, an adventure in human possibility — and incidentally a company that may be ten or twenty times as productive as that company which (as many have done) completes the first four steps and lets it go at that.

GETTING THE BALL ROLLING

But how do we learn to see and utilize others as resources? A simple and necessary first step is getting to know people better.

Here's an exercise you can use to begin meetings and other gatherings: Hold up a koosh ball and say, "When you get the ball, throw it to someone you like and say what you like about that person." If after a moment no one responds, say, "Does anyone here like somebody?" Throw the ball to the first volunteer, who will throw it to someone in the group and say something like, "I appreciate the way you always dress nicely," or, "I'm really excited about that new project you're helping me with on the team." The one who gets the ball will then throw it to someone else and repeat the process.

Generally when groups use this exercise, they'll start out with simple comments about each other — often one-liners. Then they'll move on to tell stories about something positive that exemplifies a friendship.

But eventually you'll hear appreciations that show how the person speaking depends on someone else to provide needed skills, information, perspectives and experiences. When this kind of validation appears, point it out and underline it. It's an event that will help build the habit Step Five is concerned with: seeing each other as resources.

APPRECIATE YOUR FELLOW WORKERS

If you're not in a position to try the above exercise, then before reading any further, we suggest you make a list of six to ten people you work with. Next to each name describe a quality or talent that person possesses which you find especially valuable. Reflect on what you'd miss if your colleague left to work for some other company. If there's anyone on the list who has no qualities you want to list as indispensable, replace the name with a different one. Try for at least six names, with at least one quality for each.

Then ask yourself what qualities you bring to your job that others value and depend on. See how many of these you can list. Consider whether your co-workers might value your qualities differently, depending on their experience of you, with the result that you appear to each of them a somewhat different resource.

The team might consider formalizing opportunities to appreciate one another, meanwhile keeping records of the special qualities and talents each has. It might also be useful to record developing skills, as well as new and improved qualities in each member's work — a journal of work in progress. Beyond that, things will move along a lot faster if each makes it a habit personally to point out valuable qualities in everyone else's work.

LOOK WHAT HAPPENS WHEN WE FOCUS ON THE POSITIVES

One of us was once in a writers' group that allowed members to read and then ask for the particular kind of response they wanted. When a reader did not ask for a specific response, the only kind we would give was to say what we liked in the writing we had heard.

Once a ninety year old woman read her essay in the group. It was a piece of little merit that would hardly have taxed a fourth grader. Yet we followed our rule and praised in it every little nugget of excellence we could find.

Each week this woman returned and read another piece. Within a month the quality of her work had improved so much we began to suggest how she might get some of her things published. Unfortunately, death intervened before this occurred, but her amazing growth demonstrated to all of us how a person at any age can, with proper encouragement, rapidly develop new abilities.

YOUR PERSONAL JOURNAL OF APPRECIATIONS

You might carry a journal in which you set aside a page or two for each of your fellow workers. Every time you notice a new positive quality, jot it down. Accumulate enough distinct and different qualities so you would be able to comment at length on the virtues of each of your colleagues. Your observations might include such specific examples of excellence in behavior as events, quotations, sense of purpose, and other qualities you would expect to read in a novel or short story describing someone.

What's in it for you? Since we learn the most from our peers, it is by noticing the details of others' skills that we can most effectively improve our own. As a result of the detailed awareness you'll achieve if you carry out this experiment, you'll be able to improve your own abilities in many ways you never even thought of. That, as much as anything, may help you advance in your career and achieve greater fulfillment in your personal life.

If you follow this plan, though, keep in mind one caution: people often tend not to notice excellence in others because it can overwhelm them. If I compare myself to the combined excellence of ten or twenty others, I am likely to feel extremely inferior by comparison. But no one of my colleagues has all the excellences I'm noticing. I must be content to come up to the standards set by no more than one person in the group. So compare yourself fairly and favorably with the standards set by the group as a whole. Then you'll be able to learn comfortably and easily through the simple method of noting the details of how others excel.

A second part of your journal might record every appreciation you hear of yourself or your work. Experience has shown that most of us simply don't hear the good things that are said to us. See if that's true of you. The next time someone compliments you about something, such as the attractiveness of what you're wearing, or how well you did your job — see whether, almost as a reflex, you move to discount it — not just by saying, "Well, I really didn't put much into it," but by actually pretending to yourself you didn't hear it because (in your estimation) the person probably didn't mean it anyway.

Most people are so busy reacting to negatives, they discard positives as if they had never happened. Probably, therefore, you'll have to log them in your journal every day in order to become aware of the extent of the appreciation you're getting from others.

But since it's hard to force ourselves to gather evidence that will change our self-perception, you'll no doubt be sorely tempted to drop this part of the exercise. So make a special commitment to do it even if you don't want to — and take your commitment seriously. The more modesty gets in your way, the more you're suffering from a case of poor self-esteem that needs healing. Only you can heal it, by listening to and recognizing the appreciations that come your way. Learn to accept praise with the same attentiveness you give to recognizing the good points of others. Over time, this exercise can greatly improve the way you feel about yourself.

THE POSSIBILITY OF CONFLICT

As we open ourselves to deeper understanding and appreciation of each other, we may also be setting the stage for serious conflict when misunderstandings do occur. For when we've invested our trust in another, and it seems to be violated, the hurt may run deep. In groups whose members suddenly start deepening their feeling for one another, trust and bonding may come too easily at first, without being fully earned, and without taking into account the genuine differences in values and perception that are bound to be present in any group.

The "honeymoon" of bonding with one another can create the mistaken impression that people are more in tune with each other than is actually the case. Then, when differences are discovered, a suspicion of broken trust may spread through the group, leading to a period of storming, blaming and condemnation of others, and of the group as a whole. All this happens because you're more likely to feel betrayed when you've opened your true self to the group than if you've retained your customary degree of reserve.

Abraham Maslow, along with many others, believed that survival and security are the most powerful motives of human behavior. In these times of constant and rapid change, many feel their security, sometimes their very survival threatened, making trust a much more difficult commodity to hand out freely. Survival behavior is often reactive behavior. However, the paradox of trust is that while it makes us vulnerable, at the same time it can give us the strength that comes from numbers of people working as a group.

The establishment of trust when an organization is first formed, followed by violation of trust later on is such a predictable, pervasive pattern within groups that there's a well known catch-phrase to describe it: "form — storm — norm — and perform." In the first stage, the "forming" stage, a group of people come together with a common purpose in mind. Soon they're bonded together in pursuit of that purpose, and amidst the excitement of beginning, a great many assumptions get made.

After a relatively short time, people begin to experience each other in greater depth. What they discover is that they have differences. Some of those differences may feel like moral differences, which lead to moral outrage.

Pretty soon people begin to complain about each other, blaming and pointing the finger. "So and so doesn't fulfill her responsibilities to the group." "Do you know he gave me the cold shoulder the other day, when I thought everything was just fine between us." "How can you expect a person who routinely shows up late for meetings to accomplish anything."

If the group must work closely together this sort of thing can tear it apart. At the same time, the conflicts that normally arise in group and organizational development, may engender a necessary creative tension, that if shepherded carefully could reinforce the trust level of the group.

If you've taken the Ten Step Process seriously, however, you should be protected from the destructiveness of the storming phase, because you've already learned to put a positive spin on everything, hear each other out and take risks together, and you know how to identify a problem and describe it accurately. So if storming is occurring in your group, it's time to revisit the Ten Steps Process from the beginning and discover for yourselves what it is you're failing to do that allows all this dissension to take place.

Bear in mind that the storming process is a normal part of group bonding, but that this book has been written to help you deal with and resolve it. So you should be able to go on to the next stage — norming — fairly easily. During the norming stage, you use the conflicts that have arisen to guide you towards a set of rules and practices that need to be present in order for your group to function well. Once these are worked out, you can get about your business and do a good job of performing the tasks you were created to perform.

So a built-in part of the process must be a commitment to resolve any such conflicts that may develop. The group should agree in advance that when conflict arises, bitterness and blame will be kept out of the picture. Assigning blame is the sheepish and unproductive strategy of individuals and groups who do not want to take responsibility for their actions in the world of work. When a system is not working "right", the problem usually lies in how the organization and its business practices are constructed and executed. Focusing on the positive, using the skills cultivated in the earlier Steps, will allow for a reassessment of the strengths of the group, determining what areas of genuine trust are possible. Even though this may be difficult to accomplish, the rewards from doing so will be great.

The acceptance of conflict and resolution as a normal part of the group process helps develop flexibility in dealing with each other, and also with other kinds of ambiguities that normally arise in modern organizations.

DEALING WITH CONFLICTS OF PERSONAL BELIEF

One rule that may help you avoid getting deeper than necessary into the storming phase is a rule that already prevails in polite society. It's best not to discuss politics, religion or sex. Keep the focus of team relationships on the business, and don't bring in outside issues, such as trying to campaign for increased membership in your church, or for support for a political candidate, or attendance at Tupperware parties. All these activities have their place, but they only confuse relationships in a business environment.

Of course, sensitivity to the feelings of minority groups of various kinds needs to be maintained. This sensitivity is not just some kind of bleeding heart abstraction. What is at stake here is the real feelings of real people. If any member of the group, for whatever reason, is feeling oppressed by the group as a whole, then use the Speak Out that we described in Step Three.

WHO'S WORKING THE HARDEST?

Conflicts may arise from a perception or belief that people on the team are not pulling their weight equally. Some tend to show up for work before the sun rises and are still there after it's gone down again. Others may wander in carelessly at ten o'clock in the morning, sit around reading the newspaper and drinking pop, and then perhaps lumber into some work in the early afternoon before going home about three p.m.

Such a disparity of performance can drive a team up the wall unless there's a structure and clearly defined agreements for dealing with it. Yet, if the team is self-managed, it's hard for members to confront one another, and extremely hard to get agreement by everyone about what's actually happening — precisely because individual values and perceptions may differ so much. Even though this process may be difficult, experience of having worked with dozens of self-managed workteams shows that those who have been willing to clarify and negotiate these boundary issues, have tremendously increased their likelihood of success. Those that do not work through the framework to support different working styles tend to disband or are significantly altered by upper management within somewhere between 18 and 24 months.

THE LYRICIST WHO GOOFED AROUND

Further confusing the issue is the notion of the difference between working hard and working smart. Here's an example that illustrates the difference. Lorenz Hart, who wrote the lyrics for a great many Broadway hits, among them *Pal Joey,* used to wander into the bathroom in an inebriated state, compose a lyric, and wander back out five minutes later clutching a future hit number in his trembling, alcoholic hands.

Alan Jay Lerner, another Broadway lyricist, one of whose musicals was

My Fair Lady, was by contrast the picture of respectability. He would often work for several weeks on a single lyric. In the end, both writers produced wonderful material. Yet one tossed off his work as if it were nothing, while the other labored for weeks over every semi-colon. Does anyone in the audience care?

Obviously it's more convenient for you if you can get your work done in five minutes instead of consuming several weeks arriving at the same level of achievement. But why should that matter to anyone else, as long as the work is good?

The person who's at work from sunup to sundown may have reason to be suspicious of the one who wanders in for what seems like a brief visit. Yet, given the different kinds of work styles we've noted above, both may be contributing work of equal value to the team. If the seemingly lazy one were to spend more time at it, we might see more work accomplished — or we might not. Some people seem able to work only when they're inspired, and are then very efficient. Others labor continuously, going over their work many times. In the end, it's the product that matters, not how it was produced.

So it's no easy matter to determine the true extent of each person's contribution. In the end, it will take quite a bit of insight to evaluate this issue.

BUT SOME PEOPLE REALLY ARE FREELOADING

At the same time, some of the people on the team may be along for the ride, while others are working more productively than most. Neither the most nor the least productive people may actually know who they are, for sometimes our perception of our own worth either exaggerates our importance or downgrades it. Most people err in their own favor, according to statistics which show that 75% of the population consider themselves to be in the top 25% in general quality and capacity. And in any pair of workers who are actually contributing equal amounts of time, energy and effectiveness, each person will be likely to claim having done 80% of the work. This is partly because we're much more aware of the details of what we do than of what anyone else does.

THE SELF-ESTIMATION

The resolution of this conflict will require a lot of communication. While there's no sure way to end conflict on the issue of who's contributing the most, there's a technique that seems to increase the probability a group can handle it satisfactorily. It's called the **Self-Estimation**.

The Self-Estimation can help everyone on the team assume personal responsibility for dealing with such issues. It's a process that helps people give each other feedback in a structured and non-threatening way. Four or five gather in a group and select one of their number to go first as the subject. In stage one, this person tells the group what he or she has done well on the job. In stage two, each member of the group then takes a turn to add information to this evaluation from their point of view.

Stage three moves on to an assessment of what's missing. The subject now looks at areas of performance which he or she feels can be improved. In stage four the other members of the group give their evaluation of what can be improved. The emphasis is always on positive statements, and it is always in a supportive tone.

In this way equality is preserved among peers, but a formal framework is established that allows them to give each other feedback without feeling they must take the offensive, or are being attacked. The Self-Estimation is complete when all members of the group have taken their turn as subject. If the process turns out to be lengthy, it can be broken into several meetings, to take place over a week or two.

THE RESOURCE INVENTORY

Another activity that can help teams better know each other's talents is a **Team Resource Inventory**. Here's a formal approach you might find useful as a guide to help your team improve its learning capabilities:

1. Have all team members complete the **Multiple Intelligences Checklist** (MIC) at the end of this chapter. This is not a test, but rather an easy self-appraisal which most people enjoy trying. It is also a preview of Step 6, but does not require any particular familiarity with the theory of Multiple Intelligences.
2. Have a team member, or outside person, develop a composite picture of the members of the team.
3. Conduct a team session where a dialogue takes place based on the MIC team composite.
4. Have each person look at the similarities and differences between their individual MIC results and the team picture.
5. Have the whole team evaluate the learning Strengths, Weaknesses, Opportunities, and Threats of the team as they relate to the team's learning capabilities.
6. What information does the MIC team picture provide about how to maximize the learning potential of the team?
7. What insights arise from the picture that can help prevent trouble between the team members? To what extent have the team members assisted each other in developing their individual potential?
8. Have team members negotiate contracts with each other about how they will support each other in their work. In these contracts they will spell out their learning goals and the means of reaching them. In each pair or group of three that engages in this process, it will be the

responsibility of one member to review at regular intervals how the other is doing in reaching the goals.

9. Have team members develop a list of their individual talents that didn't show up on the Resource Inventory because of an assumption they wouldn't be useful in the business. This could be things like playing golf or baking a cake. This should focus on the things they do well and enjoy.

10. Have individual team members share and discuss each person's list of talents.

11. Have them then explore how the team can use these in their daily work efforts or their team learning process.

ANOTHER TEAM RESOURCE INVENTORY

Another activity your group might find useful is the following:

1. Have each member list every talent, ability or other skill or resource he or she might contribute to a project, no matter how unrelated it may at first seem to any activity currently in the works. The goal is to list at least twenty of these, even if they don't seem particularly significant. For example, the ability to make an excellent cup of tea can be of no small value if it helps build morale in the office.

2. Each person next lists an equal number of resources the team might conceivably need under circumstances not as yet foreseen. Obviously the two lists should be different — possibly very different.

3. Next, the team lists the resources within the group — without referring to the lists already made by individual members. The object is to identify as many resources the team members may possess as they can think of. The reason for not looking at the lists already written is to stimulate the creation of new ideas folks didn't think of the first time.

4. Have the team brainstorm the largest possible number of resources that might be needed, even under unforeseen circumstances.

5. After these two team lists have been completed, check the individual lists compiled earlier, to make sure nothing has been left out.

6. Place each item from the second team list, of resources possibly needed, at the head of a separate sheet of paper. Have every member of the team sign up on as many of these sheets as appropriate. In most cases several names will be listed under each resource needed.

7. If one or more of these sheets remains blank, the team can then spend some time deciding whether this particular resource is important to it or not. If it is, the team can take whatever steps are necessary to increase its membership, so the needed resource can be acquired. (On the other hand, some of the resources listed may not be needed

at present, or in the foreseeable future. Yet if many people sign up anyway, it might be a good idea to give the matter some further thought. Suppose, for example, "playing an instrument" is listed, and twenty people sign up. That may suggest the group could benefit from spending some extra-curricular time creating a band or orchestra. The bonding that would come from such an activity could enrich the quality of group interaction. The result is not only bound to be pleasurable, but to have a favorable impact on work life.)

8. Finally, those resources possessed by the group, but not contained on the second team list, should also be placed on separate sign-up sheets. Each of these should be posted, and the group brainstorm situations under which the suggested resource might prove useful.

There are other tools available to teams that wish to develop a better knowledge of one another in order to work together more effectively. One that is very popular is the Myers-Briggs Personality Inventory. This is used to compare some very common personality traits as they interact to form complete personalities. If your group has been trained in this system, it may have met your needs for greater group understanding already. If not, you may wish to add one of the above techniques to it.

Another instrument that can be used by teams, is the Personal Profile System (DISC), which looks at a variety of behaviorial dimensions and how the team members interact with each other.

Other personality or learning styles systems you may wish to look into include the Dunn and Dunn, Kolb and Bernice McCarthy systems. All of these have had excellent results in a variety of group settings.

After you've investigated these various approaches, you may wish to combine them in your own way to meet your special needs.

REVISITING JOB DESCRIPTIONS

When you have completed activities like these, which are really extensions of Step One (assessment) at a new level of depth, it's time for members to take a new look at their job descriptions, their roles and responsibilities. This process has become more complicated during the past couple of years as traditional forms of intact workteams have expanded and evolved toward the more fluid practice of teaming: where people find themselves on three or four teams at the same time. The duration of these teaming assignments might be a short as a month and as long as a year. This kind of team "floating" places more importance on role clarity then in the past.

It should now be useful to determine how these might be changed and expanded in the light of new information. In addition, each member of the organization might keep a list of the resources provided by the others. Because of the grip old habits have on us, many may not make use of these resources any better than they did before — at least not without some prompting. Keeping the list may help overcome this barrier.

Also, it's good for someone to take on the task of follow-up, assessing from time to time how well each member has expanded his or her use of the resources the team provides. The Think and Listen is a useful tool for exploring what might be the next step in expanding the effective use of the team's resources.

At six month intervals the resource inventory exercise can be repeated. With time the membership in the group changes and people develop new values, particularly when they have an opportunity to work in a dynamic environment, so keeping updated on changes in skill level and interests can be valuable.

EXPANDING THE TEAM RESOURCES

As the use of team resources expands, it will take on a life of its own. People will soon notice how much more they appreciate each others' strengths, talents and values. There will be a stronger feeling of bonding and camaraderie, stemming from the use of strengths and skills that may have lain dormant too long. As self-esteem blossoms in this environment, each member will feel vastly more effective.

From time to time it's well to celebrate the new growth in personal appreciation. No matter how much trouble we take to think positively and appreciate each other's contributions to our work lives, there's still a great deal that remains unsaid. So it's well to take the time now and again to make sure the opportunity exists to say it all.

CELEBRATING WITH A VALIDATION CIRCLE

For that purpose we recommend an activity which, though formal, is nevertheless powerfully emotional. This activity is called a **validation circle**. It is a powerful tool for enhancing the positive atmosphere that was established in Step Two, while at the same time informally building the communication structure necessary to appreciate each other's talents and skills fully. Use of it can greatly enhance an organization's effectiveness.

As with some of the group activities described in Step Two, certain individuals may consider the validation circle — before they try it — too mushy. Nevertheless, as we said earlier, we almost invariably find that even the most hard-boiled skeptics not only get a lot out of these activities, they actually enjoy them a great deal. Reservations about them usually reflect doubts about how other people will react. When each person knows others are willing to give it a try, everyone feels free to participate.

Participants should sit comfortably and informally in a circle. When it's your turn, take your place in the center of the circle and face each person in turn. Listen carefully and attentively to what is said to you. Don't respond verbally, though you may nod, smile, laugh, perhaps even cry — as a natural expression of your appreciation for what you are hearing.

Each person in turn completes the statement, "I'm glad you're on my team because ..." or "I'm glad you worked with me on that project because ..." or "It was a pleasure teaming up with you because ..." or "It was a delight to serve with you on that committee because ..."

The validation circle works best with six to eight people at a time, but three are enough to get it going. If the group is larger than eight, we recommend you divide it into smaller units, because when there has been a lot of positive interaction it may take a long time, possibly a couple of hours, for a group of eight to say all they want to each other. As each person takes a turn in the center, eloquence of speech will tend to increase, so pretty soon one round may take quite a while. If the group is larger than eight, the time it takes may be too long to be practical.

THE BIRTHDAY CIRCLE

A variant on the validation circle can be used to celebrate only one person, with as many as you like in the circle. You might do this for your team members when it's their birthday, and turn it into a birthday circle with the phrase, "I'm glad you were born, because ..."

During your validation or birthday circle, take seriously the proposition that subtle put downs, jokes at the other person's expense, qualifications, hidden negatives and other such compromises of the process are to be avoided, no matter how natural and humorously in fun they may seem. Sometimes we're so used to joking with each other that serious appreciation is difficult, but the discipline of keeping the tone serious and sincere is important to build group strength and commitment.

Perhaps you still have a ways to go in learning to like the person you're validating, but there's no reason you can't just talk about the qualities you do like. This might have a healing effect on the relationship. Antagonisms often develop only because each person feels unappreciated by the other.

Properly used, these circles may become one of the most powerful techniques the team has for building continuous improvement. The circle serves as a feedback mechanism to provide all members with a continual updating on how each is perceived as valuable by the others. As long as the commitment to improve is maintained, everyone will continue to grow. Don't forget that people who feel valued are far more likely to give their best efforts to the group than those who do not.

Proper use and mastery of the validation circle may eventually produce one of the most powerful experiences anyone in the group has ever had. Consider the plight of one who has gone through life almost never hearing appreciation. Some families believe the only way to develop character in the young is to keep constant vigilance with negative criticism. If this has also been the philosophy of teachers, managers and fellow workers, it's possible to experience one's whole life never hearing any significant appreciation from anyone.

THIS IS A RESPONSE TO UNIVERSAL HUMAN NEEDS

And yet we all need to feel loved and valued. We also need to feel that we have some importance to our community. The process of being validated may take a while to get used to, but eventually it will sink in and start to be believed.

Then, and only then, when all the members of the organization are able to know and believe that they're good, and that other people know and recognize this, will it be time for all to address the possibility of fully committing to the challenge of personal growth and mastery.

MULTIPLE INTELLIGENCES CHECKLIST[5]

Since 1900, when Alfred Binet developed the first "intelligence test," which was to measure "I. Q.," such assessments have focused primarily on a very partial and limited definition of intelligence. Recent cognitive psychology research shows that intelligence needs to be understood more broadly and embraces more capabilities than had previously been recognized. This checklist provides a simple and easy appraisal of your multiple intelligences.

There are seventy-seven multiple intelligence characteristics listed below. Read each item and make a check-mark in column A for those that "fit" for you.

A   B

1. ____ ____ Thinks in visual images.
2. ____ ____ Learns best by acting things out, and doing them.
3. ____ ____ Is "street-smart."
4. ____ ____ Has a deep awareness of inner feelings, dreams and ideas.
5. ____ ____ Plays a musical instrument or sings during free time.
6. ____ ____ Spells words easily and accurately.
7. ____ ____ Enjoys computers and/or chemistry sets.

8. ____ ____ Learns best by seeing and observing.
9. ____ ____ Shows talent in sewing, woodworking, pottery, etc.
10. ____ ____ Enjoys loosely structured group activities where talking is permitted.
11. ____ ____ Has a quality of inner wisdom and intuitive ability.

12. ____ ____ Collects records, tapes, or compact disks.
13. ____ ____ Enjoys playing with words: puns, silly lyrics, etc.
14. ____ ____ Enjoys logical rules and formulas.

15. ____ ____ Remembers faces easily.
16. ____ ____ Has excellent fine-motor and/or large motor coordination.
17. ____ ____ Has a lot of empathy for others' feelings.
18. ____ ____ Lives in own private world, in search of personal goals.
19. ____ ____ Keeps time rhythmically to music.
20. ____ ____ Likes crossword puzzles, games like Scrabble or Hangman.
21. ____ ____ Good memory for principles and theories.

22. ____ ____ Good at doing jigsaw puzzles or mazes.
23. ____ ____ Communicates well via gestures and body language.
24. ____ ____ Often mediates conflicts for family, and/or friends, co-workers, etc.
25. ____ ____ Has strong opinions when controversial topics are discussed.
26. ____ ____ Remembers facts best when they are put to music.
27. ____ ____ Likes to spin tall tales or tell jokes and stories.
28. ____ ____ Favors science-fiction or mysteries for reading materials.

29. ____ ____ Chooses art activities or building things during free time.
30. ____ ____ Moves, taps, and fidgets when seated.
31. ____ ____ Likes being involved in group games or activities.
32. ____ ____ Independent-minded in style of dress, behavior or attitude.
33. ____ ____ Turns to music to express feelings.
34. ____ ____ Performs well on paper and pencil tests.
35. ____ ____ Gets comments like: "So brainy." "Very smart." "So quick."

36. ____ ____ Enjoys movies, slides, videos, photography, etc.
37. ____ ____ Engages in physical activities: swimming, hiking, running, tennis, golf, etc.
38. ____ ____ Socializes a great deal at work, in the neighborhood, etc.
39. ____ ____ Likes to be alone to pursue some personal interest, hobby or project.
40. ____ ____ Makes up lyrics, raps, and/or tunes.
41. ____ ____ Gets comments like: "So witty." "Very verbal." "Very intelligent."
42. ____ ____ Thinks conceptually (categorizing, making hypotheses.)

43. ____ ____ Knows where everything is located in house, office, etc.
44. ____ ____ Prefers stories with lots of action.
45. ____ ____ Understands people well.
46. ____ ____ Has a quiet, but strong sense of self-confidence.
47. ____ ____ Performance and/or composition brings comments like: "So talented." "So musical."

48. ____ ____ Thinks in words.
49. ____ ____ Learns best by exploring patterns, relationships, by actively manipulating natural environment and experimenting in orderly ways.

50. ____ ____ Enjoys machines, contraptions, and sometimes builds her/his own.
51. ____ ____ Touches people when talking to them.
52. ____ ____ Knows what is going on with co-workers (which are getting along, which aren't, etc.).
53. ____ ____ Gets comments like: "Unique personality." "Knows self well." "Insightful." "Deep."
54. ____ ____ Often sings, hums or whistles tunes to self.
55. ____ ____ Learns best by verbalizing and hearing words.
56. ____ ____ Constantly questioning and wondering about natural events ("Where does the universe end?" "When did time begin?").

57. ____ ____ Easily understands maps, charts, and diagrams.
58. ____ ____ Cleverly pantomimes people's gestures and behaviors.
59. ____ ____ Gets comments like: "Great listener." "So supportive." "Real friend." "Insightful."
60. ____ ____ In touch with his/her feelings.
61. ____ ____ Often moves and sings along with music.
62. ____ ____ Likes to write.
63. ____ ____ Enjoys brain teasers, logical puzzles and games requiring reasoning, like chess.

64. ____ ____ Daydreams a lot.
65. ____ ____ Body movements bring comments like: "So graceful." "Very athletic." "Great dancer."
66. ____ ____ Thinks by talking.
67. ____ ____ Learns best when working on independent activities.
68. ____ ____ Has strong opinions about music played around her/him.
69. ____ ____ Has good memory for names, dates, details.
70. ____ ____ Capable of highly abstract forms of logical thinking.

71. ____ ____ Artwork gets comments like: "So creative." "So talented."
72. ____ ____ Thinks best by doing, moving, and tuning into bodily sensations.
73. ____ ____ Learns best through teamwork, study groups, etc.
74. ____ ____ Has a definite personality, and strong sense of autonomy and/or discipline.
75. ____ ____ Sensitive to nonverbal environmental sounds.
76. ____ ____ Enjoys reading in free time.
77. ____ ____ Calculates mathematical problems quickly.

Once you have completed checking in column **A** those items that "fit" for you, go back to the beginning of the Checklist. You will now number the Checklist items in cycles of seven. In column **B** place the number 1 in space 1, the number 2 in the space 2, etc. When you reach space 8 place the number 1 again, the number 2 in space 9, etc. Repeat the numbers 1 through 7 until you finish with space 77, which will have a 7 in it.

Now you want to record below how many check marks you have entered for each of the seven groups. Count all the check marks identified (by your numbering in column B) as 1's. Write that total below in the line "Number of 1's = _____ **Visual/Spatial**". Repeat the process with 2's, 3's, etc.

TOTALS:

Number of 1's = _____ **Visual/Spatial**

Number of 2's = _____ **Bodily/Kinesthetic**

Number of 3's = _____ **Interpersonal**

Number of 4's = _____ **Intrapersonal**

Number of 5's = _____ **Musical**

Number of 6's = _____ **Linguistic**

Number of 7's = _____ **Logical/Mathematical**

The above totals are a snapshot portrait of your natural learning capacities. They are not a measure of I. Q., nor of any intelligence. Rather, they are intended to suggest an individual's preferred learning modes, and their relative strengths compared to one another.

The Theory of Multiple Intelligences and the characteristics of the seven intelligences will be explained in Step Six, though you will probably be able to surmise a great deal about them just by going through this questionnaire. Without going into the theory, you can use this snapshot to get a new view of yourself and of others, and use this view as part of the Team Resource Inventory described in Step Five.

PUT LEARNING POWER TO WORK

S T E P 6

We're now half way through the Ten Steps, though if you are imple-menting the first Five Steps, you are actually more than half way to the goal. In this Step we will address the core element of a Learning Organization, learning itself.

Imagine an organization in which everyone from top to bottom is either actually or potentially learning for the improvement of the organization — not just in formal ways, but anywhere at any time, without specific demands from managers or instructors. Innovation and continuous improvement occur spon-taneously, though in ways which, far from being chaotic, serve and improve the whole organization and its collective purposes. Just In Time learning has become standard. Formal training and development are still taking place, but individuals, teams, and the whole organization are passionate about teaching and learning real time.

What executive, what employee, could quarrel with such a vision? Isn't this what the times demand, what the country is clamoring for? It might be argued that it's visionary pie in the sky. But if it *could* be attained, who could object to such a goal?

WHO WOULDN'T WANT A LEARNING ORGANIZATION?

The answer is: all of us. Not necessarily deliberately nor overtly, not always consciously, but one way or another we all tend to undermine the prospects for a Learning Organization.

That, of course, is what the first Five Steps are designed to change. The assumptions and expectations that work against the development of a Learning Organization mirror those in the culture at large and those that we as individuals carry around with us. The first Five Steps aim at helping you remove these barriers by exposing and reversing the attitudes which rein-force them.

Instituting a clear-eyed, fearless assessment of where the organization is and where it is going, supporting positive interactions among individuals, encouraging thinking, risk-taking, and mutual inter-dependence — all of these steps are worthy ends in themselves. They will take any organization a long way towards good health and prosperity.

But the deeper purpose of the first Five Steps is to remove barriers to learning, and to unleash the hidden learning potential of all employees, teams, and the organization. For learning is the key to an organization's survival and success, and the capacity of its individual members to learn is both its most precious and most inexhaustible resource. Whatever throttles that capacity to learn — whether it's in the culture of the society or the group, or in the minds of individuals — strangles the organization.

ASSUMPTIONS ABOUT LEARNING

To understand how we diminish and squander the capacity to learn, we have to take a look at our assumptions about learning, how it occurs, and who is capable of learning.

When considering the fierce public debates about expanding access to the best education, and the readiness of corporations to spend billions of dollars on worker training, it might seem that there is a universal commitment to learning throughout society.

In fact, though, the debates are fueled by an assumption that runs directly counter to the belief that learning is an inexhaustible resource. For centuries we have maintained a set of assumptions about economics, all based on the premise of scarcity. The world's competitive infrastructure has been propelled by scarcity. And of course, the scarcity of some crucial resources really does threaten many societies and individuals around the world.

Unfortunately, this apprehension of scarcity has pervaded the understanding, practices and policies of learning and education in our culture. Philosophically, we view learning as a "have" and "have not" commodity system. Some people, so the mythology goes, are going to receive more educational opportunity than others, because there's only so much to go around.

Hand in hand with the commodity view of education goes the view of learning capacity as a resource in limited supply. Call it what you will — aptitude, brains, potential, intelligence. Some people, according to the prevailing view, have it; most don't.

BRAIN POWER IS NOT A SCARCE COMMODITY

Even in corporations that declare a commitment to training, these assumptions are rampant, subverting the work and the future of the organization. In particular, the assumption that learning only occurs in controlled, formal settings limits the real learning that could occur naturally as part of the work process.

A very small percentage of organizations has actually made the substantial commitment to train and develop all their employees. For the most part, however, there is an assumption that if an employee is not explicitly trained to do a particular task, he or she cannot do it. And since training and education-al opportunity have historically been confined to the top twenty-five percent of the labor force, the rest of the workers are, in effect, relegated to the status of non-learners. It's a vicious cycle: people not regarded as eligible or appropri-ate candidates for training are assumed to be unable to learn. And situations in the daily course of work which could naturally give rise to valuable learn-ing experiences are wasted.

Organizations can no longer tolerate the developmental blindness which segregates the intellectual haves from the have-nots. In the Learning Organi-zation there is a belief that everyone is of equal importance for the survival of the enterprise — and therefore learning must become an organic element of its daily operation. As Lester Thurow puts it, "Skilled people become the only sustainable competitive advantage."

To take this a step further, we can draw on a concept developed in *Unlim-ited Wealth* by Paul Zane Pilzer.[1] The growth potential of an economy can be measured by comparing the technology it is currently using and that which is available to it that it has not yet been exploited. In other words, if you're cur-rently using one percent of the technology available to you, you have a growth potential of 9900%. So for any individual we can measure the potential for economic growth by determining how much of their brain is being used in comparison with how much could be used if it were developed to its fullest capacity. Estimates of this undeveloped potential in the average human being vary from 900% to 9900% and more.

In other words, the most valuable investment you can possibly make in your business is to increase the extent to which your employees are using their brains effectively. But the currently accepted assumptions about education, intelligence and learning represent a major barrier to developing this huge eco-nomic potential. In fact, even the training that does occur is colored by these negative assumptions, which drastically reduce its effectiveness. Unfortunate-ly the trainees themselves, those deemed educable and worthy of training and advancement, have internalized the limiting expectations of the culture in which they were brought up.

CLARITY BEGINS AT HOME

We don't pretend that these assumptions are easily overcome. Both of us have spent our entire professional lives in activities motivated by our belief that all people are capable of unlimited learning. Nevertheless, we've all too often caught ourselves operating under the same limiting expectations that per-vade our society as a whole. These assumptions, it turns out are addictive in nature and overcoming them can produce severe withdrawal symptoms. So when you've had a really good learning experience which has given birth to some powerful new ideas or creative impulses, don't be surprised if you feel a little post-partem depression afterwards.

One of us was a child who couldn't draw. I knew I couldn't, because my teachers told me, and because everything I did draw reinforced the evident truth that I was woefully lacking in talent. The idea of being an artist who could exhibit in a show would have been a ridiculous dream.

Then, one magical day several decades later, in the company of thirty or so six and seven year olds, I discovered a whole new world. This was the freshly created universe in which I realized that I *could* draw. It happened under the guidance of Mona Brookes, who is famous for teaching children to draw so effectively that not only do they become top-drawer artists, they even raise their math scores as a by-product of their new skill.

In Mona's class I discovered that with a little guidance I could find wonderful joy in drawing — and at the same time I began to fantasize about actually exhibiting my paintings someday. Suddenly my eyes were lifted to the distant horizon and I could walk along the road much lighter of heart.

I have not developed my skill to the level of artistic excellence. Not yet, anyway. But a cloud of inadequacy has been lifted from my shoulders. I know I could learn to paint well if I wanted to, and so I believe in myself that much more. I look at paintings in a new way now — not just enjoying them, but also learning something from the skill exhibited by the artist. My newly won belief in myself makes me so much more than the person I was before — the person who hadn't the resources to learn the art of drawing.

TALENT IS A RESOURCE IN EVERYONE

Unfortunately, too many folks still hold low opinions of what the face in the crowd can accomplish. The myth that most people aren't very smart, and that I.Q. measurements place strict limits on what people are capable of, is much in need of retirement. Intelligence and talent can be developed in anyone, and it's safe to say that given the enormous potential of human beings, everyone you know is a serious underachiever.

Is such a claim merely wishful thinking? Japanese violin teacher Hideo Suzuki didn't think so. He challenged the myth that artists are born, not made, when he proved that he could teach any child to play musically with excellent technique. Suzuki analyzed the elements of violin playing and formulated them into a method so effective that all children, regardless of background and perceptions, could learn what he had to teach.

Rather than assume that talent is passed on genetically, we'd like to persuade you that it's built up gradually from an accumulation of effective learning experiences. Inherited differences might vary the rate of speed of our learning or the platform from which we start, but they cannot prevent us from ultimately achieving the goals that mean the most to us. Any talent, we argue, can be learned to some degree of proficiency by anyone. (Incidentally, the whole notion that behavior of any kind, including intelligence, is somehow determined by our genes is subject to serious question.)[2]

It's because the rate of learning is more rapid for some children than others that a few make headlines as prodigies. With patience, however, it is possible for anyone to learn enough of the elements of a skill to achieve mastery. The main block to success is the attitude of "Icantism", which signals the mind to slam on the brakes and disconnect the distributor.

We're also out to challenge the myth that natural talents can only be developed in the first five to seven years of life. Thousands of examples of people who achieved excellence in adulthood prove this myth false. The main reason there aren't zillions of examples of late development is that by the time we're adult, most of us are so busy earning a living we don't have time to develop new and untried skills. Can you afford to take five years off to develop your potential to be a great musician, inventor, geologist, Samaritan? To date, only the wealthy have been able to afford such luxuries. So hard are economic considerations on the development of talent that until the mid-nineteenth century only two of the great figures in English literature came from the lower classes.

THE THREE INNER BARRIERS TO LEARNING

Even when people get past the I *can't* barriers, there is still a deeper and more durable set of internal barriers which may block the ability to learn.

Human beings are born with an instinct for learning, which they lose only under duress. We could learn all the time, if we were not prevented by one of these barriers. We call them the **learning barriers**. When confronted with something that doesn't make sense, we face a **logical** barrier. If we're asked to think or do something that by our standards is unethical, we're blocked by an **ethical** barrier. And finally, if the process we're involved in makes us uncomfortable, then a **feeling** barrier inhibits our learning.

THE LOGICAL BARRIER

The first of the barriers, the logical barrier, arises when a crucial piece is missing from the presentation of something we want to learn, leaving us with no logical way to understand it. Early in life such gaps may lead to confusion in certain areas, until the missing pieces have been filled in. Virtually all of us have experienced some learning blocks of this kind.

Most of us lack important basic information about some areas of life. Unfortunately, we're usually unaware of these gaps, and how they are causing us problems. Such problems, however, can be rather simple to fix.

In one company we worked with, a manager who had spent his life in technical work was transferred to the sales department. It was assumed that somehow, on the job or elsewhere, he would learn what he needed to know. After a time it became evident that much of his work was counter-productive. For example, he would make promises he could not possibly deliver on, and he would forget to return phone calls. A customer spent several hours informing the CEO about the mistakes this man was making. Instead of firing his new sales manager, the CEO came to us for advice about what he could do.

We pointed out that the man had many highly developed technical skills, but that he had not learned many of the basics of sales management. Among other things, he hadn't learned to write down appointments in an appointment book. The CEO had just gained crucial information from a customer about what the new sales manager needed to learn. The sales manager, however, didn't know he didn't know these things.

To his great credit, the CEO began with positive expectations about the manager's capacity and eagerness to learn. By reframing the situation, the CEO saw that his manager was missing new information and skills which he could learn as successfully as he had mastered other things. Then, making analogies between the technical information the new manager had lived with for years and the new information he needed to know, the CEO was able to help him learn and apply the information and skills he had never known he needed.

There is a wide range of tacit knowledge and behavior that we usually assume people have acquired along the way, which they may indeed never have learned. We shouldn't interpret gaps in this body of tacit knowledge as a reflection on a person's capacity to learn any concept or task. That's why the positive attitudes towards others developed in Steps Two and Five are so important to a Learning Organization.

WE NEED TO KNOW WHY WE NEED TO KNOW

A logical barrier also arises when we cannot see the relevance of new information. We have a hard time learning things on command when we don't know why we're learning them. For example, a manager or shop floor worker confronted with the requirement of learning statistics might argue, "We do a good job here — everyone knows it. So why should we make all these charts to measure our results?"

The answer is, there's no reason to make them if you're not learning something from them. And right here there's a discontinuity between what passes for learning and what follows from it in many organizations. Too often people are taught skills because some consultant says they need to be taught, but no use is made later of what was learned in the training.

Not long ago, we were asked to consult on an Information Systems installation that was taking place in a corporation. The implementation had already started, and it was not going very well. We discovered that there had been no up-front conceptual training or information sessions to present the people involved in the project with the big picture reasons for the new system. There was clearly a disconnect between the implementation process and people's impressions about why the project was taking place.

So when it comes to making charts, for example, it's important that people see how the charts will help them improve their output. This can both save the company money and reduce the number of dissatisfied customers. Teams that make and use charts properly are often far more effective than those that don't because they can easily identify where a problem is coming from, and thus solve it.

THE ETHICAL BARRIER

If we are to learn something well, it must pass our personal ethical standards. Sometimes, however, what is ethical to one person is unethical to another. While these differences are to be expected, they're never unimportant. When people believe that an important principle or value is being violated, their ability to learning is compromised. Literacy trainers, for example, frequently encounter people who feel that it would be wrong for them to learn to read because their parents couldn't, and to surpass their parents would be disrespectful.

Here's an example of an ethical barrier that was causing some problems on the shop floor of a large manufacturing firm. Two expensive parts of a sizable object (call them A and B) were being manufactured. However, five times as many of part A were needed as of part B. But the molds used to cast the metal were so made that for every unit of part A it was necessary also to make a unit of part B. This meant that eighty percent of the units of part B that came from the molds had to be thrown away.

The workers on the production line were conscientiously trying to find ways to improve their work. Schooled in the values of waste management, and not wishing to put their time into manufacturing something that would only end up in the trash, they wondered why the mold could not have been made in two separate sections so it would not be necessary to throw away so many parts. The answer they got was that the molds were very expensive to make, and it was therefore actually cheaper to throw away all those units than make a new mold.

This argument was itself trashed, however, when a new set of molds came in, made the same way as the old ones had been. From that point on the workers were convinced management did not share their values after all. This is clearly an example of the kind of mindlessness that occurs in an organization where accountability is non-existent and thinking is discouraged.

THE FEELING BARRIER

The third barrier to learning is the Feeling Barrier, or Intuitive/Affective Barrier. People have difficulty learning when they feel uncomfortable with the process, or believe the knowledge could be hurtful. If they sense that their confidence or security is being jeopardized, they have learned how to protect themselves from further learning injury. As a matter of fact, this learning barrier is at the very core of people's response to most learning situations and environments. Learning itself, or a particular subject matter, may be associated with long, painful hours spent in school, and a sense of futility or failure. But when lessons are made challenging, clear, exciting and stimulating, learning not only takes place more quickly; it resides in the memory longer, which is usually enough to overcome the feeling barrier.

The greatest barrier to learning is **fear**. As we mentioned in Step One, W. Edwards Deming believed the top priority in the quality business is driving out fear. Unfortunately, fear in the work place generally goes unnoticed because no one is comfortable talking about it. So too often it can be observed only indirectly: in avoidance behavior, criticism of others, failure to support new ideas, or a general lack of excitement about work. Also we should keep in mind that though fear is a major block to communication, it increases when there is little communication, so it tends to be self-generating. Its effect is so pervasive that it may destroy a company more quickly than any other single factor.

The antidote to the feeling barrier is the cultural mind set we have been attempting to develop in the previous steps, chiefly those principles that promote safety. Maintaining positive personal relations, respecting individual thinking, and taking the onus off making mistakes free all of us to think and learn constructively.

Recognition of the learning barriers, combined with the changes in the organizational culture achieved through the first Five Steps will go a long way towards creating an organization in which learning is valued and encouraged. But the greatest incentive to inspire people to reactivate their instinctive capacity to learn comes from the successful experience of learning itself because it is natural for us to learn, and when we are not learning we feel vaguely that something is wrong. That is why one of the most therapeutic experience a person can have is to activate their capacity to learn.

WHY SUCCESSFUL LEARNING IS A POWERFUL EXPERIENCE

Over the course of our work in many organizations we have seen innumerable instances of people being turned on, even to the extent that their lives are turned around, by realizing that they are in fact capable learners. *What* they learned was not nearly as important as *that* they learned. A secretary who suddenly found she could understand math after all, a shop worker who discovered his talent for music, an executive who discovered an unsuspected but deep love for drawing and painting, a computer expert who decided that teaching others how to fly-fish was what we wanted to do — they are among many who recognized their own capability through seemingly unrelated accomplishments.

We cannot overstate the liberating and empowering momentum created by these peoples' experiences of their success as learners. Everyone in the workforce who undertakes the journey of self-discovery becomes more of an asset as a worker. The more confidence you have that you can master the unfamiliar and difficult, the more resources you can bring to each situation you must deal with in an unpredictable world.

The link between personal mastery and participation in the organization is a powerful one, for when you recognize that your personal growth is important to the whole team that works with you, you'll develop a bond with colleagues, growing out of your mutual discovery of common values and interests.

However, personal learning mastery is not achieved just by reading a few books, signing up for a yoga class and making a wish list for yourself. It involves a certain attitude or belief — that you *can* achieve mastery, and that it is important to do so. It requires the constant rehearsal of this belief, until you live and breathe it so much you can't imagine not having it. Mastery also requires a commitment to continuous improvement in every area of personal development you take seriously.

PERSONAL LEARNING MASTERY IS NOT A FRILL

Actually, those who find deep satisfaction in their work have a secret weapon. They love not only what they do, but also the learning that comes from doing, so they never have to "work" at it. They might get tired, but they won't get exhausted, because of the renewing, rejuvenating effect of new ideas. It's the best way in the world to celebrate life.

Executives and managers need to be aware of the power of these experiences — not only because of the positive effects on peoples' outlooks, but because learning is a self-generating, contagious process which has direct benefits to the larger organization. They must recognize that any positive learning experience, even unrelated to the work at hand, is far from being a frill. It is an ingredient of corporate success.

In their book *The Learning Edge*, Calhoun W. Wick and Lu Stanton Leon describe some of the qualities of executive leadership that help set the tone for a learning organization. They call these visionary individuals Learning Leaders.

Learning Leaders embody characteristics that go beyond those

commonly found in typical leaders. Learning leaders are concerned not only with their own learning but constantly are
prodding and provoking others around them to learn. . . .

By constantly stretching the abilities of those who work for
them, learning leaders create a dynamic environment that not
only places a high value on innovation and knowledge but generates the energy needed to move the organization from
contemplation to action.[3]

There are at least two vital reasons why an organization should encourage everyone in it to achieve this kind of excitement about learning. First, at
the heart of learning mastery is the experience of continuous improvement.
It's obvious that if everyone achieves continuous improvement, the value
added to the organization will constantly increase. Second, as people continuously bring more of themselves to their jobs, they reach a point where it's
possible for them to make a quantum leap in the quality of their work.

One hallmark of mastery is the phenomenon of "flow" — the worker's
ability to respond to the job interactively so that whatever happens flows from
one step to the next without pause, confusion or apparent readjustment. We all
can cite examples of people who operate this way, from athletes to craftsmen,
from furniture movers to surgeons. There can be a natural flow to their work,
almost magical to watch. They have a "feel" about what is happening. In the
work they have chosen, they are artists. Our goal for Step Six is to help all the
workers in the organization see themselves as artists at whatever they spend
most of their time doing. Achieving less than that would be a diminution of
human potential.

Organizations that take seriously the development of human potential
may want to give recognition to those who wish to undertake personal challenges. In addition, it's a good idea to offer courses at the workplace, ranging
from business-oriented subjects like computer programming and hydraulic
engineering to "soft" subjects like sight-reading music or improving at golf.
And while it is possible none of these skills will serve the organization directly, the indirect rewards of a sharpened mind allied with a more positive
self-image and improved outlook on life can pay big dividends in the long run.

HOW CORPORATIONS SUPPORT INDIVIDUAL LEARNING

Corporate support for individual personal development is not something
that comes easily to most companies. We've been too long buried in traditions
that make it seem alien or counter-intuitive to give everyone a blank check for
learning. For so many years industry tried to stamp out individual differences
and keep workers in their place, we've come to accept traditions of enforcing
conformity instead of encouraging all to develop their full potential. While a
few leading companies like IBM have been noted for doing just this, recog-

nizing individual and group learning achievements, may still come hard for many.

During the 1950's and 1960's, IBM was committed to devoting as much as twenty-five percent of worker time to training and development. It also was committed to assisting its employees in shaping careers that would most fully develop their potential. These were two major factors in its powerful ascendancy in the business world during that time period.

Louis R. Mobley, for many years director of executive training at IBM, was trained from the ground up by being given responsibility not only to be able to sell the machines the company produced, but also to repair them. In the years of his retirement, Mobley often lamented the fact that IBM had lost much of its earlier commitment to such extensive and comprehensive training at all levels of the organization. Perhaps its recent performance is an indication of the true cost of such retrenchment. Given IBM's phenomenal success during its prime years, it's somewhat surprising that other large corporations have not emulated its high level commitment to education and training, despite the fact that almost all indicators suggest the immense value and importance of doing so — now more than ever.

In fact we believe this so strongly that we'd like to make the analogy that constantly training and retraining your entire organization (provided the training is truly effective) is as important as putting oil in your car. If you don't do it, you may not notice a problem for quite a long time, but eventually the entire machine will grind to a halt and at that point there won't be much you can do about it anymore.

Nowadays it's true, many large corporations are recognizing the importance of supporting individual learning. One powerful example of what organizations are doing for their employees in relation to continuous learning was a collaborative education program between United Auto Workers and the Ford Motor Company, which involved about 20,000 employees per year.

In this program each hourly employee received a $2,000 education voucher which could be used at any local college or university. Also there was the option of earning a degree without leaving the place of employment, by taking advantage of the learning centers in some of the Ford plants. Obviously, the impact on the workplace of such a program is strong, since the workers tend to seek out opportunities to improve their value to their employer with a view towards advancement in their careers. The effect is one of empowerment, and leads to other forms of initiative in the company, so workers feel they have something to say about what goes on there.

A *New York Times* story quoted one of the workers, who said, "People consider themselves part of the process. They have a chance to make changes. They are expected to do so, and they are recognized when they do."[4] When the culture supports personal mastery, then individuals are much more inclined to develop skills that are beneficial to the organization.

WHAT ABOUT WORKPLACE TRAINING?

Of course the most obvious way corporations can promote personal mastery in the workplace is to offer training programs which enhance work-related skills and knowledge.

Though there is a continuing controversy about how much companies should be encouraged, or even required, to train their employees, there is no dispute about the need for more. *Business Week* had this to say about the value of training as an investment:

> In the long run, most economists agree with [former Labor Secretary Robert] Reich that training can be an investment that more than pays for itself. Half a dozen studies done in the late 1980's conclude that company-sponsored training programs boost workers' wages by 4% to 11% over the long run. Other studies found that the productivity gain from workers' higher skills more than pays for the higher labor costs. For instance, a 1989 study in the *Journal of Labor Economics* of large employers in the South and the Midwest found that a 10% increase in spending on training produced a 3% boost in productivity over two years, which was twice as large as the pay hikes caused by the training.
>
> As a result, many economists believe that higher corporate training budgets would create more jobs overall, even if employers were to end up footing the bill. A 1.5% training expenditure would cost companies an extra $21 billion a year and could cause them to restrain wages and hiring in the short run. But it would also generate $63 billion in new economic activity and 2.5 million new jobs over three to five years, estimates Anthony P. Carnevale, the ASTD's chief economist, who is a candidate for the Labor Dept.'s top training post. And even opponents of a mandate agree with the goal. "We don't like the idea of government forcing companies to spend 1.5% on training, but employers must invest even more than that, or they won't be able to compete," says Phyllis Eisen, a policy expert at the National Association of Manufacturers (NAM).[5]

As we shall shortly argue, almost all corporate training is regressive and produces only a fraction of the effect it could have if more up to date methods were used. We believe, for example, that while currently only 20 percent of TQM programs in industry are completely successful, that figure would be closer to 90 percent if really effective modern training methods were used in every case, provided these were combined with a corresponding culture change that leads to the empowerment and creativity needed to make TQM and other such programs work at all.

WHY MOST TRAINING DOESN'T WORK

Much traditional training is relatively rigid — lectures with flip charts and overhead projectors given to participants who are expected to sit passively and take it all in. Such an approach only reinforces the notion that whatever thinking is to be done has to come from somewhere other than the mind of the employee being trained.

Reactions against misguided training have led to the notion in some places that training is of little use and should be cut back. We disagree. There must be a great deal of training — but training of the right kind. For training, if it's any good, will lead people to discover the meaning of things in the language of their own thought process. In fact, when you put it this way, the very word "training" is a misnomer. What's needed, in short, is not so much training as education in how to activate your own capacity to learn.

Our experience with many organizations has shown that there is considerable confusion about the difference between training/education and learning. In fact you may have noticed that in the *Learning Organization Assessment* in Step 1 (and even more so in the separately published revised version of the *Assessment*), there are more questions probing this issue than any other. We believe this confusion is a major reason why the "return-on-investment" anticipated by many training programs has not materialized as promised: training has been the focus, not learning. There is a world of difference.

In *The Learning Edge*, Wick and Leon provide an excellent critique of traditional training with the following observations:[6]

1. Training doesn't tie in with the strategic business needs of the company.
2. In training, one size doesn't fit all.
3. Managers often resist training and then sabotage its implementation.
4. For those who want to apply their classroom learning, stepping back into the workplace can be a dispiriting experience.
5. If there isn't any follow-through on what was learned in the classroom, who's to know the difference?
6. Managers who try to get the most out of their off-site training usually lack support for implementation once they return to the job.

Let's consider each of these in turn:

1. Training doesn't tie in with the strategic business needs of the company. When the company has clearly determined that there's something its people must know or be able to do, then training makes sense. When there's no clear purpose, it's a waste of time.

If the purpose is to improve job skills, the following training objectives will often make sense, given the company needs and the level of skills of their personnel.

A) Workplace literacy.

B) A variety of quality improvement programs, including Total Quality Management, ISO9000 (the European quality standards that U. S. companies must meet in order to do business abroad), Just in Time Manufacturing, Statistical Process Control, Resource Planning, and other relevant skills.

C) Advanced technical training.

D) Marketing skills.

E) Entrepreneurial and intrapreneurial skills.

F) Systems thinking and ecological awareness.

G) Creativity, innovation, and problem solving skills.

F) Community development, partnering and team development skills.

G) Communications skills, with an emphasis on listening skills.

H) Visioning and imagination development skills.

I.) Networking skills.

J.) Learning Agility development for individuals and teams.

K.) Servant-Leadership development skills

David Kearns, former head of Xerox, put it this way: "We spend a great deal of money on training. Are we really utilizing that expenditure in the best way possible? I suspect that we haven't thought about it nearly as much as we should. To do that you've got to start thinking about training at the beginning of a process. We've tended often to think about it at the end."[7]

Yes, training has too often been an afterthought, because we use it to plug up holes instead of to furnish our business with the highest quality personnel. It's hard to imagine why so many companies are so unaware of the value of a strong drive for learning among their employees. Penny-wise and pound foolish. In fact, such training programs may be necessary for a company's survival.

2. In training, one size doesn't fit all. Training — and any form of education — that does not take into account the crucial differences among all learners will simply not work for many learners. Awareness of differences in learning styles should be the cornerstone of any training program.

It's possible to build flexibility into a training program so effectively that virtually everyone who takes it will achieve substantial benefits. Attempting to teach without understanding how people learn is futile. We'll explain this more fully later in this chapter.

3. Managers often resist training and then sabotage its implementa-

tion. Resistance to training can be minimized when it is introduced not by edict from above, but by a process of internal marketing that sells the training only to those who want it, or at least see its essential value to them. If the training is really effective, the number of people who want it will increase until almost the entire population has sought it out voluntarily. The key is that people come to see what a difference the training makes.

Recently, we worked with a corporations that installed a new MRPII system. MRPII (Manufacturing Resource Planning) is an inventory management system that most manufacturing corporations use. Two hundred and fifty employees had to be trained in the over-all scope of the new system. Conventional wisdom would say that such a training would be something people would want to avoid at all costs. However, the exact opposite happened. People were calling the program manager wanting to make sure they could get into one of the training sessions. The secret was that the training session was developed to match the learning needs to the participants, and provided the rare opportunity for people to learn a lot of information in a very short period of time. The training session made sense to people, and they could make direct application to their work situations.

4. For those who want to apply their classroom learning, stepping back into the workplace can be a dispiriting experience. All training should include practice in its application so its use in the workplace is guaranteed. More than that, the workplace should interface with the training so that opportunities to apply what has been learned are available to people as soon as they get back from the training. Beyond that, the managers should be trained first, believe in the training and reinforce it among the employees as they are trained. Furthermore, everything possible should be done to insure that what has been learned with still be active and current a decade later — no more Flavor of the Month syndrome.

5. If there isn't any follow-through on what was learned in the classroom, who's to know the difference? No training program should ever go unevaluated. How else can an organization know which training programs work and which do not? A company that doesn't recognize and back a valuable training program is just as blind as one that continues to offer a pointless program. So continuous improvement processes should be built into every training program, and they should involve everyone who is affected by the training, no matter how tangentially.

6. Managers who try to get the most out of their off-site training usually lack support for implementation once they return to the job. No training should be offered unless a rationale has been established for it. Such a rationale can be created when a brief sample of the training and its objectives is offered to all those who have a need to know about it. In short, a really good training involves the entire culture and often has the effect of permanently modifying that culture, at least to some degree. If this is not happening, it's time to consider how to make it happen.

SO WHAT KIND OF TRAINING DOES WORK?

Before we go on to a prime example of the kind of training that does work, we need to understand the dynamics of learning — when it occurs, why it succeeds, and how to optimize the chances that anyone will learn. Because without this understanding, most training, and indeed most education, is merely a hit-or-miss crap shoot, where success is mostly accidental and failure almost inevitable.

We should say that this was really the entry point for both of us into the whole subject of the Learning Organization. Both of us have spent many years teaching in a variety of environments — in schools, from elementary to university and adult education, and workplaces across a wide spectrum of learning cultures. We have been constantly studying, observing, and researching the learning process, from the neurological to the societal level. And what we have learned about learning is the foundation of these Ten Steps.

This understanding cannot be spelled out here in great detail, though it is implicit throughout the book and has been fully developed in the companion book, *The Everyday Genius*.[8] In order to help you understand how we approach learning, we'll give you a very brief introduction to some of the key tenets of Integrative Learning.

Integrative Learning is based on a study of how, according to neurological research, the brain operates. It also derives from observing the thinking and learning behavior of some of the adults we call geniuses, as well as the most successful learners of all: infants and children.

WHO TAUGHT YOU YOUR NATIVE LANGUAGE?

Consider first of all the fact that no matter what our learning preferences might turn out to be later in life, we all learned our native language. Babies learn virtually without instruction, but the process they use (found universally in all cultures) can be imitated in the classroom. It involves using all the senses, generating the developmental structure behind every idea explored, and having fun building models of how things work conceptually.

Learning a new language when you don't already know one is about as tough an assignment as anyone could take on, and yet virtually everyone does it. So something goes wrong afterwards that separates people who are considered "bright" from those who are not.

Why do we all succeed at this amazing intellectual feat, and then fail at such trivial, easy chores later on? Look at the way babies learn to speak and communicate. They are immersed in an atmosphere of affection and support, surrounded by people who are eager to help by joining in the play of learning and confident that they will succeed. As babies, our learning is self-directed, entirely experiential, involving our whole being. It is part of living, not a separate formal activity.

If this seems irrelevant to adult concerns, consider the characteristics of a workplace where learning and work form a continuous loop. Avice Saint in her study, *Continuous Learning Within Japanese Organizations*,[9] suggests three essential characteristics of successful learning in the workplace:

1. **Learning must come through the work itself.** Learning is an inescapable part of work and must be centered around work processes. Learning is not something separate from doing: it is one process — learning/doing.

2. **Learning must be developmental.** Traditional training was considered a corrective, a remedy for poor performance that caused errors. It was designed to bring workers "up to par."

3. **Learning means discovery.** Learning on-the-line includes improvising, trying out new methods, finding and correcting errors, and inventing new and better ways to do the work.

THE APPLICATION GAP

In traditional teaching there's a huge gap between what you learn and how you apply it. This gap is so great that studies indicate success in school is no predictor at all of success in life. While it's true that the more education you have, the better you will do, it's not true that A students necessarily do better in life than C students, or even than those who just barely made it academically. An A student may be good at absorbing information but not necessarily good at creating meaning from that information. However, it's the meaning or utility of information that allows you to make connections between school work and the real world.

To take a simple example, in teaching what two and two equals in traditional education, you are usually asked to memorize the sum of two numbers. If you memorize enough simple sums and products, you can do fairly complicated problems, because you can break them down into simpler problems, the answers to which you've memorized.

The result of this nearly universal way of teaching math is deplored by mathematician John Allen Paulos.

"You see someone who can understand anything," Paulos says, "the most complicated legal nuances, the most intricate emotional transactions, and with numbers, their eyes glaze and their gut-level common sense evaporates." Paulos attributes this to a simple fear of math fostered by an educational system that emphasizes practice without incorporating concept, by professional mathematicians who retreat into theoretical speculation, by gender myths, and by a disregard for critical thinking. "Math is thinking," he says, "thinking about numbers, about space, quantitative relationships. It's akin to logic and common sense."[10]

Having said all this, we need to point out that whatever its limitations, advanced education nevertheless has a powerful effect on the nervous system. A brain which is active and continuously involved in problem solving undergoes profound neurological development throughout life. A brain which stagnates degenerates. A dramatic piece of evidence of the importance of this is the fact that people who have university educations contract Alzheimer's disease only one fourth as often as those who don't. Extend this notion to what you're about to read in the next few paragraphs, and you'll see why there's no case on record of a person who contracted Alzheimer's after learning a foreign language at an advanced age.

Through Integrative Learning, because of its emphasis on discovery and direct experience, the learner can immediately infuse new information with personal meaning. For example, in an Integrative Learning class, if we were to ask you to learn the sum of two and two, we would use an approach that is conceptual and experiential at the same time. We might stand two students in front of the room and ask two others to come up and join them. We'd then ask the class to observe how many students we now have. Of course, the class will give the correct answer.

GETTING INTO THE CONCEPT

But there's a lot more going on here than when we memorize answers to sums. The first two people I call up in front of the room grab the attention of the rest of the class. As Johnny and Mary stand there, all sorts of ideas about how they relate to each other flood the students' minds. Then Susie and Jim join them, and again you can't help thinking about their personalities.

Children (and adults) love to think about their friends, and indeed find it impossible not to. When we put their friends into the math problems, we start a complex series of reflections that will take the children deeper and deeper into mathematical operations.

You might ask what this has to do with corporate training. It has everything to do with it. There are a great many technical concepts that are far better learned in the dramatic and experiential way described above than in the way they are usually presented. We learn best when there is no separation between the learning and the doing, when our whole being is involved — body, intellect, and emotions. We've had people act out complicated computer programs, shop floor organizational structures, statistical processes and just in time concepts of managing inventory. They have a wonderful time, and they really understand what they're learning.

One of the reasons people have trouble learning is that the information they are being asked to learn is detached from their sensory experiences. And yet the learning most of us experienced in kindergarten and early elementary school was based on the cooperation of all the essential powers of mind and body. Despite these earlier learning experiences, this natural and sensible procedure is dismissed as an obstacle to training and learning.

We have spent a great deal of time helping telecommunications companies design advanced technical training programs using the concepts developed above. In one case we informed a group of trainees for our program that at Kodak a measured improvement of twenty-seven times had occurred. This sounded like science fiction to the trainees until they actually saw the results in their own classes. Then one of them, a battle-scarred trainer of many years' experience commented, "I would think you could show an improvement of as much as fifty times."

THE CONTEXT OF EMOTIONAL EXPERIENCE

There's a fundamental fact of brain function that explains why this general approach is so important. The role of emotion in memory can be traced even to the point of physiological processing in the brain. When you have an emotional experience, you remember all sorts of details that have nothing directly to do with the experience itself. For example, when you fall in love, you remember where you were at the time, what was playing on the radio and what you were wearing. In other words, nothing is too trivial to be relevant to a powerful emotional experience.

When learning something new is part of an emotional experience, all the emotions are attached to what is learned. So if you learn to add two and two in a classroom that is ugly, with a teacher you don't like and classmates you don't care about, that's all going to affect how you feel about math for the rest of your life. But if you learn in a way that's exciting and fun, from a fascinating teacher who brings the other students into a group experience with you, then you'll have positive feelings about that subject forever after.

As a result, you'll frequently respond by thinking for yourself, anticipating what's coming in the course, and making up problems, just as people do when they're very good at teaching themselves. We call that generative learning. It produces a sense of "ownership" of the material learned. That means you feel as if you made it up yourself.

YOU'RE ONE OUT OF TWENTY BILLION

Most people don't realize, or are only vaguely aware, that we all have different ways of learning. Indeed, much of our educational system was built on the mistaken notion that there is one best way to learn. Even though everyday experience contradicts this notion, it's still widely accepted. When a student, or a spouse, or a teacher, or an employee, or a parent seems to be unable to grasp something using the same approach that works for us, we tend to assume that is a deficiency that can be overcome by simply repeating the same unsuccessful method more zealously.

Fortunately, we now have confirmation of the fact that people learn most effectively in their own individual ways. They have unique learning styles and bring to bear a variety of intelligences that are only rarely accommodated in traditional classroom settings. One can calculate the potential for about 20 billion different thinking and learning styles, simply by combining and recombining the variables we know exist in the way people function and perceive things. The chances that there's anyone else out there who thinks exactly the way you do are vanishingly small — and even if someone else did, you certainly couldn't locate that person within your lifetime.

So, given that you and everyone you associate with has a unique way of processing information, how can anything be presented in a way that's acceptable to everyone?

THE THEORY OF MULTIPLE INTELLIGENCES

Let's look now a little more closely at one of the theoretical bases of Integrative Learning, so we'll better understand what kind of training succeeds. One recent set of findings that has helped people understand the rationale of Integrative Learning is the theory of Multiple Intelligences.

Well-publicized studies in brain research conducted by Howard Gardner of Harvard University demonstrate that there are many different intelligences present in every human brain. He has identified at least seven, several of which are not currently measured by standardized tests, and has recently offered some additional ones as well. We all possess Multiple Intelligences. Their relative strengths vary from person to person, partly because of the different ways we have all developed as a result of our learning experiences.

MEET THE SEVEN PARTS OF YOUR BRAIN

If you've completed the *Multiple Intelligences Checklist* at the end of Step Five, you've already begun to recognize your own distinctive mix of intelligences. The seven intelligences originally identified by Gardner are:

Linguistic: Your sensitivity to the meaning and order of words, whether you're speaking, writing or studying the structure of language itself. This applies to the full range of language use from the emotional and expressive to the more formal and scientific.

Logical/Mathematical: Your intelligence for conceptualizing in math and science and in dealing with complex logical systems. This involves the use of symbols and abstract reasoning.

Visual/Spatial: Your ability to perceive the visual world accurately, or to recreate or alter it on paper, in the mind, or in direction and distance. Non-sighted people also have a strong spatial sense, which helps them think about moving around in the world without the input of sight. The way we organize our spatial world powerfully influences the essential structure of our thinking.

Bodily/Kinesthetic: This is your capacity for hands-on learning. It's the ability to use your body skillfully for self-expression or toward a goal — like dancing, acting, and athletics. Some of the world's greatest thinkers (among them Einstein) have had to feel their ideas in their bodies in order to think effectively. We've found that all ideas can be symbolized in abstract forms that can be represented in movement, much in the manner of modern dance. When ideas are translated this way the richness of their connotations and applications becomes much more apparent.

Musical: Even if you're tone deaf and can't carry a tune in a bucket, you have some ability to understand and/or create music. Your rhythmical and harmonic sense are very important in resolving some problems that may seem to have nothing to do with music.

Interpersonal: Your perception and understanding of other individuals — their moods, desires, and willingness to interact with you. Essentially this intelligence allows us to become the other person, much as an actor might, in order to understand how the world looks from the other's point of view. This is essential for most communications skills. It is the intelligence that is called for, more than ever before, for leaders and managers.

Intrapersonal: Your understanding of yourself, how you think and feel and what you want out of life. This is perhaps the least well developed skill in most educational contexts, but it is the one that can produce the most valuable jumps in learning, since your ability to identify with what you are learning is all-important. It is the reflective learning process that is so sorely missing in most organizations.

GETTING THE BEST OUT OF YOUR BRAIN

We come into the world possessing these seven different routes for discovering the world. They are our receptors of the full sensory range of the physical world. Through them we make sense of the universe, from the abstract logic of mathematics to the intricate social text of human interactions. As babies we engage the world with the full set of intelligences operating. Infants engage their linguistic, kinesthetic, visual, musical, logical, interpersonal and intrapersonal intelligences all at once. That's why they are such expert learners.

It's hard to get the best out of any resource if you use only a small part of it, and the human brain is no exception. If as a society — beginning with our educational system — we have been measuring only two forms of human intelligence (the logical/mathematical and the linguistic) and have largely ignored the other five, we have not been performing or learning as efficiently as we can.

IT'S A MATTER OF SURVIVAL

In a survival situation you would need to use all your intelligences and sensory inputs to stay alive. Speaking of survival, even zoo animals will activate otherwise untapped intelligences to make their lives more interesting in captivity. In the absence of the stimulation they would have in the wild, a number of elephants in several different zoos have taken up the art of painting, and their paintings have been selling at rather good prices. And, perhaps even more surprisingly, their works appear to have enough individual character and style to set one elephant artist apart from another. It would seem obvious, then, that if even animals need their intellectual fix, we humans, if caught up in humdrum jobs, ought to have some extra stimulation to keep our brains fit.

So, given that obviously biological need, plus the increasing complexity of today's world, doesn't it make sense to use and further develop as much of your brain power as possible? Here, then, we have another powerful rationale for a robust, exciting and creative program in any organization that hopes to become a Learning Organization.

It's probably true that the most important survival need of the modern organization is for learning that is relevant, quick and powerful in its impact, learning which will make a permanent impression on the organization, changing its operational capacity, in order to deal with the ever shifting challenges of an increasingly global marketplace. If so, a deeper understanding of how we learn is a powerful leg up in the struggle for survival.

ENTER, THE LEARNING LEADERS

So what does the best kind of training actually look like in practice? It begins with teams trained in the principles of Integrative Learning who can effectively apply this understanding to any course that serves the purposes of the corporation. These teams, which we call the Learning Leaders, become an extremely powerful tool for stimulating the thinking that will ultimately result in a Learning Organization. We've worked with such teams both as units in large corporations and in a consortium combining several smaller companies. Either way, the principles are the same. Much of this model was built in collaboration with Ron Heidke, then head of manufacturing in Kodak Park.

When one of us worked with the Learning Leaders at Kodak, I watched them create a revolution within the areas of their company in which they worked. In a mere eighteen months they had not only trained nine thousand people, they had also won the respect and support of the two human resources groups within Kodak Park. That was because they were raising the effectiveness of technical training in their company to a degree that, when measured by different yardsticks, ranges up to 2700 percent.

These teams were made up of people drawn from throughout the company, not necessarily experienced or professional trainers. Yet, far from rejecting them as unqualified amateurs, their co-workers paid them the respect of using their services and taking on much of the learning process they developed for further proliferation throughout the company. The fact that many of the company leaders remained unaware of this revolution only adds to the evidence of their success, for, apart from the championing of Heidke, they achieved it largely without support from the top, and used it to stage a quiet revolution that offended virtually no one and led to none of the reprisals that so often greet innovative programs when a conservative management learns about them. In addition, as we mentioned earlier, the Learning Leaders, even without full recognition of management, are believed to have saved their company at least ten million dollars the first year.

THE MODEL OF THE LEARNING LEADERS

Here's how you can use the Learning Leaders model to capture the essence of much that is in the Ten Step Process and build it into a style of working, doing business and living well that can ultimately permeate your whole organization.

The organization must first commit itself to a clear, high-priority learning goal. Perhaps the goal is to adopt a new quality program and make sure it's fully implemented. Or perhaps it's to upgrade skills in a certain area, or to develop a literacy program. Whatever the goal, if it is well chosen and well administered, it can transform your company. Keep it narrow and focused at first, to make sure it succeeds.

The second step is to determine how many people are to be trained, and what the extent of the training will be. If it's only a couple of dozen, then it would be good to join in a consortium with other companies seeking similar results and develop a jointly owned training program.

If, however, those that need internal training number in the hundreds or the thousands, it makes sense to develop the training internally. In this case, set a target date for completion, and decide how many training sessions must be held by that time. This will determine the number of Learning Leaders you will need.

The team should be large enough to develop and deliver all the training courses needed, and in addition take care of the other business aspects of their program. For example, to train 10,000 people in a year and a half at Kodak, we concluded that the team should be composed of slightly more than twenty people. Interestingly enough, when we've worked with substantially smaller corporations or lesser demands for training, we've still ended up with about that number of learning leaders, but when the demand is much smaller, then the learning leaders combine their duties in that role with other jobs in the company, so they're not working full time in training. That may actually be an advantage, since they continuously return to the perspective of the employee who would technically be on the receiving end of training in order to do a better job. In other words, they frequently step away from the perspective of the trainer to that of the worker.

QUALIFICATIONS TO RECRUIT FOR

Once the number is determined, it's time to start recruiting. Let's say, for the sake of our example, that you're going to train twenty people. In that case you should look at about thirty or forty possible candidates.

What qualities should you look for in a candidate for this training? We've drawn up a list of promising characteristics. You probably will not find more than a handful of these qualities in any one applicant, but if you can select a team in which most of them are present, you'll have a much stronger team. Also, publication of these criteria will tell applicants something about what will be expected of them, and help in the selection process.

Here are some of the qualifications we use in selecting a team of Learning Leaders:

1. **Cross-disciplined awareness of math-science and liberal arts.** (Many of the tools for effective training are derived from the liberal arts. Therefore, a background in music, art, literature or drama is helpful when combined with the necessary technical background needed for the subject matter of the training.)

2. **Empathy to cross-cultural orientation**. (The trainer should be sensitive to the values of different cultures, in order to preserve the safety in all groups. Otherwise it's too easy to make careless comments that may turn certain people off — fatal when you're trying to get them to accept new ideas or a new culture.)

3. **Ability to respond to confrontational questions comfortably**. (In many groups, as soon as a more permissive attitude is allowed, previously controlled hostilities may tend to surface. A good trainer can respond to such confrontations without taking it personally, and also without creating situations that disturb other learners in the group.)

4. **Ability to reframe**. (Oftentimes the material may seem difficult to the participants, and the trainer should be skilled at helping them feel comfortable when they're not immediately successful at understanding something.)

5. **Comfort with emotional outbursts**. (In the current business environment, change can be threatening; so there may be times when people become emotional because of it. An effective trainer can handle such outbursts sympathetically and supportively, while not letting them take over the proceedings.)

6. **Awareness of edu-economics**. (It's helpful to understand the relationship between education and economics, so as to be able to justify the notion that good training is an important investment. Also this will help in evaluating the impact of training on the economic condition of the organization.)

7. **Business acumen**. (Whatever the subject of the training, if it's in the context of business, the trainer must be able to help the participants think through the business objectives they're involved with.)

8. **Strong marketing ability**. (Teaching is a form of marketing. You have to sell the ideas you're teaching. Beyond that, the trainers will need to sell their programs throughout the organization, and that will require some marketing ability.)

9. **Ability to think on your feet**. (No two classes are the same. By the time the training is ready to go, it will be an interactive experience improvised against the background of the course structure. Every classroom moment will be a unique experience that will require a fresh response.)

10. **Ability to take criticism**. (The Learning Leaders will work together as a team, and will need to critique each other. In addition, participants in the course will often critique or question it. Good trainers do not become defensive under these circumstances.)

11. **Sense of paradox**. (There are many paradoxes in the learning process. For example, the more you know about something, the more aware you become of how little you know. Or, in order to reduce the number of mistakes you have to increase the tolerance for them. People who are too controlling and by-the-book will have difficulty handling these subtleties.)

12. **Artistic experience**. (Teaching is an art. Any background of artistic experience, such as drawing, playing an instrument, or experience with theater, helps as a background for understanding the art of teaching.)

13. **Regard for quantification process**. (It's always important to be able to generalize, but in the end generalizations must be backed up with notions of quantity. That's particularly important in industry. Many of the programs to be offered will emphasize the importance of quantifying things.)

14. **Knowledge of how to translate course material into Integrative Learning process**. (While this will be conveyed in the training of the trainers, some people intuitively understand what it takes to get a point across, while others tend to think everything needs to be over-explained.)

15. **Belief in the teachability of all people**. (Most people will espouse this belief, but few will stand by it firmly when, on the front lines, they confront someone who seems to be an exception.)

16. **Ability to think like a child**. (A child is someone who is alive to learning possibilities. The magic of childhood enlivens everything. Any sub-

ject, no matter how boring it may seem, can be brought to life by one who can think with the magic of childhood.)

17. **Proactive orientation**. (Learning Leaders need to anticipate problems and solve them before they occur.)

18. **Sense of humor**. (The classroom should be fun. A stand up comic can make a good teacher. However, the best approach is to let the class develop their own sources of laughter. You can't do this very well if you don't have a sense of humor yourself.)

19. **Sense of universal patterns and relationships**. (Everything in the universe is related to everything else. When you're explaining something obscure, you often need to be able to come up rather quickly with an everyday analogy.)

20. **Sensitivity to special needs**. (Everyone learns differently. But some people have unique needs that one must respond to. The person in your class who's in a wheel chair may not be able to participate in some of the activities. You can still do the activities, but find a way to make that person feel included. Someone else may have unusual difficulty with some of the material. Be creative in helping out.)

21. **Ability to recognize and respect individual value in individual people, as well as ethnic groups and unusual orientations**. (The goal of the trainer is to help all people discover their unique value. This will be done, of course, in the context of the subject matter, but the glow will effect everything else as well.)

22. **Ability to admit mistakes**. (Sometimes you'll make a mistake in front of the room. You should be comfortable admitting it and then getting on with things. You can even, on occasion, use your mistake as a teaching opportunity.)

23. **Flexible thinking**. (There are many different good solutions to most problems. Don't lock into one way to get something done, but do insist on quality.)

24. **Lack of need for immediate closure**. Sense of the open-endedness of life. No hard and fast answers. (Creativity is often destroyed by premature closure. Part of the magic of Integrative Learning is its ability to allow people to grapple with a question for some time before they decide what it means. Quick answers are not always the best.)

25. **Willingness and ability to listen sensitively**. (All of us think we're good listeners, but the question is do our spouses, children and employees agree with us? The person who's most critical of your listening ability is probably the truest measure of your effectiveness in this area.)

26. **Ability to interpret research findings in the light of practical application**. (There's lots of good research and you should know what it is. But how does it truly enlighten the matter at hand?)

27. **Willingness to conduct research to improve training practices**. (There are an infinite variety of ways to approach a problem. Some of them haven't been researched yet. The team of Learning Leaders, or even one of the teams they train, may need to get into the research business occasionally to find out what works best.)

We repeat that you probably won't find more than a handful of these qualities in any one candidate, but a team whose members possess them will be much better able to accomplish its mission.

YOU WON'T NEED EXPERIENCED TEACHERS

Incidentally, it's not necessary that the people selected for the Learning Leaders have any previous experience in training or teaching. Sometimes it's better if they don't, because they won't have to break the previous habits established with traditional teaching. But they should all very much want to be part of the team. Drafting people who would truly rather not be in front of the room spells death to any such project.

TRAINING THE TRAINERS

The next step is training your trainers in Integrative Learning. There are a variety of trainers who are capable of providing this instruction.[11] Once you've located your expert and made the appropriate arrangements, plan to present a day-long sampler for at least twenty of the people you think might be good candidates for the Learning Leaders team. Observe how these people react to the activities presented. Some of them, once they see what's involved, may opt out. Others may reveal behaviors that just won't work out. You'll also probably see some people who show promise of being strong leaders in the new project.

When you've selected your team, set them up with facilities and resources to design and deliver courses. They should also be prepared and encouraged to act as consultants for each other. When they're ready to spend full time on the project, begin with a forty-hour training.

It takes at least forty hours of instruction for most people to understand the basic structure and philosophy of Integrative Learning, but once digested it can easily be applied to teach anything from the most complex technological subjects to the simplest material such as phone-answering procedures. With this background, the team can get started on course design. After they've been at it for two or three weeks, have a follow-up session to refine their knowledge of Integrative Learning. Supplemental follow-up sessions may be helpful from time to time, as well as some consulting on course design.

In addition, you'll want to give the team specialized training in the material they're expected to teach. If it's Total Quality Management or Workplace

Literacy, put them in the hands of a subject matter expert, so they're able to work professionally with the content they're supposed to teach.

GETTING THE TEAM LAUNCHED

When you've done all this, it's time for the Learning Leaders to prove what they can do. Their goal is to offer the training your organization needs with such thoroughness and flair that they create a demand for their services. People in the organization will want to participate in this exciting new learning process. And you should expect improvement in the quality of performance of those who have taken the courses taught by the Learning Leaders. We've found that when the process is working well that improvement is monumental and present throughout the entire group that has been trained. In fact, we feel comfortable picking people who've been trained off the shop floor at random and asking them what they're doing with the training they've received. The answers to this question should be enthusiastic, detailed and precise, and generally you should get different answers from just about everyone.

If you organize everything well, you should have your Learning Leaders functioning effectively within the first six months, and you should see substantially better implementation of the course material than would be the case if traditional training were used. In fact, it might be useful to run an experiment, comparing the work of the Learning Leaders with the work of traditional instructors in the material being taught. Study both the evaluations of the two groups and the results they produce over time. But avoid placing too much emphasis on competition here, as that can be divisive.

Also, make sure that the groups have sufficient access to follow-up in the areas in which they are being trained, so the training can really be successful. Training that is too scrimpy or superficial will inevitably be far less effective, and thus far more expensive in the long run.

THE GREATEST BENEFITS WERE UNEXPECTED . . .

In addition to improved success rates in mastering the course material, we have observed other beneficial effects that are sometimes quite surprising. Often these side effects are, if anything, as important and beneficial as the course material itself.

An illuminating example of this occurred when the Kodak Learning Leaders did their first run on a Total Quality Management course. The course was designed to be taught in two parts of two days each, separated by a week. At the time, they were still a little unsure of themselves. When they concluded the first two days, the director of the division they were training told them the course was a failure and he'd like to take over the second half of the course himself.

When the trainers asked the director to please let them finish the course they had designed, he reluctantly agreed. But after the course was completed and the director saw the results, he changed his tune. Now he said he'd like to have his people take any course they taught, whether it was relevant to his needs or not. He had discovered, first of all, that the learning of the quality concepts was truly outstanding. The side effects of the training, however, impressed him even more: his group was more productive, more independent and more cooperative than they had ever been before.

These changes were very similar to the ones we mentioned earlier as being documented in a report on training at Bell Atlantic.[12] Upon completion of Integrative-Accelerated Learning based courses, the supervisors at Bell Atlantic noted remarkable improvement in critical areas quite apart from the subject matter of the courses: professional confidence, problem-solving ability, ability to work without supervision, accuracy, speed, use of reference materials, ability to give complete information, personal accountability, and people skills.

. . . BUT NO MYSTERY

We asked the Learning Leaders what had happened to turn the skeptical director around. Why had their TQM course seemed so inadequate at the end of the first unit, and so powerful at the end of the second? One of the trainers compared the reactions at the halfway point to the feeling you have after reading only half of a good mystery. The clues and the story lines haven't been connected, and there's a sense of nothing being resolved. But by the time you get to the last page, there's a feeling of surprise and delight at how well it all fits together.

What actually happened was this: The learners were presented with a number of experiences designed to activate *their own* prior understanding of quality, and how it works. Since everyone learns differently, this approach seemed chaotic from the point of view of a linear thinker. So by the end of the second day the division director was convinced not only that nothing really serious was being taught, but that nothing had jelled out of what had been taught.

But when the next two days of the course were completed, the workers immediately began to use what they had learned. They had thoroughly understood the material because they were able to encounter and absorb it in ways that were appropriate to them individually. In addition, they began to behave in rather different ways from before. All of a sudden they were initiating new ideas and processes themselves, working together better as teams, and solving problems much more creatively.

WHEN STUDENTS ARE EMPOWERED

When students of any age feel empowered to learn, the results are always exhilarating, sometimes even unnerving. At Kodak, when instructor Ed White presented a new Integrative Learning version of a course in basic electronics he'd been teaching for years, he was jolted by the students' positive response. Suddenly, they began inventing problems that jumped ahead of his course plans. For the first time, line workers from the shop floor were really thinking about and playing with the concepts and information he was teaching. Once he adjusted, he found his students' new level of learning and involvement stimulating and delightful.

This kind of breakthrough not only can, but must take place in courses like Total Quality Management, or MRPII, a course in Management Resource planning that's been taught in about 100,000 corporations with approximately 11% success. Look at these courses through the eyes of traditional curriculum developers, and you're guaranteed to be asleep in half an hour. But look at them through the eyes of Integrative Learning, and you're rethinking your whole life, even changing the way you relate to your spouse and talk with your children. Suddenly you see yourself and your potential in a new way and you want to solve new problems and create new possibilities. That's what happens when your mind's power to learn has been reawakened.

MAP OUT THE VISION

S T E P 7

"One of the great bogus concepts wafting through management suites," writes management consultant Allan Cox, "is something called *'consensus'*: solving problems through unanimity. As a concept it's a failure — and in the end, that's what it produces, too: failure and mediocrity in performance, accountability, options, even commitment to the project. Something that is everyone's task becomes nobody's task."[1]

And yet teams are essential, because a truly comprehensive vision of an organization's resources and how they can ensure success depends on teamwork. Teams must learn to deal with a variety of points of view. "This strategy spins on the ability of a company to manage diversity."

PITFALLS OF GROUP INTERACTIONS

Consensus often leads to an appallingly mediocre state of affairs in which *the collective I.Q. of the group is likely to be lower than that of the individual with the lowest I.Q. in the group*. That's because conflicts tend to be resolved downward. If someone has an idea and anyone else objects, it is dropped. Therefore, the only ideas likely to be seriously considered are those acceptable to everyone, and these ideas are usually commonplace, unchallenging, and in many cases already widely accepted anyway. This tendency for groups to function at the level of their lowest common denominator leads to cynicism about "groupthink".

It's like what they've done to peanut butter, which is to apply the baby food approach to adult cuisine. One of us used to love the kind of peanut butter that was oily when you first opened the jar and gradually dried out as you got near the bottom. Every sandwich was a slightly different experience. The homogenized peanut butter on the market now doesn't taste as good, and isn't anything like the interesting experience one can have with a jar of "natural" peanut butter that changes its character each time you use some of it. It's another chapter in the "one size fits all" approach to food we've come to accept at the expense of experiencing food as nature provided it in the first place.

Just so, forcing a group to arrive at consensus drains the character out of the group, robbing its ideas of interest or effectiveness. It's like draining all the nutrients out of the food before you eat it.

Because of this nearly universal emphasis on consensus people get used to going along with the group, no matter what their feelings. This leads to another wasteful byproduct of groupthink, the Abilene Paradox. Jerry Harvey in his book *The Abilene Paradox*,[2] tells the story of his family's misguided trip to Abilene. They were all pleasantly ensconced on his in-laws' porch when the suggestion was made to drive the fifty-three miles to Abilene. Off they went in an unairconditioned 1958 Buick, through a dust storm and 104 degree heat. The trip consumed four exhausting hours and accomplished nothing. While everyone was complaining about it afterwards, it came to light that not one of those who'd taken the trip had had any desire to go in the first place. Everyone had gone along simply because everyone else was going along too.

It may seem at first as if the lowest common denominator and the Abilene Paradox are opposites. In one case people do what no one wants; in the other, nothing gets done unless everyone agrees. Actually, they're both results of the same cause. When people communicate only about formal transactions without reference to their feelings, there's no way of knowing what the group really wants, or might be capable of achieving.

And yet, despite the lowest common denominator effect and going along to get along, we also believe that humans in groups *can* learn to function intelligently. It is our goal for Step Seven to help you establish a kind of group learning that achieves synergy in place of paralysis or chaos.

THE BASIS FOR GROUP SYNERGY

As we've progressed through the previous steps, we've already developed self-assessment, positive attitudes, safety for thinking, readiness to risk, the capacity for seeing each other as resources, and desire to learn and continuously improve. These provide a firm foundation for what must happen now. For when self-esteem is well established in each person in the group, everyone will also have learned to think in terms of a personal future that is related to the future of the organization. Then the future of the group as a whole can begin its process of natural evolution through the achievement of the shared vision.

This evolution of a shared vision cannot be a mechanical process. It must involve the total personality of each member of the group. For without strong convictions, synergy is impossible. At stake are personal feelings and values, opinions about how things should be, and territorial imperatives. For we can share our territory with friends, but only if we feel they can comfortably share our values and convictions — or at least understand them and support our right to have them.

Thus the negotiating that will take place during Step Seven may be complex, but can also be very illuminating. When many well-defined personalities come together, they must often struggle within themselves as much as among themselves. What will happen is the emergence of a deepening sense of possibility for all as individual visions are synergized into a shared vision.

TOWARDS A SYNERGISTIC SHARED VISION

When human feeling is taken into account and negotiated, you can achieve a new level of synergy that gives everyone more than anyone was bargaining for. A shared vision created through synergy rather than consensus integrates the contribution of everyone into a new, much richer possibility than any individual or small group could have achieved alone.

George Land believes that, "Growth is first a discovery and sharing of commonality and then an exchange of differences. In such a situation, any system is susceptible to bringing people together in a way that can be greatly growth-facilitating."[3]

Thus a synergistic process will take any group beyond what a particular person, working alone, would be capable of. Through the magic of synthesizing its ideas to a level of complexity and richness no one had previously thought of, the group may rise beyond the capacity of its individuals to something surprisingly original, unique and powerful.

COLLECTIVE INTELLIGENCE HAS BUILT OUR WORLD

It should be easy to see the potential. After all, modern culture depends on the collective intelligence of individuals working together. Every kind of technology we use represents the combined efforts of from dozens to hundreds or thousands of minds whose ideas and inventions have accumulated over many centuries. Cars, telephones, computers, you name it — all are synergistic results of group effort.

Even the Nobel Prize is often awarded to a team who, working together, produced something no individual working alone would have been capable of. Scientific progress itself represents a true synergy of the thinking of hundreds or thousands of individuals, many of them forever lost to history.

Margaret Mead said, "Never doubt that a small group of thoughtful, committed citizens can change the world. Indeed, it's the only thing that ever has."

LEARNING ORGANIZATIONS ARE A PRODUCT
OF SHARED TALENTS AND VISIONS

As we've continued to emphasize, a Learning Organization can exist only to the extent that many creative minds come together in a common enterprise and give it their best — not by watering down or compromising their talents, their insights, their ideas or their skills, but by synergizing them into an organic structure that goes far beyond what any individual would be capable of.

A truly shared vision should engage the commitment and unique resources of disparate individuals. We cannot work effectively as a team if we merely duplicate each others' efforts. We must retain our individuality, recognizing at the same time that we cannot be effective if we're working at cross purposes. When a group of people are all committed both to personal mastery and to the purposes of the organization itself, then synergy seems to follow quite easily.

THE VISION MUST BELONG TO EVERYONE

So let's get clear on the importance of organizational purpose. If the purpose of the organization is, for example, transportation, then every member must be personally committed to the value of providing transport. They must know the uses of what they do themselves, as well as the value that can be created by their team working together to provide the best possible transportation for everyone.

If the organization produces steel pipes, the commitment to steel pipe making must be solid throughout the enterprise. We've heard reports of a trash collector and junk dealer on the west coast whose office is filled with things that remind him of trash. Even the ash trays and lamps are in the shape of garbage cans.

We all know that transportation is not the most important thing in the world, nor are steel pipes — and certainly not junk. So how can we argue that any of them is?

The guiding impulse behind any successful business or service is that society cannot function as well without it — or, conversely, functions better if it is present. Anyone who lived through the sanitation strike in New York City would agree that trash collection can seem like the most important thing in the world. It's this essential nature of the service or product that must be seen by every member of the organization as having central importance. All must have pride in what they are doing — not because it is more important than what other organizations are doing — but because it is in its own way unique, special, or essential. And from pride comes commitment to quality.

For these reasons, it makes good sense to teach everyone the organization's history, so it will be clear how it was built and in what arenas it has struggled and succeeded. This knowledge of history will be a great help in thinking about the future and understanding the potential of the organization. As this sense of the past leading into the future grows, employee identification with the company's future will grow stronger too.

A company that loses contact with its past as each new person is hired, can easily get off track. Just as good citizens must know the history of their country, so good employees must know the history of their company.

A GLIMPSE OF COMPANY HISTORY

The importance of a shared knowledge of the organization's history was brought home to us while participating in a middle manager development program entitled *Yesterday, Today and Tomorrow*. The "yesterday" component was introduced by a video that traced the company's one hundred year history, beginning with its founding. The video helped participants understand key events that shaped the company's growth and explained its philosophy of product development.

The participants appreciated this opportunity to examine their roots. It helped them understand how company history shaped their work. As a result of this knowledge, participants said they could more clearly sense where the company should be going, and better define their role in that process. "Now, I understand better why we do some of the things we do today," one of them said. "I never knew that the development of that product was because of World War II." "Being involved in the space program that long certainly makes a difference in ways I didn't know about."

When there's a shared sense of the past, the future becomes more comprehensible. Yet understandably, each person's view of that corporate future can be substantially different.

AVOIDING ORGANIZATIONAL CANCER

Just as your body is made up of many different parts with different purposes, all of which must coordinate perfectly if you are to go about your business, so a corporation or any other organization, if it is to function at full power, must achieve a similar concatenation of purposes. Each person serves a somewhat different function, and therefore must have a somewhat different purpose and vision — yet all must work together to achieve a whole which is organically related.

In the body the emergence of cells which go about their business without regard for the whole is the disease we call cancer. In an organization a group may work against the purposes of the whole — and thus form a kind of organizational cancer.

Indeed, in many modern corporations that's just what happens. As individual divisions are valued entirely on their profitability, and not on their contribution to the dynamic of the entire corporate organism, they may actually work at cross purposes, canceling each other out. For example, the sales and marketing department may sell what the operations division has not geared up to produce, causing cost overruns, late deliveries and other disasters. Yet sales and marketing may continue unabashedly to sell what is really not available.

HOW ALL GIVE UNIQUELY TO THE ORGANIZATION

As the vision of the whole comes into focus, it will be clearer how individuals or groups are interdependent and must work together for the good of the organization. Thus accounting will be alert to cost-cutting that may lead to false economies as opposed to true savings. As a result, people will not lose sales because their travel budgets are cut, the quality of manufactured products will not decline because inferior parts are ordered, and the highest paid and most valued members of the company will not seek out jobs with the competition, which knows much better how to pay them what they're worth.

On a level closer to the guts of strategic planning, two different divisions will not exhaust their energies in competition with each other, trying to get out products so similar that they tend to drive each other off the market.

The librarian will learn not to be so concerned about the possible loss of books and materials that they become all but inaccessible. Instead, he or she will develop new ways to promote the library as a primary communications tool for the whole organization.

Thus, as each division and each individual brings the whole company's vision and mission more clearly into focus, they will coordinate their efforts so the best interests of all are served.

FINDING THE UNIFYING ACTION OF THE ORGANIZATION

The Russian actor/director Constantine Stanislavsky revolutionized acting by instructing the actor to look for the central motive of his or her character, which could be simply stated in an infinitive phrase. With this key thought, all the various lines which had otherwise been parroted unrealistically, and characters who had otherwise been played woodenly were brought together into a coherent performance. This approach has been the foundation of virtually all actor training since. Most of the actors who star on stage and screen today have learned to find the central motivating force of their characters in relation to the general action (or mission) of the script through use of the infinitive phrase as a focusing, motivating concept.

Much of the disorganization of business can be brought under control by the same process of finding the unifying action or mission and particularizing it in the mind and behavior of everyone in the organization. This alignment of purpose is very different from the old school of mechanistic scientific management, in which most people kept their sights focused very narrowly on only their part of the process, rather than on its overriding purpose and goals. This unifying purpose, summed up in a phrase — as in: "to provide widgets perfectly suited to customer needs in a timely fashion", or: "to improve the understanding and use of documentation by all customers" — is easy to generalize and play out in many different ways throughout the organization as a whole.

We must cease thinking of an organization as though it were a machine, and start thinking of it as an organism. While manufacturing may produce machines, it has never done so by an inert, mechanical process. Instead, it operates systemically, and indeed organically. Like an anthill, or a rain forest, any human organization is made up largely of interdependent living elements, which coordinate in a mosaic that is much more complex than the linear structure of a machine. This is true of any human community: business, manufacturing plant, non-profit or service organization.

THE ART OF FINDING YOUR PLACE

In such a community each person must find and develop a role. No two roles can be the same, and thus each role must fully develop the talents of the person who has found it. In a sense each job must be created in the image of the person who holds it.

This is analogous to what occurs in a living organism, whose structure maximizes the value of all of its parts. And, difficult though it may appear to be, the same process should occur in the evolution of a Learning Organization, where the fullest use of the individual's resources best serves the purpose of the entire organization.

The process is also similar to the staging of a play, an analogy we will pursue more closely in Step Ten. When a director casts a play, it's not possible to get good results unless the actor cast in each part has the resources to play that part well, and is also challenged by the part. It won't do to give a great actor a completely mundane role, nor will it work to push people beyond their capacity. So the selection of actors for the roles they are to play is the beginning of a sensitive and complex process.

But the casting of the play is only the beginning. From the first rehearsal until the play closes, the exploration of each part continues. If that exploration deepens each actor's understanding of his or her own part, something of value is achieved, but not necessarily an ensemble performance. It is bringing all the parts together so that each actor understands the contribution of the part to the whole that creates the most effective performance.

As we'll see in more detail in Step Ten, just such an ensemble can be created in a Learning Organization. All the actors come to understand the relationship of their parts to the whole. Once that understanding is achieved, the creative process begins.

FINDING FREEDOM IN ESTABLISHING THE BOUNDARIES

The paradox here is that in the very act of binding yourself more closely to your company through a shared vision and the agreed-upon processes that follow from it, you achieve the greatest freedom and independence. This is the point where you see most clearly the unique nature of your contribution — where it begins and ends — and also how that contribution can be enriched, using the tools that only you have, to enrich it.

Understanding the big picture of the organization of which you're a part

— while at the same time seeing very clearly your unique contribution to it — creates an ideal lifetime learning opportunity. It is your chance to become most competent, most professional and most fully yourself.

THE VALUE OF NON-STRUCTURED STRUCTURES

The kind of environment we are describing, one that fulfills the maximum learning needs of the people in it, is, in effect, a non-structured, or chaordic, structure. That is, it provides parameters within which operations take place, but does not specify the operations themselves. This is an extension of the concept mentioned in Step Three, **minimum critical specification**.

One way to think about this concept is to reflect on how the rules of a game function. Football, for example, consists of a field, a ball, a set of specific ways the ball can and cannot be moved around the field, and a set of points and penalties for certain actions. But these rules do not specify the best way of playing the game. That is where the excitement of competitive sports originates: finding the best strategies for excellent play.

Similarly, whether on the shop floor, in leading a seminar, in developing a marketing strategy or in figuring out better ways of getting a product rapidly from the drawing board to production, think in terms of masterfully playing the game. Non-structured structures are the game rules that catalyze original thought in developing the particular ways to achieve a goal.

When everyone in the organization possesses a clear mental map of these non-structured structures, everyone can feel ownership in the company. That's because you can feel ownership only when you understand the importance of your contribution to the whole structure. All the members of the organization need to work out that understanding in their own terms.

When they do, everyone will know what actions are and are not permitted, just as they do when playing a game; but they will be left to their own devices to continuously decide how to improve the effectiveness of their actions. This will put excitement back into the tasks of business or manufacturing, for each employee can contribute to the design that will improve the performances of whatever jobs are to be done.

ENTER MIND MAPPING

We now want to introduce a powerful graphic tool that will help the members of your organization to achieve a shared vision, and also to understand their part in the scheme of things. Called **Group Mind Mapping**, it derives its strength from its rootedness in visual thinking, and from the cooperative process which brings it into being.

For those of us (about 30%) who need to interpret the world in visual terms, Mind Mapping is a particularly valuable tool. Visual learners need to see the relationships among the ideas they are learning and thinking about.

Only when they've got clear pictures to work with can they build a bridge of understanding with the subject under discussion, and thus become fully identified with it and motivated to use it in their work.

Many seminar leaders and human resource people are not visual learners. If you are among them, you may be somewhat impatient with Mind Mapping. This is unfortunate, because a high percentage of the people human resource folks must deal with are visual learners and would benefit greatly from learning to use Mind Maps.

A Mind Map represents, through visual symbolism, the relationships between ideas, projects, goals, and so on, much in the way that a map shows geographical relationships. In case you haven't seen a Mind Map before, we've provided an example using many of the concepts in this book. This, we should say, is only one of the innumerable possible ways you could mind map these ideas.

As you can see by studying the Mind Map, the main idea is located centrally — in the form of a picture or symbol, or in words — like the center of a city on a road map. Various lines (highways) branch out of the main idea (the city): each with its own name. They depict one possible arrangement of the interrelationships among ideas. At a glance, we have a diagram which represents a global overview of many ideas.

MIND MAPS ARE NEUROLOGICALLY BASED

Mind Maps are a byproduct and record of real thinking. They are the graphic reflection of connections made and relationships understood. Let's consider why Mind Mapping is capable of recording our thoughts in a more flexible and immediate way than words alone.

Your brain stores visual information more effectively than it stores words. Generally speaking, visual images and memories are richer and more vivid than abstract concepts. However, it's not necessary that these images be in the form of posters or pictures. A vivid image that you imagine in your own mind can be more memorable than a picture you view passively. So a lecturer who uses vivid, concrete images that encourage you to actively visualize can strongly impress your memory. As graphic designers and advertisers well know, words themselves can be made more memorable when they are presented in visually exciting ways.

However they're used, visual components relate more easily to the other ideas and information you already remember than abstract concepts do, because images activate more areas of the brain. Even the most striking word-images can be used so often that their original meaning all but disappears. But pictures, though they too can become clichéd, tend to leave a lasting impression on the mind. A picture automatically reminds you of the thing it stands for.

PUT A DINOSAUR IN YOUR TANK

If I ask you to imagine a dinosaur inside your gas tank, I haven't just given you a convenient mnemonic device to remember that your car is run by fossil fuels created from prehistoric animals and plants. The picture I've given your mind to play with may also raise questions like how many dinosaurs had to die so you could get to work in the morning — the kind of question that breathes life into recently articulated concerns about the real cost of fossil fuels.

It may be, too, that the image will encourage you to think about what happens to the dinosaur when it departs from its multi-million year old resting place inside the earth and takes up new residence in the atmosphere. It may occur to you that every year you have to breathe a few more long dead dinosaurs than you did the year before.

So the use of visual imagery not only makes things more vivid and easy to remember, it invites your mind to play with them more freely and creatively than it can if confronted only by a stream of words. This makes it seem more natural to think about the implications of ideas and explore how they can be applied in new, more powerful ways.

In fact, recent brain research suggests that language is an offshoot of a very small subset of the visual part of the brain. This means that for all the value language has in encoding thoughts and making communication possible, the brain is far better equipped to deal with and integrate visual images than words. That's probably why ideas expressed in visual terms are literally thousands of times more memorable than the same ideas expressed in words without any visual components at all. Research even suggests that language cannot operate without a subliminal form of visualization accompanying every semantic unit in every sentence.

MADISON AVENUE GOT THERE FIRST

Advertisers, of course, long ago realized that if they want to rouse customers to action, they have to do much more than talk about their products. Pictures, music and suggestions are blended to entice the buyer into an attractive and imaginary world of wish fulfillment. As television commercials have become more sophisticated, they've tended to rely ever more heavily on the playful association of images. Many times we are not sure what the advertisement is selling. We are drawn in by the visual power of the message, which is the intention of the commercial.

That's why making visible the relationships among the various components of a subject is such a powerful way to energize the mind and deepen the level of communication. And that's why a Mind Map invites you to think about a subject from many more angles than you would if you were making linear outlines. It is an enriched process that automatically stimulates the brain to make connections that initially seems disjointed and irrelevant. However, the exact opposite is what is really taking place. We are on an archeological expedition to figure out how the multiple piece of the puzzle fit together.

Educational theorist Leslie Hart is not alone in observing that logical thinking is not natural to the brain.[4] Although it can use logic, the brain is much more comfortable discovering patterns and interrelationships than logical sequences. It looks for clues — often in the form of disjointed, seemingly disconnected pieces of information, and has a subtle, but not always logical, capacity to make meaning out of what seem to be fragmented elements.

The fact that Hart is right in this is reinforced by the discovery that the routing process of the neurology of the brain assures that all of our decisions are made in the midbrain where no logic or linguistic elements can operate. In other words, it has always been literally impossible for anyone to make a purely rational decision. All decisions are made with reference to emotional components of experience which are then rationalized retroactively after the decision is actually made.

While this accounts for the fact that juries are far more influenced by emotion than by reason, which accounts for the strange behavior of lawyers, it also means that when we have made a significant decision about life, the basic motivation, founded in emotion, is there to support it. Wonderfully, the commitment to our new found passion is automatic and indisputable. It is intuitive, correct.

The Mind Map reinforces the natural processes of the brain by melding disparate and seemingly separated ideas and concepts into a workable graphically represented whole. This gives the brain the raw material it can later use to make better logical connections among the patterns it has discovered.

THE VALUE OF THE BIG PICTURE

Once your brain has the big picture, it will easily fill in details. The most common way to do a jigsaw puzzle is to begin by filling in the frame, then to sort the other pieces into categories based on similarity, so they'll form substructures. Most people can do this much better if they have access to the picture that will emerge when the puzzle is all put together. In the same way, a global picture or understanding of a subject helps connect assortments of facts so you can better understand and organize them. Over and over again, we find that a lack of commitment to change among organizations is often undergirded by a crucial lack of understanding among the members about the overall context of their work, they haven't been supplied with the big picture of the initiatives they're involved in.

According to some researchers, coordinating the big picture with its details gives your right and left brain practice working as partners in whole brain processing. Thus they learn to process, store and recall information more efficiently.

In this relationship, the left brain is involved in maintaining without question the course that has been chosen. It is left to the right brain to sense a need for a change in course and to signal the left brain to steer in a different direction or abandon ship.

When we discourage the right brain from playing a role in our organizational structures, we often condemn the organization to stay the course long after it is wise to do so, and thereby assure its early demise.

All these values come to the fore when Mind Mapping is used. It is easy as well as powerful, because it involves more of your brain in the thinking process than more traditional methods of gathering information.

TRY IT, EVEN IF IT'S NOT FOR YOU

One of us is a logical/mathematical learner who prefers sequential outlines to Mind Maps. Nevertheless, I teach Mind Mapping in all my seminars, and have learned to use it comfortably. My experience may be like that of many other seminar leaders: Mind Mapping is uncomfortable at first and may seem a bit childish and unstructured. Yet, as we practice using it, we find there are many things we have been able to do with it that no other tool could have helped us do as effectively.

This is particularly true for personal brainstorming, which you can use when you want to do an inventory of your ideas on a given subject. I frequently use Mind Mapping this way to explore possible ideas for a new book or article, or to help me design a workshop or seminar, or even a short talk. Sometimes I use it to explore new career possibilities, usually in consultation with a client. I've even used it to plan the way I'd like to organize things in my household. For such purposes, I find that Mind Mapping is an outstanding way to explore my own thinking.

Logical/mathematical learners will probably find, as I have, that the more you encourage yourself to use Mind Mapping to develop your visual learning skills, the more your logical/mathematical style of thinking will grow and benefit from it. That's because when we strengthen a weaker component of our mental process, the stronger ones seem to gain even greater benefits as a result.

THINKING: A HIDDEN AGENDA

Another benefit you'll receive from Mind Mapping (along with other methods you discover for symbolizing ideas or words through visual representations) is sharper thinking. Translating words into visual images requires you to think about what they mean. Reshuffling memorized definitions seldom produces new insights. However, when the brain is required to move information from one system of mental processing to another, thought is the inevitable consequence. The successful reconfiguration of information and ideas uses the natural skill of pattern detection. The brain loves to make sense out of seemingly disjointed and fragmented pieces of information. The brain functions best when it has a Sherlock Holmes type puzzle or problem to solve.

For example, if you are asked to draw a picture representing your idea about democracy, you're forced to decide what democracy means to you, or else you can't proceed. But if you're asked what kind of political system we have, and you reply "a democratic system" there's no way for your listener to know what you think that means.

So accustomed are we to throwing words around without relation to their meaning that we can spend hours saying very complicated things to one another that upon closer inspection turn out to mean nothing at all.

Physicist Richard Feynman relates the story of sitting in a faculty meeting at a university and asking what a particular word meant. He was told to be quiet, because "everybody knows what that means."

"Well, tell me," he said.

Someone gave a definition. Another person immediately contradicted it, and soon the whole meeting fell apart in an argument about what it was they had so comfortably been discussing before the awful question was popped.

THE POWER OF VISUAL MEMORY

We have at least three kinds of memory: conceptual, emotional and rote. Notions retained in our conceptual and emotional memories operate more actively in our thought process than those retained in rote memory. Generally speaking, conceptual and emotional memory are more likely to have images associated with them than rote memory. That's because we can more easily manipulate images in our minds and associate them with other images than we can manipulate words.

In addition, images are easier to remember than words. Thus, in most cases conceptual and emotional memory are more likely to stay with us than rote memory. You might think it silly if we asked you what a chair is: the concept of a chair is so much a part of you it's hard to even imagine forgetting it. Your notion of chair is crowded with endless experiences of seeing different kinds of chairs, sitting in them, valuing them as symbols of one sort or another, and so on. But if we ask you what formula determines the area of a circle (a very much simpler concept than that of a chair) we're more likely to cause you a little discomfort.

In "How We Remember What We See,"[5] Ralph N. Haber addresses the matter of image recall. In one study, people were shown 2,500 photographs at the rate of one every second. An hour later, shown the same pictures in mirror images that were paired with similar pictures not previously shown, subjects were able to identify 85% to 95% of the pictures by choosing the correct one from each pair.

Our remarkably accurate visual memory is further explored by Peter Russell in *The Brain Book*, using reports from two additional research projects.[6] The earlier observations are confirmed and extended with experiments testing people's short term recall of simple spoken words. Words like bicycle and dog are repeated three times. After one hour, the subjects correctly identified the words 33% of the time. Those people who were able to create separate visual images for the words had a recall rate of 46%. Those who produced more elaborate interpretive images had a recall rate of 71%. Those who created detailed interactive impressions, (for example, picturing the dog riding on a bicycle), had a recall rate of 95%.

So if you store information in your mind in a visual form, you're guaranteeing that it will remain alive in your imagination and continue to connect with other ideas. And if *you* make the pictures yourself, particularly if your mental pictures are highly dramatic ones, you are even more likely to remember well.

Furthermore, if you create mental pictures to represent a set of words, as you are invited to do when making a Mind Map, you're automatically thinking about what they mean and storing them in your mind in a vivid and dynamic format. You cannot do this without thinking about the implications of the ideas themselves, and thus actually beginning to use them. The information is locked into your long term memory. It is like throwing cooked spaghetti on the wall to see if it sticks. The power of the visual symbol provides a brain compatible connection that makes the information you are learning stick.

Harvard Psychologist David C. McClelland studied the causes of developing economic trends, and found that the most reliable predictors of them were the children's stories that were popular a generation or two before the trends appeared. That's because children's stories are so full of imagery, detail and experience that they mold our way of seeing the world.

During the early years of this century the Horatio Alger books were very popular among boys. These were found to contain powerful suggestions causing their readers to develop a strong form of achievement motivation. Boys who grew up reading those books were inspired to become entrepreneurs.

The same is true of the children's story, *The Little Engine That Could,* first published early in the century, which is practically a textbook in entrepreneurialism. Compare it in detail with Tootle, another popular train story, published in the post-World War II years, which teaches you to stay on the tracks no matter what, and you'll see why the tremendous economic growth early in the century took a downturn shortly after mid-century as America's economic promise was not fulfilled nearly as well as had been predicted.

Thus we learn the tremendous impact that stories can have on our thinking. An organization that wants to grow and prosper needs to invent stories (having much in common with popular children's stories) that convey the vision, mission, main strategies and anticipated development of the company. It's in the stories that we tell that we most powerfully build our futures. The stories, of course, can be spun off the Mind Maps we're recommending here; and perhaps, in a workshop format can be turned into skits and other performances that capture the essence of the developing vision.

MOVING TOWARD SYNERGY WITH GROUP MIND MAPPING

We have found that Mind Mapping techniques can help organize group thinking at a high level of synergy. Most organizations we've worked with haven't previously discovered this tool. And even people who have used such techniques individually doubt that it would be possible to combine several Mind Maps into one. Nevertheless, the process of Group Mind Mapping is easy to learn and helps the group bond in synergy. When people learn not only how similar their thinking is, but also how much more forcefully they can address a problem when the whole group contributes, their sense of what's possible is enhanced.

We first tried Group Mind Mapping as part of a training at a large corporation. We had previously asked the participants to make Mind Maps depicting the information systems they used in their departments. After that, they were to gather in small groups and pool the wisdom of their Mind Maps. There was a lot of overlap, yet each department also had systems unique to it which the other divisions didn't necessarily understand.

The participants regarded what we were preparing to do with a great deal of skepticism. After all, they protested, we had just been convincing them that everyone has a unique way of structuring ideas, and touting Mind Maps as highly personal visual representations of an individual's ideas. If the Mind Map represents such a personalized viewpoint, how can two or more people combine their Mind Maps?

GROUP SYNERGY AT WORK

Nevertheless, one by one the groups began to take fire. As the participants discovered how their ideas could be interwoven with those of others in the group, they shared a powerful new experience. They began to see what it was like to experience group synergy.

The goal was to create an overview showing how all the departmental information systems interconnected, while highlighting the special role played by each. The process required that each group explain its unique systems to the others present, and often this led to a greater understanding of their significance, even by the group that was using them.

Repeatedly, we overheard people probing more deeply into how the company really functioned. They were grappling with the hidden agendas, the infrastructure, and the culture. We heard a lot about how risk-taking, while nominally encouraged, was in fact discouraged through management's actual responses to people who took risks. Lights seemed to be going on in people's heads about what they were dealing with, partly because many things were being discussed that had been known and understood only privately before.

There's something wonderful about discovering you're not alone in your perception of how things around you actually work. Everywhere the participants seemed to be making breakthroughs in understanding as they pictured cause and effect relationships, and noticed where loopholes had cost time and effort that need not have been wasted. They clarified the bottlenecks and stonewalling activities.

It was clear that they were communicating about all these things, and many others like them, as they never had before. Never again, we thought, would they be content to let sleeping dogs lie. Some of the company processes were being restructured right before our eyes.

BREAKTHROUGHS FROM GROUP MIND MAPPING

Afterwards some people said they had learned more about themselves and each other, and about how their company worked, during that two hour process than in their entire previous experience with one another. As the days went on, we were able to guide this newly informed set of insights into well structured strategic plans and vision statements that would radically reorganize the way each division or company thought about itself and its appropriate modes of operation.

When a group experiences the Group Mind Mapping exercise we've described, it is not unusual to hear comments like, "If our organization is really in this big a mess, how come we're able to stay in business?" When this happens, don't despair, and don't let the group despair either. Realizing that you're in a mess is the first step towards cleaning it up. All you've done is revisit Step One for a little while, and that's important to do more or less continuously as you keep moving forward. It's not an overnight job you'll find you have to do, but a journey of a thousand miles . . . .

The breakthrough that folks are most likely to experience from sharing the maps is a new recognition that it's possible to understand the processes, infrastructure and culture that keep the organization functioning. Once you understand these, and can identify how they work, you are well on the way to redesigning them so they will work better. The result of this improved management will be that all have a better chance of getting their needs met while doing a good job.

BALANCING COMPETING FORCES

Group Mind Mapping is an excellent tool for organizational goal-setting and strategic planning precisely because it heightens awareness of the delicate balance between the individual and the group. Since each individual is responsible for some part of the total future of the organization, all the different responsibilities must dovetail properly with one another. When a group works together to articulate a shared vision through several rounds of Group Mind Mapping, it increases the likelihood that all views are taken into account, and that each individual has a clearer understanding of his or her role in the long-term evolution of the organization.

The executive mangement team of a large government agency were developing their strategic plan for the following year. They were taught Mind Mapping, and over a period of three days developed five "pictures" representing the primary focus areas of their plan — no words, no lists, just visual illustrations to encapsulate their ideas. Of course, they also developed the corresponding strategies, goals, and time lines needed to fulfill plan. The important and exciting part is that they firmly believed they achieved about two months worth of work in those three days. They also published their Mind Map results for the rest of the organization.

There is another balance that must be maintained in strategic planning: when you are thinking about the future, you need to remind yourself continuously of the current reality. Mind Mapping can be used to bridge the gap between the present and future.

When working with a client or during our seminars we sometimes ask people to make separate Mind Maps of the current reality and of the desired future state of their organization. The exercise helps create a realistic awareness of the tension between where you are now and where you are trying to go. In clarifying the differences between the present and the objective you are aiming for, you are providing a non-structured structure for getting there. Benchmarks seem natural, and are almost intuitively recognized even before they are specified. The goal of all this is to notice there's a path you have to follow to get from one place, or state, to another, and that you'll have to discover that path as you go. Don't be distressed by the fact that there's going to be an awful lot of backtracking, going off in the wrong direction or down blind alleys. That's all in the nature of moving through uncharted territory, which is what you'll be doing if you're truly forging ahead. Sailors know that getting from point A to point B requires a lot of tacking back and forth. And every time you get on an airplane you are off-course 90% of the time. Through pilot skill and computer technology, the airplane is able to make continuous course corrections in order to arrive at its pre-determined destination.

AN UNUSUAL SUCCESS STORY

In 1990 the Susan Lindgren School in St. Louis Park, Minnesota, conducted an interesting strategic planning project.[7] They used Group Mind Mapping to synthesize the collective input of more than five hundred stakeholders, which included students, parents, staff members, district administration, and business people.

Participants were asked to draw two Mind Map pictures on a large sheet of flipchart paper. On the top half of the paper they Mind Mapped their "ideal school." On the bottom half they Mind Mapped the current reality of the school. Then working in small groups, participants integrated their "ideal school" visions with the school's current reality and came up with a composite Mind Map. Out of this shared visioning process, seven vision statements were developed, which, taken together, aided the school site council to set goals and objectives for the future.

The seven vision statements were:
* Promoting self-esteem throughout the school community.
* Respecting differences in people.
* Valuing cooperative learning.
* Addressing all learning styles.
* Inviting students to have a voice in school decisions.
* Strengthening parent involvement.
* Supporting "bottom-up" management.

The school mission that emerged from this shared visioning process was: "To provide an integrated education for all learners in a cooperative learning environment that promotes success through decentralized democratic stakeholder partnerships." The school linked its goals with its shared vision and created four committees. The school council structured an agreement with the school district to control their own budget so they can fund their particular goals.

In December, 1992, Susan Lindgren School received the National School Excellence Award. The principal told us the auditing board that reviewed the school had said the Mind Map-based shared visioning process played a major role in the decision to give the award to this school.

DESIGNING SELF-MANAGED TEAMS

In another corporate training program, we worked with a team of ten people designated by the Vice President of Manufacturing to research how the factory workforce could implement Self-Managed Work Teams. When we first brought the team together, we needed to create a sense of purpose and cohesion among the members. As they bonded with one another, we hoped it would be easier to facilitate the creation of vision, goals and team responsibilities.

One of the methods used to assist in this team development process was Group Mind Mapping. Here are the steps we followed during one of the early team-building sessions. The whole process took about half a day:
1. We showed the participants a number of Mind Mapping samples taken from books on creativity and learning, along with illustrations that had been developed in our other workshops. (*The Brain Book* by Peter Russell was our major source.)
2. We asked the participants to Mind Map their ideas about how trees grow. This subject was placed in the middle of the page. The partic-

ipants spent the next few minutes building a Group Mind Map, which we facilitated.

3. A brief discussion followed about the whys and hows of Mind Mapping.

4. We gave each participant a large sheet of flipchart paper. We asked them to divide their sheets in half. On the top half, using the colored magic markers provided, they were to write *Barriers*. In this section they were to express all the things that would get in the way of successfully establishing Self-Managed Work Teams.

5. On the bottom half of the paper the participants were asked to write: *Workables*. These are the things about an organization that make implementing Self-Managed Work Teams achievable.

6. When they were finished with their Mind Maps, the participants were asked to combine into groups of two or three with others who were also finished, and share their Mind Maps with each other, discussing the differences between them. Each group was then to agree on a Group Mind Map developed from their individual Mind Maps. We then paired two small groups into a larger group and repeated the process.

7. When a final Group Mind Map was agreed upon, we debriefed the whole process up to this point.

8. From the Group Mind Map the team strategized their course toward the goal of establishing Self-Managed Work Teams.

9. For the last exercise of the half day session, the participants individually showed their original Mind Maps to the whole group and briefly talked about what insights they had about the team, and the project they were about to undertake.

10. Copies of the final Mind Map were sent to each member. Members were also invited to keep their original Mind Map as a reference point, and to share its content with fellow workers who might see it.

The Mind Map that was developed during this session provided a constant visual record and benchmark of the work being undertaken. The Mind Mapping process provided a simple way to figure out what was important to each person, and to all of them collectively, and to build in a relatively short time a common base from which to work. Of course, the group had further work to do in refining their vision and goals, but this experience provided a jump start, greatly assisted by using Mind Maps as a vehicle.

COMPLETE DIRECTIONS YOU CAN FOLLOW

For our grand finale, we offer an example of the use of Mind Mapping with a financial department in a large corporation. This Mind Mapping model has been used in many different settings, with factory workers, support function staffs, engineers, self-managed work teams, and management development workshops. It is a generic summary of how groups of all types can use Group Mind Mapping to achieve synergy in goal-setting, visioning, developing mission statements and process redesign.

In what follows we give a complete outline of the workshop so you can either reproduce it if you wish, or modify it to suit your needs.

In this case, the Finance Director was interested in making a difference within his department. He decided to start with the department's supervisor and management — a total of eighteen people. The department had previously had a traditional management style that was highly controlling, risk-avoiding, and inflexible in serving the organization. The purpose of the workshop was to assist the group in finding shared values, a statement of purpose, and a means of bringing management together so they could work as a team more effectively than ever before.

The expected outcomes were to develop a vision statement, along with a maximum of seven goals that could be presented to the whole department for clarification and acceptance. The Director did not want the workshop conducted in the customary way, which would have been to have the team talk all day long, put their ideas on a flipchart, assign a couple of people to write up the results, publish the results for the department, and forget about them until the following year.

The innovative learning development process instead focused on Mind Mapping as its chief tool. We developed the material in the following sequence:

1. We presented the day's agenda and the desired outcomes.
2. We asked the participants to select a topic we could use to demonstrate Mind Mapping. Someone said, "Making Chocolate Chip Cookies."
3. We placed the subject in the middle of the flipchart, and circled it in a bright color. A number of small pictures of chocolate chip cookies were drawn inside the circle.
4. With the aid of the participants' input, we created a Mind Map. This took two or three minutes. For another five minutes we answered questions about how Mind Mapping works.
5. We gave each participant a large sheet of flipchart paper. We instructed them to fold their papers in half.
6. On the top half of the paper, we asked them to write: *Current Reality*. On the bottom half: *Vision*. For this purpose we provided them with boxes of multi-colored magic markers.
7. We then asked them to create a Mind Map, preferably with pictures only, of the Current Reality of their department. We asked them not to talk with each other during this phase of the activity.

8. When the participants finished their Current Reality Mind Maps, we asked them to create a Mind Map of their vision of the department. When these in turn were finished, we asked them to hang their Mind Maps on the wall.

9. We then asked the participants to look at all the Mind Maps, without talking, and to answer the following questions:
   a. What are the common themes in the Current Reality?
   b. What are the common themes in the Vision?
   c. What don't you understand that you would like to clarify?

10. Once everyone had the opportunity to review all the Mind Maps, people began to ask each other questions like these about their Mind Maps: "What does this picture mean?" "How come your colors in the Current Reality are so murky?" "Why are these stick people in a circle?" "What is the meaning of the sun coming up over the horizon?"

11. After they had explored and discussed each others' Mind Maps, the participants listed the common theme that they saw in the Current Reality and Vision Mind Maps. These common themes were anthologized on two separate charts.

12. A couple of times people were asked to review again the Mind Maps hanging on the wall, to see if there was anything they had missed that was important to them.

13. Once the two lists were completed, the group began a gap analysis between the two lists. If anyone encountered a difference, we encouraged that person to go back to the Mind Maps in search of further clarity. A great deal of flow occurred between examining the lists, discussion, and input from the Mind Maps. We had thus provided multi-modal avenues that allowed people individually and collectively to explore and clarify the issues that were important to them.

14. The team spent the rest of the day working on their Current Reality description, comparing it with their ideal working Vision, and then developing critical success factors that they could all commit to for the following year.

15. At the end of the day's session the participants were invited to take their Mind Maps with them, so they could hang them up in their offices or work areas. The Mind Maps would provide them with a starting point for dialogue during meetings, or when people stopped by to talk. They also provided a constant reminder of their thinking and feelings at one point in time — a simple personal form of benchmarking.

The Mind Mapping process described here is a highly effective tool to assist a team to draw out of its members what they are thinking and feeling about the issues, conflicts, situations and goals they must deal with on a day to day basis.

The more traditional approach, of spending a great deal of time in discussion, including some small group sessions, leading to a lot of listing of ideas, narrows the whole learning and development process. Therefore it fails to engage the multiple capacities of a diverse group.

Mind Mapping provides the opportunity for all participants to be active in the learning and development process, to be respected for their unique individual perspectives, and to build a collective outcome that is both dynamic and productive.

ONWARD AND UPWARD

Effective as the Mind Maps are, however, they still remain somewhat abstract. We haven't used them to explore fully how all the relationships and actions will work out in practice. To achieve that, in the next chapter we'll move on to an even more powerful tool.

Meanwhile, let's reflect once more on the fact that Step Seven is about vision. All of us have some vision of life that guides us as we move forward from day to day. For some, that vision is limited to uninspired survival issues: "I'm going to do my best not to step in something today and to be able to go to bed with a full stomach." Such a visionary approach to life suggests little that is far reaching about how our lives can be shaped towards a better future.

It's been found that a very large percentage of the population views the world in this way.

A company made up of people whose vision goes no further will be severely compromised in their ability to learn and grow as their people necessarily won't be able to get very far beyond just trying to do what they are told.

But a company that develops vision in its employees by the methods we have examined here, provided it has taken the time to work through the preceding six steps adequately, will be one which offers a much richer life experience to all of its people.

It will also be one in which the people tend to align around the company vision rather than giggle about it in the bathrooms, as so often happens now. My vision cannot be your vision, however. It can only have something in common with it. So in the chaordic company, where the concept of minimum critical specification is understood, all the individual visions will have found their common ground in a rich and powerful shared vision towards which all the members of the organization can feel profound loyalty and commitment.

BRING THE VISION TO LIFE

S T E P   8

Back in the 1960's Richard Held performed an experiment at MIT which demonstrated with stunning clarity a surprising point about the way the mind works.

Held placed two kittens on a carousel about two feet in diameter and open at the top. The wall surrounding the carousel was papered with a colorful design. One kitten rested on a carriage attached to a pole passing through the center of the carousel, and thus rode around it as if on a merry-go-round. Its legs tucked under it, the kitten rode in comfort around the carousel, observing its surroundings from that position, for two weeks.

The second kitten was placed in a comfortable harness connected to the central pole. As he walked, the pole turned and the first kitten's carriage was set in motion. Thus, the two kittens were exposed to the same visual stimuli for two weeks.

When the kittens were removed from the carousel at the end of this time period and allowed to run free, the kitten that could walk as he viewed his surroundings demonstrated completely normal behavior. But the one who rode in the carriage was, temporarily, functionally blind: stumbling along in the grass, he slowly accomplished the tedious task of connecting his visual input with the action of his body, until he too acquired normal vision.

Held's famous experiment shows graphically how important kinesthetic input is to the interpretation of vision. Anyone who has ever watched a baby gradually learning to coordinate body and eye movements has seen this link being made in the human brain. For without the coordination of our bodies we cannot build a meaningful response to visual input. This truth has powerful implications for learning and education in general, and for the successful creation of a Learning Organization in particular.

THE HIGH COST OF NEGLECTING
THE KINESTHETIC INTELLIGENCE

In Step Six we referred briefly to Howard Gardner's Theory of Multiple Intelligences, which derives from the observation that all people possess a variety of intelligences. We noted that only two of these intelligences, the linguistic and the logical/analytical are regularly called upon in traditional education. The process of thinking with our bodies, our kinesthetic intelligence, is the most neglected in our schools.

Yet for a sizable percentage of the population who are primarily kinesthetic learners it is almost impossible to understand anything until it has been processed in some way as a physical, action oriented, kinesthetic experience. The sad neglect of our kinesthetic learners is so severe that they comprise about eighty percent of all school dropouts. These same students, with slight changes in their classroom experience, could become outstanding students and achieve great academic success. Ken and Rita Dunn,[1] researchers in learning styles, believe that a large proportion of students who have been labeled as learning disabled, are designated so because they are primarily kinesthetic and tactile learners, and are not given the opportunities during their schools years to learn in these physical ways.

We have found in the training of school teachers and the design of curricula that this problem is fairly easy to correct. When courses in any subject are taught using techniques like those we will be describing in Step Eight to represent basic concepts, the kinesthetic learners are soon able to translate these concepts into linguistic and visual expressions. Suddenly students who had been failing become successful and proceed with their studies, showing as much intelligence as their fellow students.

A high degree of kinesthetic intelligence is often found in athletes, dancers, and others who are drawn to sports and activities that require excellent mind-body coordination. But, contrary to the notion that most of us have of 'intellectual' activity, abstract thinking can also be enhanced and illuminated by kinesthetic intelligence. Albert Einstein's reliance on thought experiments where he vividly imagined himself moving through time and space is well known. In fact the biographer of Richard Feynman, another Nobel Prize winning theoretical physicist, points out that physicists have recognized

> that Einstein's great work had sprung from physical intuition and that when Einstein stopped creating it was because "he stopped thinking in concrete physical images and became a manipulator of equations." Intuition was not just visual but also auditory and kinesthetic. Those who watched Feynman in moments of intense concentration came away with a strong, even disturbing sense of the physicality of the process, as though his brain did not stop with the gray matter but extended through every muscle in his body.[2]

Ironically, the kinesthetic intelligence — so little respected and inadequately cultivated in the academic classroom — is highly valuable in industry. Many jobs require the same kind of thinking that it takes to do well in competitive sports. In the understanding of how things fit together physically the kinesthetic thinker shines. Seldom or never is this ability called for or trained in the classroom. No wonder it's so often true that people who are highly successful in business did not do well in school.

INDUSTRY NEEDS TO LEARN HOW TO APPRECIATE
ITS KINESTHETIC LEARNERS

But even in industry the outlook for strongly kinesthetic learners is usually not very bright. For many employees, the workplace offers merely a continuation of the kind of disappointing experience they had in school. These same workers, if they were trained with an eye to their kinesthetic intelligence, could shine among their peers and move forward brilliantly in their careers.

In a Learning Organization, this waste of human potential can be eliminated. Individuals who are predominantly kinesthetic learners should be as capable as all other learners to harness their full intelligence. And all of us should bring the benefits of this too little understood intelligence to bear in everything we do, to make a living and to increase the usefulness and meaning of our lives.

STEP INTO ACTION

In Step Eight we'll be exploring the most unusual, and in a sense the most unorthodox of our Ten Steps, particularly through a technique we call Kinesthetic Modeling. For many it will at first seem a challenge — at least until they have a chance to try it out for themselves. For much of what we wish to convey can best be understood and confirmed by direct experience. It must, in fact, be learned kinesthetically. As we bring our physical actions more fully in line with our creative thought processes, we begin to enjoy many things that used to seem like hard work. Used properly, Kinesthetic Modeling is non-threatening, non-judgmental, and extremely enlightening.

It can also teach us a great deal about communication, particularly the 93% of communication which is non-verbal. As we become more aware of the gestures, tones of voice, and signals our actions are constantly sending, we might want to consider how we unwittingly send messages we are not aware of. For our bodies tend to be much more honest and revealing than the smokescreen of words we often send out to disguise what we're really thinking. As we learn, by using Kinesthetic Modeling, to be clearer about our thoughts and our communication process, new possibilities begin to emerge.

MIND MAPPING WITH OUR BODIES

In Step Seven, we used Mind Mapping as a way of visualizing, displaying, and manipulating information that is more dynamic and flexible than our usual linear, logical/analytical thinking. There are, however, many activities, processes, and relationships that can best be clarified and improved by going one step further, taking the time actually to get ourselves into the Mind Mapping — physically, in three dimensions.

What does it mean to turn Mind Maps into Kinesthetic Models? An illuminating experience we had will suggest how this can be achieved.

WELFARE RECIPIENTS LEARN
TO UNDERSTAND THE BUREAUCRACY

We were recently asked to teach unemployed people how to plan upwardly mobile careers for themselves. In the process of recruiting people for this class we found it necessary to work with several different state agencies, all of which had regulations and requirements affecting our clients. For people on assistance to get child care, transportation to and from the class and other necessary types of aid, they had to fill out many forms and deal with numbers of different people in the social services system. Many of the participants in the class were impatient with this process and critical of the system that supported them.

To improve communication and good will between the government agencies and the clients in our classes, we invited the providers into the classroom and asked them to help us create a Kinesthetic Model which would represent all the relationships between people, systems, regulations and funding sources that were necessary in order to make it possible for our students to enroll in our program.

One by one, the student participants took their places in the middle of the room. Each represented an agency, or a person within that agency. As each student stepped forward, the corresponding person from the agency explained his or her role in the process. When there was a direct relationship between two agencies, the students representing these agencies would indicate this by shaking hands or in some other way acting out the connection implied by the relationship. Variations of the handshake could be as simple as linking arms or placing a hand on another person's shoulder, or use colored yarn or lengths of rope.

When all the components of the bureaucratic machine were in place, one of the participants acted out the role of the application which had to move from station to station through the system. As this movement was staged, and the process that took place at each station was described and acted out, the participants understood for the first time why all the bureaucratic processes were necessary. As they learned to understand the process, they became eager to express their appreciation to the people who were attempting to administer it for their benefit. The agency people also enjoyed the experience and were pleased at this opportunity to explain the process to the people whom they served.

This example suggests an immediate use to which Kinesthetic Models can be put in building a Learning Organization.

GETTING STARTED IN YOUR ORGANIZATION

Every organization has divisions with different functions and responsibilities. Each division has established its own typical processes of communication. Often no single person in the organization fully understands what all the divisions do, or how the communication processes work. In the same way that the welfare recipients learned how the social services system is supposed to work, the management of any organization can show the employees how it is organized by having everyone involved act out these relationships in the manner we have just described.

You'll find that this experience, (which need take only a few minutes to enact) makes clear to everyone present just how the system is supposed to work, and how the parts of it are related.

SEEING HOW THINGS COULD WORK

But this is only a prelude. Kinesthetic Modeling can be either a static representation of relationships, or a dynamic ballet of ongoing interactions. It is also extremely useful as a means of exploring possible changes in the processes, structures and systems that make up your organization, many of which have been taken for granted so long they've become virtually invisible. But if you enact them, critique them and explore ways they can be transformed, you will get to the heart of what makes your organization work, and by helping it to become conscious of its own structure you will be taking one of the most important steps needed to make it a Learning Organization.

For example, if you're developing a quality program and the one thing you're certain of is that the old way of doing things is no longer satisfactory, you can begin by creating a Kinesthetic Model that represents the current reality. You can then ask for suggestions for change in the process. As each change is suggested, you can have the participants model it by altering their positions and interactions with each other. This provides the participants the opportunity to test out different solutions for bringing about the changes they are looking for. Doing three to five different models generally provides insights and solutions they might not have otherwise thought about.

Kinesthetic Modeling is also an effective way of introducing and previewing new concepts and processes. It can quickly convey not just the procedures, but the underlying rationale behind a newly adopted process. When we present the Ten Step Process in our public lectures, we often explain the steps first and then have members of the audience create models of them to show how they interact with each other. Usually about half of those present say they didn't really understand what we were talking about until we introduced the modeling process. What is happening is that multiple channels of learning are being used, which increases everyone's ability to understand at a deeper more visceral level.

MODELING A JUST-IN-TIME PROCESS

Suppose, for example, you want to replace a very large inventory with a Just-In-Time process of ordering only what is needed for a given lot of manufacturing. In our trainings, we've often represented the Just-In-Time process by having individuals in the group portray the inventory of raw materials to be used in manufacturing. We ask them to enact the various processes these materials will go through in manufacturing. To represent the current state, they are bunched together as a heavily overstocked inventory. To represent the new way of ordering materials only when they're needed, we have the group representing inventory stand outside in the hall and come in one by one when they are actually needed in the manufacturing process. Simple as this model is, it gets the point across much more quickly than lectures and diagrams possibly could. Furthermore, once the trainees have actually walked through the process they understand precisely how it is supposed to work.

WHY THIS METHOD OF LEARNING IS SO EFFECTIVE

You still might be wondering why modeling is better than just describing the process, or showing a film about it — particularly if you understand the process well yourself and are used to explaining it to people. Our experience has demonstrated that when you explain a process to someone else, you may see in your own mind exactly what it is you are trying to describe. But the listener, who has little or no experience following your line of reasoning, has a much more difficult time seeing the pictures that are in your head. What the Kinesthetic Models do is take the pictures that are in the head of the instructor and create them in living three-dimensional color where everyone can see and experience them clearly. And for those who learn best kinesthetically, the chance to walk through the process makes it clearer than any explanation ever can.

We have found that many people simply cannot understand an idea unless they've either acted it out with their own bodies or watched someone else participate in a process with which they can empathize. Once they get it, and are from then on able to walk through it mentally, they understand it very well. Lecturing and showing films, however, isn't going to create the understanding they need.

USING THE PROCESS FOR GROUP DISCOVERY

The example of Just-in-Time manufacturing is simple. It involves a change from one way of doing things to another. From the point of view of the instructor or manager, there is never any doubt about what the change will be. Often, however, better quality must be obtained by processes that haven't yet been created.

In the group Mind Mapping activity of Step Seven, we showed how these new processes may be discovered as a result of group synergy. But as long as they remain in the form that Mind Mapping gives them, they haven't yet taken on three-dimensional reality. Kinesthetic Modeling can give them that reality, by bringing the process fully to life.

When a group works in this way, a great deal of exploration and back-tracking is likely to occur as the group searches for the model that will work best to achieve what they want. There is probably no other activity that lends itself to this exploratory process quite as effectively as Kinesthetic Modeling. As the group searches for a better way of representing the desired process, participants spontaneously raise and answer questions that might never come up in a more two-dimensional presentation.

OTHER USES OF KINESTHETIC MODELING

Because it is such a powerful means of improving understanding and communication, Kinesthetic Modeling has been successfully used in a variety of fields. Family therapist Virginia Satir, who called this practice human sculpting, discovered that when members of a family sculpt the relationships among themselves, they can develop a deeper understanding of those relationships than would otherwise be possible.

More recently, in classrooms around the country teachers are finding that when students act out the relationships among various aspects of a subject, the group's understanding of the subject's structure is greatly strengthened. These findings are consistent whether the subject is multiplication, the diagramming of a sentence, the geographical relationships between the states of the U. S., the way characters interact in a novel, how to put a paragraph together, the best way of organizing ideas in a debate, how reactions take place in a test tube, or how a computer program works. In short, there really isn't any school subject which cannot be explored with Kinesthetic Models. And when that exploration takes place a great deal of potential confusion is identified and cleared up.

The Richard Feynman anecdote about confusion in the definition of words which we related in Step Seven illustrates a problem that frequently arises in communications. Often we think we understand each other when we don't. The Kinesthetic Modeling activity, by asking us to create a symbolic representation of our understanding of an idea or process, forces us to pin down definitions and underlying concepts that can cause confusion when not fully understood and agreed to. That's one reason the appropriate use of Kinesthetic Models at the appropriate time can save enormous amounts of time in a strategic planning process. Indeed, some organizations literally spend months in strategic planning when, with the use of Kinesthetic Modeling they might well reduce the amount of time needed to no more than a few days. We've seen several actual instances of this time reduction in under-standing taking place in various kinds of organizations.

A TOOL FOR TEAM-BUILDING

When you create a new team, you can use Kinesthetic Modeling to develop the structure around which the team can be built. The goal is to stop the endless talk and get on with things. To explore ideas, we model them. Doing so helps us to be more innovative, creative, flexible, and responsive. The role played by the Modeling is to infuse the emerging learning environment with life — an essential ingredient in creating the Learning Organization. It's a form of active learning that helps people step into new roles and relationships with deeper understanding of their consequences, implications and effects.

During a team-building workshop for a team of twenty-five factory workers and their supervisors, we asked the participants to construct a Kinesthetic Model representing the way they currently saw themselves working together. One person volunteered to start the process by standing in the middle of the room. We had him assume a physical stance to represent feelings about how the team worked together. Then another person took a position in relation to the first. And so the process continued, until all twenty-five had placed themselves in the location they felt expressed their view.

During the five to ten minutes this took, we asked the participants not to talk, but instead to think about what was happening, and as the Model took shape, what its symbolism communicated about their manner of working together. Once the Model was completed, anyone who wanted to start could share thoughts, feelings and insights about the group's effectiveness as a team. We, the facilitators, made no observations of our own. We encouraged the participants to share whatever they wanted to say. Some chose to say nothing.

We listed the comments on a flip chart. Then they took a break. When they returned, they started the Modeling process again. This time they were to construct a symbol of how they would like to work together under ideal circumstances. Again we listed thoughts and feelings on the flipchart.

As a result, the team began to have a sort of distilled or crystallized experience of how they presently worked together and how they would like their working relationship to be improved. The Kinesthetic Modeling process provided them with a dramatic means for making this important issue come alive for everyone in the group. It provided them with a shared learning experience on which to base further discussion and dialogue designed to create a shared vision and a plan of action.

Kinesthetic Modeling can thus be considered an option expander. It summons resources and capabilities in the organization that can go untapped in more verbally oriented brain-storming and problem-solving formats. It also cuts through the confusion and fuzzy thinking that can sometimes be masked with words: actions often speak not only more loudly but more clearly than words.

And yet in another and quite wonderful way, the Kinesthetic Models increase the degree of fuzzy thinking. It's been found that fuzzy thinking is essential to being able to function in the world. It's the basis of abstract conceptualization that allows you to see one tree, for example, as being like another. If you couldn't fuzz out the differences between various trees, you'd treat each of them as a unique species and the world would be loaded down with unidentified foreign objects.

By using the Kinesthetic Models to symbolize relationships, we can see a wide range of applications that are revealed in the process. A handshake, for example, can represent an equal relationship. Sometimes equality in relationships is desirable, and sometimes it is not. I wouldn't want a brain surgeon to operate on me if I thought we were exactly equal in our relationship.

By using the handshake as a symbol of equality and other simple enactments as symbols of different kinds of inequality, we can examine in the abstract how people and other things properly relate as a systemic interaction is built. We can move the various components around and consider their significance quite easily, because of the very element of fuzzy thinking that allows us to see a great many different analogous situations growing out of the same symbolic relationship.

GETTING WORK FLOW INTO THE PICTURE

Kinesthetic Modeling is also a good tool for focusing on more specific and localized aspects of organizational procedures, and testing out changes that might improve them.

Any workplace is made up of thousands of interactions, many of which are personal. Some of these interactions involve the flow of work, or the shared understanding of how things should be done. For example, when you walk into an office for the first time it makes a difference whether you are greeted by a receptionist or a decision-maker. The receptionist is little better than a telephone — a way of making a connection between you and someone else. The decision-maker can immediately open up a new relationship between you and the company you're dealing with.

However, let's suppose that a person moves from the role of receptionist to decision-maker. In this case, a lot of things will have to change. The decision-maker out front will be able to handle many problems, and thus deflect them from the awareness of the inner office. But as a result, the person in the inner office will no longer be as accessible.

Once the former receptionist has become an executive, what if some of the decisions are not made well? What if people who wish to have access to the inner office no longer can? How many relationships that had already existed are going to change, and what will be the effect of the change?

We've found that you can talk about these sorts of changes forever and never really understand the labyrinth of consequences that will follow from implementing them. But as we demonstrated at the beginning of this chapter, if you involve people's bodies in the process, many things become clear much sooner.

For example, if you act out a skit that shows some of the things that could happen as a result of the change, everyone will have a clearer idea of the consequences.

KINESTHETIC MODELING CAN ILLUMINATE RELATIONSHIPS

You can also do the whole thing non-verbally as well, symbolizing the relationships with Kinesthetic Modeling. To dramatize the change in the role of the receptionist we just discussed, you might try this: The receptionist automatically ushers you into the inner office. A symbolic gesture of moving you along might be the obvious way of expressing that. The decision-maker redirects, blocks, and only sometimes ushers in. Thus the symbolic gestures must now be more complex.

As the people involved in building the new Model try to find the appropriate gestures to express their roles, the depth of their understanding grows. When we discussed Mind Mapping, we pointed out how the process of translating words into visual representations activates different intelligences and stimulates the brain. By building Kinesthetic Models, we further deepen the thought process. That's because relationships and their implications must now be expressed through actions, not abstractions, and this cannot be done unless the meanings that underlie them are explored. The resultant thinking can be even more powerful, subtle and flexible than it was in the case of the Mind Maps.

The subtle shifts of tone and movement that occur as the Kinesthetic Modeling continues to be explored will give much greater depth and understanding to the relationships under review. People will become attuned to each other's point of view as they never have before. But this will only be true if the group has already mastered Mind Maps and taken them as far as they will go in helping to define relationships and vision. Use of Kinesthetic Models before the group is ready for them is likely to be a confusing waste of time.

TRANSLATING VISION INTO ACTION

When it comes to making your vision work in the actual world, you have to have means of translating words that express goals and ideals into actual ways of doing things. Kinesthetic Models can provide the framework for accomplishing this. Trying to show how you're going to model a concept with people's bodies, you'll inevitably get into all sorts of discussions about what the ideas really mean. These discussions are necessary if you are going to produce the results you want.

For example, the organizational vision may assert that "the customer is king." An attempt at modeling this statement could begin with a customer standing in the middle of the floor with a crown on her head, and everyone else bowing before her. But is this the way the relationship should go? The people who are kowtowing may find it difficult to think in that position. Maybe the customer doesn't know exactly what she wants. How do you help a queen explore her thinking? Maybe we should change the phrase to something like: "The customer is the person we focus our attention on, using all our ingenuity to provide her with the tools to get what she wants."

Incidentally, this is one of the areas in which librarians require a great deal of training. Many people who ask for help in libraries really don't know how to express very well what it is they are looking for. The effective librarian draws out of the client information that will help to define the real need.

Yet businesses often fail to do this same thing because they are so awestruck by the customer that they don't take the leadership that may build a far better relationship than simply doing what is asked.

These sorts of subtleties tend to come up in the discussion when you look critically at what you've modeled and consider the implications of it. Often you can make an important discovery about how you can operate more effectively by exploring kinesthetic models in this way.

When discussions of this sort take place, a great deal of clarification is achieved in a relatively short time. Sometimes you can clarify in a couple of hours of this activity what you might otherwise spend months wrestling with, not really sure what you are trying to accomplish.

THE ROLE OF BODY LANGUAGE

The issues we've been addressing so far in our consideration of Kinesthetic Modeling are those of explanation, comprehension and clarification. In every case, what we have been trying to establish is a group agreement about actual meanings, structures, processes and so forth.

There's another dimension of understanding and communication, however, which can also be improved with the aid of Kinesthetic Modeling: the emotional element that inevitably accompanies communication. As we pursue this next topic, we're aware that some of our readers may already have a great deal of experience in the area of non-verbal communication. It is also a subject that was crucial in Step Two, on promoting positive interactions within an organization, for it's through understanding how our tone of voice and body language affect others that we can most powerfully move towards conveying a positive message in all situations.

Only 7% of our communication process is conveyed in the words that we use. Another 38% is in the tone of voice. But a whopping 55% is in our body language. A great deal of this communication is outside our consciousness.

Therefore it's well to consider the consequences of not understanding what our body language conveys when we communicate with each other.

So now we're going to address the question of the feelings that lie behind the relationships that are being communicated in Kinesthetic Models.

THE EMOTIONAL DIMENSIONS OF COMMUNICATION

It's one thing to say that you and I both fulfill functions in an organization, but quite another to discuss how we feel about those functions. It's just as important that I feel reasonably positive about my work as that I have a thorough understanding of what it is.

If I like my job but don't understand it well, I'll spend a lot of time doing what's not really needed. On the other hand, if I understand my job but don't like it, I'll give it less than my best effort and probably do it rather inefficiently. In either case, the work suffers, and so does the worker.

To achieve the highly productive state in which everyone can feel positive about the overall system and their role in it, we have to be aware of the emotional dimensions of the communication within the system. As we will see, the emotional components are often subtle and may not actually enter anyone's consciousness, but they are critical nevertheless. So there must be congruence between the behavior someone exhibits and the attitudes, values, words, and judgments that person is known to have.

Congruence of behavior is an important concept — it can make or break an organization. If what I say and what I do are not congruent, I will soon breed distrust among those I deal with. As the succinct popular saying puts it, I have to walk my talk.

Thus, in Step Eight we are concentrating on the relationship between these two very powerful aspects of how people express themselves in the kinesthetic motions of their bodies. In other words, we need to explore not only how people communicate the meaning of something, but also how they communicate their attitude towards it. Kinesthetic Modeling is a valuable tool in both these essential areas. We have seen it used to represent an actual or proposed process or system. Now we will explore its use in supporting congruence in the behavior of people in the system.

WHAT NOT TO DO WHEN YOU'RE STOPPED FOR SPEEDING

We once read that when stopped by the police, it's a good idea to get out of the car and face the policeman. By doing so you put yourself at eye level, and command a different kind of response. Policemen leaning down and looking at you through the window cause you to cower behind the wheel, waiting for their judgment of your conduct. But they are more likely to give a judgment tempered with mercy if they see you on the same level as themselves — at least so the theory went.

After several years of waiting for the opportunity, one of us was finally able to try out this theory in practice. I had been pulled over for turning right on red in New York City where, unbeknownst to me, the rule was different from most other places. As the lights flashed behind us, I got out of the car and started to walk back to the police car, while at the same time the police-man walked towards me. "Get back in your car, sir," he said.

I immediately realized that he understood the point as well as I did, and wanted to establish just the relationship with me that I wished to avoid. I also realized something the author had apparently not considered — that in this day and age my actions might be interpreted as threatening to him. This also was part of the rapid, unspoken kinesthetic communication between us.

The relationship a police officer establishes with you by leaning down and looking into your window as you sit there illustrates the effectiveness of physically expressed communication. How you and I place ourselves physically in relation to each other says a great deal about the psychological exchange we are having.

WE SAY MANY THINGS WITHOUT SPEAKING

Just about every aspect of physical behavior in communication is a factor in delineating the relationship between the various people involved. In seminars, for example, there's a great difference between a classroom in which people sit in rows facing the instructor and one in which they sit around in a semi-circle, able to maintain eye contact with each other. Our daily lives are full of these messages, though we seldom pay conscious attention to what they mean.

Over time organizations develop a wide range of signals and symbols which express a great deal of unspoken information. These involve the space that people occupy, the way they approach each other when meeting, the way they position themselves to talk to one another, organizational rituals small and large, and so on. These behaviors signify a great deal about our relation-ships and convey information and attitudes about which we may not be consciously thinking, but which we nevertheless take very seriously.

We are all highly attuned to the innumerable and richly varied forms of non-verbal communication. It comes naturally. Paradoxically, however, though we are all very sensitive to other people's body language, and very practiced at picking up the subtle meanings of tones of voice and gestures, we are often quite unaware of the incongruity between what we ourselves say and what we think, between what we mean to say and what we actually commu-nicate.

BLOWING IT WITH YOUR BODY LANGUAGE

We once gave a workshop in which as a concluding exercise the participants were supposed to demonstrate what they had learned. One participant left us wishing we had never even held the workshop. He made such a withering condemnation of everything we had advocated that the entire room was in a state of shock from his attack.

"Let me tell you," he began, "what I've learned here. I've learned to redesign an entire course in five minutes. And as if that weren't enough, I've also learned — " and he went on with a litany that was almost too painful to listen to.

That night as we discussed what he had said, it seemed that apart from his sarcasm everything he had described made sense. Imagine our surprise the next day when the organizers of the workshop told us our sarcastic friend was actually a true believer: he had thought the workshop was one of the greatest learning experiences he'd ever had, and he couldn't wait to get started applying the new insights he'd gained.

Only then did it become clear that everyone present had listened to his tone of voice and watched his body language and *completely ignored his words*. Because he expressed himself in a sarcastic tone, it didn't matter what he said. Words of the highest praise sounded like bitter condemnation.

WHY WE HAVE TROUBLE LISTENING TO OURSELVES

You may have noticed from time to time that it is possible to read aloud without paying attention to the words you are reading, just as it is possible to walk or drive a car without noticing where you are going. You might even, though more rarely, have noticed during a conversation that you have been partially unaware of what you were saying. (Sometimes we catch ourselves with the mental note: "What did I say *that* for?")

In the brain, the organizer of speech does not connect directly to the organizer of listening. In other words, we have to learn to listen to what we are saying because we don't *automatically* do so. How many times have you heard someone deny having said something you clearly heard that person say? In *Julius Caesar* two of the conspirators are arguing, and one accuses the other of having said he was the better of the two. To which the other replies, "I said an elder soldier, not a better." If you go back and read the scene again, you'll notice he said both of these things. So in Shakespeare's plays, just as in real life, people often don't know what they themselves have said.

The problem is further complicated not only by our failure to listen to *what* we're saying, but by our obliviousness to *how* we're saying it. Facial expressions, body language and tone of voice, all too clear and imposing to others, may be hidden from the speaker. Thus we may, on occasion, say and do fairly complicated things completely outside our own awareness. The shouted remark, "I'm not raising my voice," is one common example. One of us once watched a person cross the room while smoking and stoop and blow smoke in the face of someone else, as a gesture of hatred. When the group later confronted this woman with what we had all seen her do, she flatly denied having done it.

Such instances of lack of congruence between what we intend and what we actually communicate can be trivial, even comical. But they can also be critically important to the success of any enterprise. Effective communication is crucial to any organization. In a Learning Organization, we must communicate about how we communicate.

Often there's a communication credibility gap between what the leaders of an organization say they are going to do, and what they actually do implement. Such incongruity only serves to sabotage any possible successful creation of a Learning Organization.

THE STORY OF EDWARD

Some years ago we worked with a division director in a large corporation. We'll call him Edward. Edward's understanding of chemistry was remarkable. Where others might study a problem for days, Edward could solve it in a few hours. As a result he quite naturally fell into the pattern of always having to be the clearing house for everyone's problems.

Managing a group of about seventy-five workers kept Edward very busy. He'd wander around looking over shoulders, giving advice, and making it clear he knew very well who did and didn't measure up. Consequently, no one in the division believed there was any point in trying to be an original thinker. Edward would and could solve everything, they thought, so they would automatically wait for him to do what he was quite certain he did best.

The trouble was that for all Edward's brilliance, not even he could equal all the thinking potential of a large well-organized group. The net result of Edward's behavior, therefore, was a considerable loss in the total effectiveness of the division.

When we talked with Edward, we discovered that his notion of management was that the man in charge (he couldn't imagine a woman in this role) had to be responsible for everything. We began by pointing out to Edward that when he stood behind one of his people on the floor, the fear level skyrocketed, and the worker for that very reason nearly always became less efficient. Thus in the very process of trying to increase the efficiency of his workers he was in fact lowering it. Not surprisingly, we told him, no one enjoyed working for him and nearly everyone came to work in a state of numbed anxiety.

Edward was dumbfounded. It had never occurred to him that his behavior might have such an effect. Furthermore, there was no evidence of this visible to him, since everyone who felt fear concealed it and tried to look at ease and in control. In the hard-nosed culture of Edward's division, the fear of admitting that you were afraid was the greatest fear of all.

EDWARD SEES THE PROBLEM . . .

Because Edward was so brilliant, his mind went right to work on the problem we'd presented to him. He could see that his management style was preventing his team from becoming more effective. However, he believed control was an either/or proposition. It seemed to him that if he didn't stay on top of everything, he might as well go out and play golf all day and leave the floor to manage itself.

We posed a problem for Edward to solve. "Suppose," we said, "that your objective was to have everything happen exactly the way you want it (or even better than that) but in such a way that all your employees actually believed they were in charge and had thought of everything themselves?" For a while Edward was unable to understand what we were getting at. It seemed like a paradox to him. If you try to control by not controlling —- you can only give up control — or so he thought.

Then we discussed how ninety-three percent of communication is in the nonverbal realm. By specifying the types of outcomes he wanted, and by encouraging (mostly with body language) those behaviors most likely to lead to such outcomes, he might still be able to get the results he wanted. The difference would be that the people doing the work would feel they had played a significant role in the successful outcome.

We reminded Edward of the maxim that it's better to give a starving person a fishing pole than a fish. It was true, we said, that the first few times he probed a problem in the manner we indicated the results might not prove cost effective. We were certain, though, that after a while his teams would learn to solve problems for themselves and eventually to achieve even better solutions than he might have thought of. Once the teams had complete confidence in themselves, Edward could bring his suggestions into play if they were still needed.

Eventually Edward became convinced that such an approach made sense. He needed to shift his focus from getting the immediate problem solved to creating a shop in which the solution of problems was, in general, more efficient. Part of what he would have to do was change the way he would walk into a room.

. . . AND FINDS THE SOLUTION

When we talked to Edward a few weeks after this conversation he described a change that had occurred. "It used to be," he said, "that I would walk on the floor and everyone would scurry back to what they were doing, like cockroaches running from the light. But now it's different. If people are engaged in legitimate problem-solving discussions, they continue them, and it's only the ones that have been wasting time that still try to run and hide what they were doing."

We asked Edward what had caused this change. He said he'd been thinking about the problem a lot, and he'd tried standing a little farther away from people while he watched them work, and always asking them open-ended questions about their work. He'd also tried softening his manner and speaking more slowly. As he spoke and acted in this new way, people seemed to be more comfortable around him.

"I still feel a little stiff about it," he said. "I'm not used to it yet, and I have to form a lot of new habits. I probably fall back into my old ways when I get worried or there's a crisis. But I'm learning to play down my tendency to dominate people, and I find I can listen to them more and hear them better when I do that."

An interesting sidelight on this story is that Edward had been stuck in a middle management position for longer than he should have been, given his capabilities. Shortly after that last conversation, his career started to advance, and now he holds a much more influential position within his company. After a few false starts, he has become an expert on the concept of giving away your power in order to increase it.

IT'S IN OUR CULTURE

The Edwards of the world, we find, are pretty widely distributed in organizations, primarily because most managers have grown up with a controlling management style. Such a style is often focused on putting out fires, getting short term results and maintaining control at all costs.

In a recent interview of a CEO of a large corporation, it was obvious that he still operated with the obsolete belief that it was not possible to really develop people. It was just not worth the effort. He thought the only lasting solution was to keep turning people over within the organization, and bringing people in from the outside until you found the "right" people.

Modern managers are learning to be the kinds of facilitators, coaches and teachers Edward has now become. Meanwhile, many of the old school are learning to change their style of nonverbal communication so they're less confrontational and more perceptive and supportive. As a result, smiles have replaced frowns in many offices and on many shop floors.

But such occasional conversions are not enough. In Step Eight we're not just looking for congruence in individual communication style, we're out to change the organization as a whole. For only when such behaviors are stabilized through the whole company can we have a Learning Organization.

WHY YOU DON'T WANT TO SEE YOURSELF ON VIDEO

The peculiar way we route information through our brains produces effects we cannot directly monitor. That's why it's so often true that people are surprised and sometimes disturbed by the sound of their own voice on a tape recorder. Beyond that, it can be deeply disturbing to watch yourself on video tape performing some professional function you've carried out for years, under the illusion you were doing everything just right. Imagine what it would be like for the trainee we were describing, who blew his whole presentation with his body language, to watch a video tape of the talk which we had so completely misinterpreted.

Sometimes the damage a presenter does to his or her own message can be quite dramatic. Recently we watched a video tape of a presenter who so over-reacted to every contribution from the group that he seemed to be turning a quiet little discussion into a Cecil B. De Mille epic. The group who had attended his session brought in the tape to show to their colleagues because they thought it was so funny. Yet if you analyzed what this presenter was actually saying, it made perfectly good sense. It was the ham acting that did him in, and probably was undermining his whole career.

The disparity is seldom this dramatic, but most people have some degree of incongruity in their tone and body language when they communicate. That's one reason good actors are so rare. For the actor is a professional expert on making body and tone of voice conform to the ideas and feelings being communicated. Just as we've all had teachers who stood in front of the room and in a flat, nasal voice told us how interesting their subject was, so we've all had managers who told us how well loved they were while we wondered what boot camp they were trained in.

WE NEED FEEDBACK WE CAN LEARN FROM

Recognizing how you're coming across to others often requires a long process of trial and error. During that process you have to have some way of getting feedback on how you're doing. It shouldn't be necessary to have someone tell you you've failed miserably at communicating your ideas. Nor should you be allowed — or allow yourself — to go on antagonizing people when you think you're having the opposite effect.

It's much better if we can learn from others how our tone of voice and body language are affecting them without having to feel traumatized by the experience. At the same time, this kind of feedback, even when given with the best of intentions, can be hard to take, and some people react unpredictably when suddenly given more feedback about how they're coming across than they are ready to handle. So we advise treading lightly when exploring issues of non-verbal communication, unless you're skilled and experienced at it.

It's definitely true, though, that gentle feedback about a few simple aspects of communication style can be extremely productive. This can best be accomplished by pursuing the matter impersonally in such a way that individuals are at liberty to make those discoveries they can handle with reasonable comfort.

And in fact, except in extreme cases, a few simple changes might be all that are needed. One of the ways we do become aware of our effect on others is through a gradually increased understanding of cause and effect relationships. I know that if I punch you in the nose there will be consequences. Much of my behavior is ruled by just such perceptions.

A SKIT TO SEE THE 93%

You can explore this phenomenon with an exercise in heightening awareness of non-verbal communication, which we often do in workshops, and which is always entertaining and enlightening. It requires no special preparation or paraphernalia. To do this exercise, ask for two volunteers. Have them do a skit with the following scenario:

Two old friends meet after a long separation and talk about old times. While they are doing so, an argument develops, which leads to an intense conflict. Pretty soon the old friends are screaming at each other in threatening tones. But soon enough they find a way to resolve the conflict, and the skit ends with a renewal and strengthening of their friendship.

The participants perform this skit by using numbers as their only verbal language. They count sequentially from one to one hundred, giving the numbers the same kind of animation they would have given real dialogue. By the time they reach fifty in the sequence, they are in the middle of their conflict and are screaming and gesticulating at each other. But all has been resolved by the time they reach one hundred. As the skit concludes, they are happily enjoying their friendship once again .

During the skit, the numbers are grouped and inflected like actual words or phrases of conversation. In order to avoid confusion and needless distraction, each actor begins counting where the other left off, and all the numbers in the sequence are spoken without repetition. This allows all the concentration to be on the tone of voice and physical gestures that appear in any real conversation.

If you've never tried this before, you'll be surprised at how easy it is to do, and how dramatic the effect of it can be. After the skit is performed, ask for comments from the participants. When everyone has reacted to the experience, often by noticing how lifelike it was, and how much you can tell about the events that happened without any words to guide you, it's time to take the next step.

COACHING COMMUNICATIONS SKILLS

This is the point where the actors in the skit can learn about how they come across to others — how well their non-verbal communication matches their intentions, and how effective that communication is.

Call the actors back in front of the room and revisit some part of the scene that was just acted, for example during the escalating argument. After a few exchanges, stop the actors and ask one of them what specific things in the other's behavior might cause feelings of anger or other forms of discomfort. One of them might say to the other something like, "When you spoke to me at that moment you weren't looking at me, and you had your arms folded. Also you were shouting."

Next ask the other actor what the body language and tone of voice described were meant to communicate. You might get an answer like "firmness" or "I was determined to show *her*." The question then is, is this the message that came across? And if not, why not? And what did come across?

The `script' of the skit at that moment called for expressing anger. But now you can experiment with isolating and changing the emotional content of the actors' kinesthetic language. "Is there any other way you can express your feelings without doing the things your partner finds off-putting? For example, can you leave your hands more or less hanging at your sides, look her straight in the eye and speak in a quiet voice, but still be firm?"

Pursue this line of thought for a while. Try several different ways of getting the point across without arousing fear or some other undesirable reaction in the listener. Then work with the other actor for a while, selecting a different point in the scene and exploring how the second person might also change tone and body language in getting an essential point across.

Everyone watching is bound to learn something from this exercise. For many there will be a whole new insight about communication.

IS THIS A LEARNING ORGANIZATION — OR ACTING SCHOOL?

There's a general impression that when you talk, you are expressing your personality, and to talk in a different manner would violate your basic nature.

Yet the way we speak in tone and body language is somewhat arbitrary, like the way we dress. We have many choices about how to communicate something without straying outside the bounds of our basic personality. But since most people have never before received any instruction in making such choices, they've formed the impression that there's basically only one way they can respond to any given situation.

Often, when you try to communicate with someone on this issue you'll get a response like, "That's just the way I am," "that's how I express myself," or "I really couldn't do that and still be sincere."

But these comments are only defenses against learning something new and potentially very useful. Everyone understands how you can learn ballroom dancing, karate or tennis, and thus teach your body some new tricks. It's pretty widely accepted, also, that you can take a course in journalism and creative writing and acquire some new verbal tricks for expressing yourself effectively on paper. It's equally true that you can learn how to control yourself internally when communicating with someone else in order to get the reaction you want. This doesn't involve compromising anything in your basic nature, it simply increases your vocabulary of non-verbal communication techniques.

By working with a couple of participants as we've suggested, first letting one coach the other towards more accurate expression and then taking an example from the other actor's communication and going through a similar coaching process, you can help all the participants see that there are many different ways of getting a point across. It's easy to learn to distinguish in a situation like this between what is helpful and what just gets in the way.

This approach is safe because we're dealing with volunteers acting out a fictitious situation, not real people doing the things they actually do in real life. The actor is only playing a role. As people watch an activity like the one we've described, they can make their own personal and private judgments about what they themselves often do that confuses the communication process. In this area we all have a lot to learn, and an accusing finger need be pointed at no one.

FALLOUT FROM THE EXERCISE

Once when we did this exercise, a woman told us of a situation that had occurred where she worked. Two people who seemed to relate well enough to one another in social situations always became tense and angry when they worked together. Finally a co-worker explored the situation with them and found the source of the problem.

The first woman said that when the second woman laid a book down on the table she always slammed it, as if she were angry. This made the first woman nervous, causing her to speak in a loud, critical tone. If the slamming of things could be stopped, the relationship would be much easier for her, she said. The second woman confessed she'd had no idea she'd been slamming books down, and that she would certainly try to stop doing it, since she gained nothing from the results. She was able to change her behavior, and from then on the two workers got along together very well.

In another instance a woman noticed the man who assisted her was uncomfortable around her. After we had done the exercise described above, he went to her and said that she always gave him an order when she wanted him to do something. "Couldn't you phrase it as a question, such as 'Would you move the chairs now?' I'd feel better that way," he said. Her response was she'd had no idea she was giving out orders, but she might have gotten in the habit a long time ago and did it without thinking about it. She found it easy to change the way she phrased her requests, so the man who worked for her would feel more comfortable.

There are thousands of such irritations and misunderstandings large and small that may arise between people who are not aware of their body language and tone of voice. By becoming more conscious in these areas, we can facilitate our relationships with others and build a more successful work environment.

A WORD ABOUT DISCOMFORT WITH KINESTHETIC MODELING

Before you plunge into exploring Kinesthetic Modeling more fully, at least one further reminder and caveat is in order. In 'polite society,' overt physical expression is often discouraged, even frowned upon. It's not surprising, therefore, that any activity asking people to think and explore through the medium of the body may occasionally meet with some resistance and discomfort on the part of a few participants. If this should happen, just back off a little.

Once any feelings of resistance have been overcome through gradual acclimatization to the idea that we really do think with our bodies just as much as with our minds, and that modern organizations depend on our ability to do so, we can internalize a new dimension of communications that will make possible group understandings that might have been achieved in no other way.

In fact, physical interactions have long been a staple of organizational training. Rugged outdoor adventure in which trust is built by working with a team to overcome a physical challenge can have powerful effects in team building. The techniques of training in the martial arts are frequently employed in team-building seminars. And methods for increasing awareness of the body's internal state are being taught as an integral part of employee health and accident prevention programs.

Compared to these, Kinesthetic Modeling is tame and simple enough. All we ask is that people symbolize the professional relationships between them through the kinds of gestures often used in activities like charades.

Under the conditions that will prevail when the organization has signed off on the previous Seven Steps, however, the kind of exploration we use Kinesthetic Models to accomplish can produce many revelations. As a result it can become much easier to make useful adjustments in the way things are normally done. As the group continues to explore, for perhaps several hours, the implications of the Models they create, additional new insights may be captured in revised and updated Mind Maps. Over time, the Models can be revisited and redone until the team has developed a harmonious style of communication so natural and comfortable that a great deal of it literally goes without saying.

With the kind of thinking and discussion Kinesthetic Modeling generates, the organization will unconsciously learn a great deal about systems thinking. In the next Step, we will see where that can lead.

CONNECT THE SYSTEMS

S T E P   9

Everyone has seen a Rube Goldberg machine — one of those elaborate contraptions that's designed to do something very simple in an apparently complex and funny way. The Rube Goldberg machine may be a parody of a system, but it's funny because it mirrors the way some of the systems we have to deal with actually work.

For example, there are many situations in industry which work like this: A machine breaks down. The machine operator understands it well and could probably fix it in five minutes, but the system requires him to do something different.

He has to fill out a form which will be passed around among a variety of officials who have to sign off on it. Eventually it will reach a decision maker who, in due time, will send instructions to the maintenance department that this machine needs to be scheduled for repair.

Meanwhile the operator sits around for two or three days until the repair person shows up, at which point the operator shows the repair person what is wrong and tells him how to fix it.

We learned about this particular example from a machine operator who had on several occasions experienced just what we've described. When people talk in a derogatory way about "the system", it's this kind of nonsense they usually mean.

Such systems, designed by bureaucratic imaginations, are designed to slow things down and make everything more complicated. Sometimes, when they show up under government influence, they're the result of conflicts in the legislative process itself. We remember the restaurateur who told us that if he conformed to certain requirements of the health code, he was in violation of the building code.

Systems that lead to such results are actually what we might call anti-systems. That is, like the Rube Goldberg machine, they make otherwise simple things very complicated.

WHAT'S VITAL IN SYSTEMS THEORY

Systems theory, on the other hand, is supposed to help us see how the interacting elements in a complex situation work together to make something happen. A system is anything so designed that if you change the operation of one part of it, every other part is affected as well. Looked at from this point of view, systems thinking is essential to the success of any organization.

Peter Senge identifies systems thinking as the fifth discipline of organizational learning. W. Edwards Deming argued that when things go wrong in an organization it's virtually never the fault of individuals, it's the fault of the systems that dictate how individuals behave.

But systems thinking, though a fundamental principle of effective organizations, can too easily be honored and then ignored like other principles enshrined in organizational policy, or like the fabled contents of the college course, which passes from the textbook through the lectures of the professor into the notebooks of the students without passing through the minds of anyone.

We too are convinced that systems thinking is vital to any organization. In fact, if you have been proceeding through the previous eight Steps to a Learning Organization, particularly the last two, you will already have encountered systems thinking. You will have — as befits a Learning Organization — tried it, practiced it, even played with it in action.

For the group Mind Mapping and Kinesthetic Modeling activities of Steps Seven and Eight are basically the exploration and enactment, in two and three dimensions, of systems. They could not be accomplished without invoking systems thinking. Step Nine connects the thought processes behind those activities — to make the organization more fully aware of the power and relevance of systems thinking, and to extend its use through all phases of an organization's life.

WHERE YOU FIRST ENCOUNTERED SYSTEMS THINKING

We've all learned a great deal about systems thinking without knowing it. We learned much of what we know very early in life.

Every family, as Virginia Satir pointed out, is a system because what happens to one person in the family affects everyone else.

In every family all kinds of interactions take place on a systemic level. Each of the family members has a role to play, a role that is worked out carefully over a period of years and is balanced with all the other roles in the family.

As an experiential introduction to systems thinking we often divide seminar members into groups of five and ask them to pick roles to play in an ad hoc family. The family may consist of members of any type, but each person takes a role within his or her own sex. When the members have decided their roles in the family, we ask them to select a topic of concern, such as where to go on a vacation. We then give them about five minutes to work on this topic, playing out their various roles in the discussion that ensues.

At the end of five minutes we ask them to stop where they are and move one seat to the right. They will now take on the role of the person who was previously sitting in that seat.

After the group members have rotated in this way through all five seats, they return to their original seat.

What people learn from this exercise is how to see a discussion from all points of view. In other words, when we are part of a system we have a role to play, but we often fail to notice how that role interacts with the roles played by other people. By playing all the roles, we can get a feeling for how the system itself works.

One of the things to notice about family systems is that when we leave the family, we take our family system with us. We now react to situations outside the family as if they were occurring inside the family. We continue to play in other contexts the role we have played in our own family.

Of course over time changes take place, but the influence of the family is never lost.

So in an organization you are never dealing only with the people present. You are also dealing with all the family systems that each individual was once a member of. This enormously complicates the process of getting anything done. Only as people learn to step out of their own customary roles and see how things look from other perspectives, can a truly systemic way of interacting and doing business be developed.

SYSTEMS THINKING AND THE LEARNING ORGANIZATION

The Learning Organization exemplifies systems thinking in two particularly remarkable ways. First, the Ten Step process emphasizes the human element as an essential component of any system within an organization, and of the overall system which is the organization. The human element — people's potential, their emotions, their elusive means of communication, their motivations — is the essential but frequently unpredictable and messy element that is often left out of systems planning, not to mention the programs of business and organizational experts. But a Learning Organization, as we have seen, begins with the recognition that the human element must be taken into account, and provides occasions and tools for doing so. This enormously reduces the liability of the systems developed, while increasing their profitability to the organization.

Second, a Learning Organization is itself an effective system — a system that learns. As we shall see in this chapter, a Learning Organization can be structured so it processes information from its day-to-day and long term activities in order to learn, grow, and flourish. To show how organizations can develop and sustain this capacity, we will begin by taking another look at what is meant by systems thinking.

WHAT WE ALREADY KNOW ABOUT SYSTEMS

Whenever a group of elements is so interconnected that, as we have said, a change in one part produces a change in the whole structure, you have a system. A book is not a system, because ripping out one page in no way affects what's printed on the other pages. However the interaction between the reader and the book is systemic, and the omission of the page may effect a change in the reader's total reaction. But a computer program is a system all by itself, because if you change one element of it, you run the risk of changing the way the program itself works in every respect. That's why computer viruses are so damaging, and so aptly named. Like organic viruses, they attack the program at a systems level.

The average person already understands systems thinking when it occurs in certain familiar situations. For example, we know that if the heating and electricity go off in a vacant house during winter, the pipes may freeze, break, and later flood the house with water. But other effects may be less predictable. The ice in the freezer could melt and overflow onto the floor. The water may leak into the closet below where summer clothes are stored, causing them to mildew. Meanwhile, the burglar alarm isn't working, so the house is more vulnerable to robbery. These kinds of problems have led to the development of "smart" houses, which are even more systemic in their operation, but can be controlled more easily at a distance.

From small, localized events complicated effects ensue and proliferate. If we're agitated, our nervous system may cause insomnia, memory loss and other nervous disorders. And since our body is itself a system, other less readily apparent effects may result, such as indigestion and perhaps even ulcers. If the weather system brings a cold front together with a warm front, the result may be a heavy fog, which could close airports and interfere with the transportation system, which may in turn disrupt the political system, because a candidate arrives too late to give an important speech. This, in turn, could affect the welfare system or the prison system, which could lead to a rise in the crime rate, affecting the community system as a whole. What we're looking at here is the famous story of the loose nail in the horseshoe which caused the fall of a nation.

THE LESSONS OF THE STOVE

One reason many of us have some difficulty understanding the full implications of systems thinking is that our strongest experiences of cause and effect from early infancy tend to be narrow and oversimplified.

Illustration: As a curious child of three, you receive a painful burn when you put your hand on the red hot heating unit of a stove. The lesson is immediate, tangible and unambiguous. The chances you'll repeat this particular blunder are slim. The painful burn provides a simple, yet powerful lesson.

The lesson learned, however, is not just that if you put your hand on a stove, you will get burned. It is more general than that. You have learned that a particular action has a single, highly decisive result.

Because this learning experience is so intense and basic, it tends to establish a fundamental pattern in your thinking. Whenever something breaks down, you look for the cause of the breakdown. Because you are so certain that a simple breakdown had a simple cause, you are immediately on the trail of that one cause. After all, the hot burner on the stove was the cause of the burned hand, which means that forever after you will avoid hot burners.

In many management systems today, a similar process takes place: for example, something goes wrong with an information system. The boss says to himself, "I have the answer, it's what I'm getting paid for." So he moves in to control the situation, and fix the problem. Once the problem is fixed the boss feels assured that things are back to normal. Besides, he saved his department once again. He begins to think that his people don't know what they used to know, and he wonders what personnel changes he'll have to make. Of course, about six months later, something similar goes wrong, because the glitch is the result of a system inefficiency not the fault of the people involved.

This manager and department are caught in the vicious cycle of simple cause and effect solutions. Work continues to get done, but the underlying dynamics and system disconnections are never addressed and resolved. Their motto could be something like: No snowflake in an avalanche ever feels responsible.

WHAT FROGS DON'T KNOW ABOUT BOILING WATER

In this respect, a human being is a little like a frog. If you put a frog in scalding water, it will jump out right away. But if you put the frog in cold water and warm it up gradually, the frog, lulled into comfortable relaxation by the gradually increasing heat, won't get the message that it's time to jump out until it's too late. By the time the water is hot enough to hurt, the frog's system is already so damaged it can no longer jump. At that point the frog has no alternative but to sit there and quietly cook.

Both the frog and the human being tend not to react unless the problem is immediately apparent. When the cause is more slowly-developing, or more complex, they may not respond until it's too late. And even then, in their haste to solve the problem, they are likely to look for the simple, but superficial quick fix. For example, when a relationship is in trouble, we tend to blame someone (usually the other person) for causing the problem. When there's a breakdown in a government process, we look around for someone to vote out of office. We are searching for the perfect elected official to solve our problems. And when a job doesn't go well at work, we look for the one culprit who presumably caused all the trouble.

The crucial lesson to bear in mind is that the whole system is causing whatever the problem is and it is not the fault of any particular person or function. As the Walt Kelly cartoon character Pogo so well points out, "We have met the enemy and he is us."

So we're not only looking for a single cause for the effect we don't like, we're also looking for a highly visible cause. The same notion lurks behind much of our everyday thinking, even, for example, about our health and our own bodily systems. Most of us, when something is wrong with our health, will look for the single pill or operation to solve the problem. And the belief in the quick fix, the magic potion, is not confined just to the patient. The medical establishment has also bought, and sold, this concept. Meanwhile persistent and routine bad habits which lead to more gradual breakdowns of health are quietly ignored, or even actively sought out, as in the case of substance abuse.

The trouble with this kind of thinking is that it ignores the highly interactive process that complicates the relationship between cause and effect whenever a system is involved. When we deal with anything as complex as an organization, there's virtually never a time when a particular result can be said to be caused by a particular person or event.

Think how fruitless it is, therefore, when the quarterly earnings drop forty million dollars, for the CEO to get up in front of the assembled managers and read them the riot act. Whatever caused the sudden drop-off in profits, it isn't simply the managers. When a whole system is causing a problem, then the problem cannot be the fault of any particular person. To address the problem, we have to change the system. For that reason it is important to see people in terms of their interactions, not in terms of their individual behavior. Their interactions often are themselves systems which can be redesigned.

Despite individual and even group brilliance, systematic breakdowns will occur whenever people are unable to pull their diverse functions and talents into a productive and workable whole. Failure to pull together guarantees the continued segmenting of the system.

Any organization will struggle with Systems Thinking if the people involved don't fully understand how their work integrates with the whole. Unfortunately, there is a greater tendency for people to see others and themselves as helpless reactors rather than as active participants in shaping their futures. Seeing the interrelationships of all the parts rather than just isolated cause-effect chain reactions is essential for full understanding and also for successful adaptation to the rapid and constant change that's taking place in all organizations.

So, don't be a boiled frog. Healthy systems tend not to overreact to the natural small changes that are introduced to the system. The critical factor is to stay on top of change by being able to identify and respond to those changes that will bring about a crisis if left undetected. The rule is: Clarity is power; your head in the sand is dangerous.

LEARNING TO MANIPULATE SYSTEMS

The Mind Mapping and Kinesthetic Modeling activities we've discussed are two flexible tools that allow us not only to understand, but actually to experience restructuring the systems that affect us. Restructuring with maps and models is a preview and practice for organizational restructuring.

Their purpose is to help everyone become aware not only of how the organization is systemically interactive, but also how the structure can be changed to make it more effective. This sets in motion thought processes that can lead to formulating necessary changes, while helping people understand why those changes are being made, so the responsibility and motivation for making them is spread throughout the organization.

We often use Kinesthetic Modeling with teams who are exploring their interactions in order to analyze the bottle-necks in their system. First the team lists the various ways they function in the organization. Someone stands in the middle of the room to represent one of the listed functions and then invites another team member to come forward to represent another function. These two people are handed a ball of colored yarn, and they decide how they are linked together. Then another person, representing a third function, joins the interactions, and the linking process continues until all the functions are connected together with the yarn.

The group then explores the represented interconnections they have build, and analyzes the obvious relationships, and the workability of their team. They are also asked to explore the underlying assumptions to the systems' structures they have built.

Once they have gotten a clear understanding of the current interchanges in their system, they are asked to reconfigure themselves into a system that they believe would provide greater workability and fulfillment of their objectives.

This process provides the participants (in many cases for the first time) a visual representation of their system and engenders a dialogue to evaluate its effectiveness; deciding what works and what is missing within their unique structure

Let's take a closer look at the thought processes that are compatible with systems thinking, and how they differ from those that are not compatible.

TRY THESE QUICK THOUGHT EXPERIMENTS

To better understand this distinction, let's perform two thought experiments.

First, determine how many times the word "flag" appears in the "Star Spangled Banner." Don't read any further until you've tried it.

Your next task is mentally to visit your living room and count the lamps there. Again, don't read any further until you've done this.

You may notice a difference in the way you approached these two tasks. If you are like most people, you ran a check on the words of the song, taking them in order, one word at a time, looking for the target word. You probably did not throw the whole text up on your mental screen and pick out the single word you wanted.

But when it comes to visiting your living room, that's exactly how you can operate. In your mind's eye you can imagine yourself actually present in a three-dimensional room and look around it until you've found all the lamps. Unlike the words in the song, you can take them in any order, starting any-where, and you don't even have to go around the room in sequence unless you want to. You can also ignore everything in the room that's not a lamp, even though you can clearly see it while you're ignoring it. This mental operation simulates what you do in real life while actually looking at a room.

The difference between the techniques you probably brought to bear on these two tasks throws light on the most basic ways we process information. It is the difference between linear and global thinking.

LINEAR VS. GLOBAL THINKING

Some problems are best solved by taking things in a linear sequence. For example, it would be unwise to try to proofread a page like this one by jump-ing around and spot checking. Your best bet is to take the text one word at a time until you've checked every word. That's not to say that someone might not develop the talent of just "knowing" where the incorrect words are. But accounting for this "knowing" would be difficult within a linear framework.

When you're choosing a book to read, however, it's most unlikely that you'll start at one end of the shelf and move all the way across, checking each book until you come to the other end. More likely you'll seek out that part of the shelf that reflects your interests, or perhaps you will simply be drawn to a book that catches your attention.

MUCH OF OUR THINKING IS GLOBAL AND SYSTEMIC

Most of the things we do in life are done this way: not by rigorously checking things out in linear sequence, but by jumping around, following hunches and making judgments on the basis of a relatively small amount of conscious processing of information.

When we operate in a rigorous linear framework, we're probably activating one of the main functions of the left hemisphere of our neocortex, which is designed to help us bring order and logic to things. When we operate more globally, we're likely to be using the right hemisphere of the neocortex.

From an academic perspective it seems as if the best way to operate is to check everything carefully and in the right order, because by comparison any other way seems sloppy, inconsistent and undisciplined. But in fact relatively few problems can be effectively solved with the kind of linear inspection you probably brought to bear on the "Star Spangled Banner". Remember that phrase we found among the star pharmacologists: "Take a flier on this."

Most of the time we're forced to make judgments on the basis of incomplete information, because the situation is so complex that it would be impossible to get complete information. Nutritional analysis, for example, is one instance. The interaction among the foods you eat is so complex that, except in the cases of food problems which really have only one cause, it's almost impossible to tell through any sort of logical analysis what the best foods to eat with each other might be, and in what order they're best eaten.

Linear thinking can often get us into trouble, because we move from one step to the next without taking into account the whole scope of the interactive properties of the situation. Let's look at a real life example of this dilemma.

THE IDEAL EMPLOYEE
WHO THREW THE SYSTEM OUT OF BALANCE

A manager noticed that one of his employees was so dedicated to her job that she was never absent. As a result, she hadn't taken any sick leave, and at the end of the year lost the opportunity to have some time off which virtually everyone else had taken advantage of that year. The manager, feeling that this devoted employee had been cheated, decided to pass a new regulation: anyone who came to work every work day would be paid for an extra week at the end of the year. In other words, his model employee could actually earn fifty-three weeks of pay in one year.

The manager's thinking in this situation was linear. He saw what he perceived to be a problem of unfairness and he took the next step, which was to find a solution to that problem. He did not consider placing the problem in a larger context and looking at all the possible interactions it might lead to. In short, his thinking in this situation resembled the thinking you applied to looking for the word "flag" in the "Star Spangled Banner."

But had the manager mentally walked around in the problem the way you mentally walked around in your living room counting the lamps, he might have anticipated something like the result which actually followed. Once the regulation was passed, all the employees behaved in a somewhat unexpected way. They reasoned that they were earning enough during the year, but since there was that extra week being paid for, they could simply take a week off without loss of pay. So the company, by rewarding one person for exemplary behavior, ended up encouraging indolence in others, and costing itself a bundle in the process.

Such unexpected results are typical when solutions don't take the total system into account . Most of the time when something goes wrong we run off in pursuit of the elusive quick fix. Because so many quick fixes really do work, at least temporarily for specific problems, we tend to ignore what's still going on under the surface — and may return to haunt us — after the quick fix has been applied.

HOW QUICK FIXES LEAVE THEIR MARK ON AN ORGANIZATION

For better or for worse, anything that happens in an organization is the result of many different causes interacting among themselves. Often none of the individual causes is itself a bad thing — it is simply that the events, people, structures or other factors that have come together do not interact in a desirable fashion.

If you think about how your organization has grown over the years, you'll notice many ways in which the quick fixes of its past have been preserved in its behavior today. Perhaps ten years ago someone slipped on a greasy floor and sued the company for the resulting injuries. This event has led to regulations about conduct on the job, some of which are necessary, and some of which may be causing needless blocks to progress.

Perhaps when the company was first started it was quite small. Manufacturing was done in a small building. Stock was kept in another small building across town. Today, even though manufacturing and storage occur in the same building, the distance between the two is much greater than it needs to be, and considerable time and energy are wasted transporting things from one part of the building to another. When the activities were all consolidated into one building, people were so used to thinking about wide separation between manufacturing and the stock room, that no one considered bringing them closer together and thus taking advantage of the new possibilities that consolidation created.

Because your company "just grew," you've learned to adapt to all sorts of stresses that arose in your systems along the way, many of which have since become invisible to you. Our bodies do the same thing, adapting to injuries or stresses, incorporating the adaptation and retaining it often long after the original injury has healed.

But if you and other members of your organization look around in order to discover these relics of old stresses, you will begin to notice them. Then you will observe that here a process can be simplified from five steps to two, there a management approval can be obtained much more simply than by going through six people to get signatures on papers no one reads, and elsewhere you'll notice that what is being printed out and filed in file cabinets could be stored on computer disks instead.

Most organizations could benefit from this kind of examination. But great care and consideration must be brought to the task. Because of old habits and a tendency toward simplistic thinking, revision is best accomplished by first describing the actual systems operating in the company and then modeling them as systems. Afterward you can think about redesigning and simplifying them. You'll want to do so, though, while taking into account the unforeseen undesirable changes that may occur if you take the flaws out of the system you've got now.

TWENTY QUESTIONS ABOUT YOUR SYSTEMS

So now it is time to look at your own organization with the new perspective of a search for systems. All of your people can join in by describing the systems they participate in. To begin with, we recommend forming a committee of about five people to identify and report on the various systems operating in your organization. Here's a checklist for starters:

1. What system is used for answering the telephones?
2. What system is used for billing?
3. How are these two systems connected?
4. What system is used for strategic planning?
5. What system is used for performance evaluation?
6. What system is used to decide who is best equipped to make new things happen in the company?
7. What overall production system do you use?
8. What's your system of marketing?
9. In what ways do these systems interface and influence each other?
10. How are records kept in your organization?
11. What is the most necessary kind of information that tends to be unavailable?
12. What kind of system redesign would make this necessary information available?
13. How do you know whether a system is effective or not?
14. If you want to improve a system, how do you get the information you'll need in order to do so?
15. How do you discover the need for a system where there isn't any system yet in operation?
16. How do people redesign their systems so they can improve their work environment?
17. What learning systems do you use in your company?
18. How do the systems in your company learn?

19. What are all the different ways communications take place in your organization?
20. What systems exist for handling grievances of all types?

These questions are intentionally somewhat random, and are certainly not meant to be inclusive. They're meant to get you thinking about how you could question yourself and the members of your organization about the systems you're using. If you have groups working with these questions in the process of redesigning something, have them come up with additional questions to add to the list.

GENERATE YOUR OWN SYSTEMS THEORY

As you think about the systems in your organization which can be brought into clearer view by these questions, and consider them in the light of what we have been saying about systems in general, you will begin envisioning possible systems that might make things around you work better. Thus you will be building your own systems theory.

In case you don't think you can do this, let us note for starters that you already have a theory of business, a theory of communication with other people, and a theory of language. Even if you couldn't sit down and write out these theories, they are implicit in everything you do. Your theories enable you to make your way in the world because they allow you to predict and anticipate the consequences of various actions.

Your own systems theory will naturally derive from and apply to the specifics of your organization. There's no way any outside source can provide you with all the information you'll need to redesign the systems you work with. Every organization operates under very specific conditions. It is exactly this specificity that must be grasped and evaluated to determine the nature of your systems and how they could work better.

You already know how to use Mind Mapping to visually describe any given system, strategy or process your organization may currently be using. And you already know how to use Kinesthetic Modeling to explore the implications of each of these in greater depth, and also to explore what really happens when logical analysis and human feelings meet. Both of these methods are invaluable for clarifying the systems which are already in place in an organization. They help explain behavior and procedures that otherwise might appear to be incomprehensible.

SIX GUIDEPOSTS FOR BUILDING YOUR OWN SYSTEMS THEORY

As you begin to think about streamlining the systems in your environment, you'll necessarily confront issues which systems in general must address. Without trying to cover all the ins and outs of systems theory, we'd like to highlight certain key points about effective systems which are particularly relevant to a Learning Organization. As you think about these points, think also about how, by addressing them, you will be able to create systems that are themselves capable of learning and transforming.

1. **Memory**: Good systems keep track of themselves. If your systems are designed to remember the important things that happen in your organization, you're off to a good start.

Probably your organization is good at recording data it needs in order to survive an audit. But many organizations regard audits as a necessary evil, instead of an opportunity to establish and maintain information gathering and remembering systems. In many cases data from some part of the system could prove useful to other parts of the system. You might want to improve ways to provide immediate access to the memory for anyone with a need to know.

A key here is to constantly look for the weak spots in the feedback systems you have within the organization, departments, and teams. When you locate one of these points spend your time improving them.

2. **Purpose**: The purpose of each system must be defined. By knowing quite clearly what each system is supposed to accomplish, you can make its operations more efficient, for then you can eliminate from the system everything that fails to contribute to the fulfillment of its goal. If you find something that has to be eliminated for this reason, but nevertheless provides some other benefit, you can create a new system to preserve that particular benefit, and define the purpose of that system accordingly.

3. **Rules**: Articulate the rules according to which a system operates.

To devise these rules, you have to comprehend the full scope of the system. This includes knowledge of the total web of relationships within the system. It means having a capacity to predict consequences of various changes. It means knowing which points should be informed with feedback, what and where checks and balances should be introduced.

It is vital that the rules being made can be enforced. Many times a whole system is placed at high risk when the larger organizational system tries to over-control the smaller sub-systems. Trying to enforce unenforceable rules and regulations will only further fragment the whole organization.

The founding fathers of our country were excellent systemic thinkers without necessarily knowing it. Experienced with the tyrannical rule of England and enlightened by some revolutionary egalitarian principles, they constructed a system of government equipped with the necessary rules to keep the power of government balanced among three branches and firmly in the hands of the people. They accomplished this feat through the foresight of systemic thinking. They understood the complex workings of a state and created the rules that would keep it running.

Any system can be structured just as carefully through this global, systemic approach. Then rules can be devised to promote the most efficient workings of the system. For example, suppose you wanted to devise a set of rules for keeping a customer. Based on knowledge of your product, knowledge of the kind of service your customers expect and other particular conditions in your organization, you could develop a system of customer service. This might require that all your employees graduate from a courtesy course. Or it could mean that everyone on your staff would be continually learning more about how to trouble-shoot the problems brought in by customers.

4. **Continuous improvement**: Keep revising the rules of the system to continuously improve operations.

By defining and then restructuring your systems' operating rules, you can continuously improve the systems themselves. Sometimes a bit of trial and error is necessary to accommodate all the dimensions and relationships within a system. Rules and processes should be amenable to change as long as the changes better fulfill the goal of the system.

Having said that, it is also necessary to realize that every improvement may create new problems. Every new technology has generated unanticipated problems. The car solved the problem of horse manure pollution, and created air pollution. The freedom of the Internet increased the speed of sharing information world-wide, but created a problem of privacy.

It's important to anticipate any ancillary problems that will be introduced with new improvements; evaluating whether the anticipated new problems are worth the risk, or whether it might just be better to live with the present problems in the system. Continuous improvement does not mean change for change sake, which is what happens in organizations many times. Because of systems dynamics, sometimes the cure is worth than the disease.

5. **Feedback**: Systems may need monitoring and regulating.

Think about designing into each system sources of feedback — so you'll know how well the system is meeting its goals. For if a system can learn that it is inefficient, it can be designed to sound the alarm when it needs intervention. You might, for example, develop a statistical process control to alert you to the number of customers you are losing each month. Then you could explore procedures that will help you in retaining and gaining customers.

You might develop a means of determining how many times the phone is answered within the first two rings and the call handled smoothly, in order to determine where there is need for improvement in the way the phones are answered. Some systems can be made to self-regulate, learning to adjust themselves in response to feedback in the system. A heating or cooling system for instance will regulate room temperature in response to feedback from the thermostat. The sources of feedback within the system and the program of responses to that feedback can be designed to allow systems themselves to learn and transform. Teaching your systems to learn is a giant step toward creating a Learning Organization.

This transformation of systems goes on all the time throughout nature, and is an essential ingredient of the learning process. To learn something, you have to understand it. Then you must synthesize that knowledge with other knowledge you already have. This synthesizing is really a recasting of all systems of knowing that the new knowledge affects. Only after restructuring has occurred can the learner act as a result of what has been learned.

The same process applies to the Learning Organization, which can learn only when it transforms its systems by incorporating into itself new and better structures.

As we learn more and more about how systems work and how they can be changed, the power of each individual to effect such a change is increased. And it is with consideration of the individual that we come to the last guidepost to keep in mind when thinking about how systems should be structured.

6. **Human behavior is part of the system**: Good systems encourage people to act in the most positive and effective ways. Systems that fail to do so are squandering their greatest and most vital resource. If people are hampered because the system controls too many choices, the people will try to outwit the system.

Understanding and respecting the human dynamics of systems, is one of the greatest, most difficult, and rewarding challenges facing today's leadership; placing great demands on the interpersonal skills and sensitivities of most executives and managers.

The principles of human learning and human behavior we've discussed have been shown in innumerable cases to bring out the best in people. When the members of your organization are accountable, interact positively, think on the job, take risks, work cooperatively, seek personal mastery, align themselves with the group's vision and think systemically, they will function as vital participants in all of the systems.

After all, the way your systems function will determine your organization's capacity to be a Learning Organization. For only when the systems favor the learning of every individual — and also when the systems themselves have the capacity to learn — can the organization cease to treat people as cogs in the machine, and instead turn to them as primary sources for new solutions and creative ways of doing things.

WE KNOW HOW TO RESPOND TO SYSTEMS
LONG BEFORE WE CAN DESIGN THEM

The learning instinct in all human beings is so strong that the mastery and transformation of a system is always among the most rewarding experiences life has to offer. Consider, for example, one astounding feat of systems thinking which you have already accomplished: the mastery of your own native language. When you learned your native language, you deciphered, internalized, and mastered an exceedingly complex system of communication. You did so not because you wanted rewards and recognition, but because the natural bent of your mind was to learn to communicate.

Throughout your life, whether you are trying to learn a new skill or build a friendship, mastering the dynamics of systems will open up new opportunities for you — some of which may well transform your life. And how do you do that? You understand the rules, you practice the necessary skills, and you perfect strategies for success. Through this ongoing process, you become a master of the system.

Much of this activity is not consciously planned. That is, you don't set out to play a game of tennis so you can master and transform a system, you play it because it's fun. If you look closely at activities you enjoy — playing cards, making a new friend, going for a ride in the country, or doing whatever you love to do best — you're likely to find that in reality you're deepening your understanding or skill in some system, while seeking strategies to transform it. In short, many of the most rewarding things we do in life are the very things we most need to do in an organization to make it truly a Learning Organization.

THE IMPORTANCE OF INTRINSIC MOTIVATION

Thus an environment that is designed to bring out the best in people can do so effectively without any extrinsic motivation. There is no need to give people prizes or bonuses or to shower rewards on them. What they do need is the opportunity to do something deeply meaningful and transforming in their work life.

Interestingly enough, the failure to meet this need has been connected to the disappointing results of quality programs in some American corporations. Karen Bemowski has observed that the attitude towards quality in our society is largely negative because people so often hear about it when it's missing in a product or service.[1] Similarly, many quality programs in large companies emphasize the absence of quality, treating it as something missing that must be supplied.

Americans do not respond well to this approach, because they like to see themselves as achieving excellence in their own unique way. They do, however, usually respond well to a quality program (or any other type of corporate endeavor) which gives them responsibility and accountability, while at the same time allowing them the opportunity to express their uniqueness.

Bemowski's advice to organizations, therefore, is to reward successful teams by giving them the wherewithal to pursue the goals they have set for themselves. We've observed the wisdom of this in the organizations we've worked with. Often people will develop a program they believe in while working on their own time. All they ask of the organization is that it support them, once the program has proven its excellence, by developing and promoting their project further.

So often it's wise to give people the tools for personal or organizational improvement. This approach will work far better than giving them recognition or bonuses. Furthermore, it's important that the new tools be provided as soon as possible after the success has been achieved. This will keep the team moving forward with the energy and emotion it has developed up to that point.

W. Edwards Deming believed that our cultural practice of motivating people with grades, bonuses, and other rewards has the effect of killing off the intrinsic motivations of learning and working. Alfie Kohn has explored this belief in several well written and influential books. From a systems point of view, the loss of intrinsic motivations means that each point of origin of potential knowledge in the system is functioning at a low level of efficiency, so the system as a whole becomes ever more inefficient. In plain English, the result is that both the worker and the work suffer.

So a system that aims to achieve the highest efficiency and the maximum use of its resources must be based upon sound insights into what makes people tick. A Learning Organization, by relying upon, reinforcing and rewarding behavior that people feel intrinsically motivated to perform, is positioned for success.

And when it's well designed and on the path to success, it's time to focus on keeping it oiled well enough so that the final step, the achievement of a mature interaction of all elements of the system, becomes reachable.

GET THE SHOW
ON THE ROAD

S T E P   1 0

When Sam Walton used to fly into one of his stores and visit the employees on the floor, he was like a director dropping in on the run of his play and giving notes to the actors. There was drama in his surprise visit, and the drama he created with his personality was designed to inspire drama in his employees, to refresh and crystallize the unifying vision of their enterprise.

What we mean by drama, as we approach it in Step Ten, is not something insincere, artificial or remote from actual experience. It is that heightening of life that always comes about when a thing is done supremely well. This quality of drama is the interplay between science and art, the movement from the careful study of a how a thing is put together and mastered, to the aesthetic sense of what it is to feel that thing, that system, that production, that culture. In this Step the organization takes up residence in the heart and soul of every one of its members.

That's why we suggest you think of the Learning Organization as a new type of drama, a culmination of our shaping of the type of organization that will succeed in the twenty-first century. The old show has just about finished its run and will soon be closing. The time has come to get the new show on the road.

PUTTING IT ALL TOGETHER

Up until now in the Ten Step process we've been laying the foundation for everything to come together as it should in this final Step. We've been coaching, doing exercises, building a culture, and in many other ways providing the basic tools with which an organization may structure its success. But the first nine Steps do not, in themselves, coalesce the character and vision of an organization to the point where they are internalized by everyone connected with it. Taken collectively, they still lack the unifying force that ties everything together.

Step Ten may be the most indispensable, for it is here that everything culminates — here we experience most clearly not only the unifying force that ties the organization together, but also the overlapping energy between the organization and life itself. Our goal now is to internalize all we have learned, and to express it through the particular forms of action into which we have chosen to direct our life energy.

THE POWER OF GUIDING METAPHORS

The images we use to describe our activities deeply influence the way we see ourselves and the way we behave. Most organizations have some kind of image or guiding metaphor which focuses and energizes their actions. These images can be relatively subtle and even unstated; or else overt and highly elaborated. But in either case, they can greatly affect everything that happens in the organization. In a Learning Organization, this is particularly important, since everything that happens must happen throughout the company and involve all personnel.

Probably the most frequent and recognizable example of such a guiding metaphor is *war*. Businesses and groups that see themselves as engaged in mortal *combat* for scarce rewards tend to promote the same kind of attitude inside and outside their organizations. *Campaigns* and *crusades* are somewhat more limited variations on this theme. Similar to war, but less terminal, is the metaphor of *sports*, which can inspire the participants to supreme effort and teamwork for the sake of *victory*. On the darker side as a guiding metaphor is the struggle for *survival*, in which continued existence and life itself are constantly at stake. *Kill* or *be killed*. What all these different metaphors have in common is a zero sum game That is, that there have to be winners and losers.

GREAT OPPORTUNITIES FOR PLUS SUM GAMES

The universe isn't like that, though. It's a plus sum game. Its resources are not limited, and one of the glories of modern industry is that innovation actually increases the available resources of the world at a mind boggling pace. This means that if we use what we have, we can raise the standard of living for everyone on the planet. That greatly increases the available markets, incidentally, because the more people can earn and raise their standard of living, the more they'll want to buy. So industry can, by raising the standards of living of all employees, actually create richer and richer possibilities for everyone while building markets that greatly enhance the bottom line. This plus sum aspect of industry underscores the dynamic need for creating Learning Organizations, because a Learning Organization is committed to increasing win-ability for everyone

THE LEARNING ORGANIZATION AND
A RAPIDLY GROWING ECONOMY

One vital and powerful example of using the plus sum process, is the incredible growth rate of the Springfield Remanufacturing Company, which developed the Great Game of Business, and maintains its growth at 15% per year (astronomical compared to the average) while having spun out seventeen subsidiary businesses in not much more than a decade. What you have with the Great Game of Business is both a theory and a tool for enormously increasing the potential for worldwide economic growth, stability and productivity.

But it all depends on learning and on management that realizes the tremendous hidden potential and resources already within their organizations and then acts to unleash the natural learning power and capacities at hand.

So it's time to put aside the zero sum stories and metaphors and replace them with plus sum stories and metaphors. Drama and, more generally, the arts, fall into this category. So do social development paradigms, education and learning paradigms and quality enhancement paradigms. And so, in the end, do the very best business plans ever developed.

So we propose, for the last step of our Ten Step process, that a Learning Organization explore *drama* as a guiding metaphor, because it is a plus sum game, because it is oriented towards rapid and dynamic change, and because it is a powerful medium that the organization can use to focus and energize its internal activities and its approach to the world at large. In this suggestion we are in league with shapers of opinion among the top executives of leading corporations, such as Total Quality Management expert Barry Sheehy, who strongly promotes the drama metaphor because it adds so much excitement and energy to the enterprise. For those who seek to inaugurate a new way of doing business, this way of envisioning their venture can be a very powerful tool.

DRAMA AS A GUIDING METAPHOR

If your first thoughts suggest that beyond some show biz sizzle, there is little common ground between the "serious" world of organizations and the "play-acting" of a drama, give the matter some additional thought. For looked at objectively and with imagination there is a great deal that organizations can learn from the individual and group activity that goes into putting on a successful show.

"All the world's a stage," said Shakespeare, "and all the men and women merely players." When we are at our best we are playing most intensely the roles that life has given us to play, whether it be in rising to some challenge, or in a quiet moment of intimacy with a family member, or pulling off a practical joke at a party. And we are also frequently, and consciously, preparing for roles that we want to act. It's not just actors who rehearse and perfect their parts. Brain surgeons and basketball players, engineers and expectant mothers, writers and welders, astronauts and economists: all are rehearsing parts they want to play.

Beyond the individual perspective, the model of a dramatic production is a useful one to a Learning Organization both in how the organization sees itself, and in how it is seen by others. The drama model suggests the degree of cooperation and mastery within the organization necessary for peak performance. And, from the outside — to the audience, the customer — it suggests the distinctive uniqueness of a successful enterprise.

The excitement of drama, both for the performers and the audience, creates its own additional energy. For in the molding of the drama all the participants come together in a unified effort. They understand the way each of their contributions fits the whole, and share in the excitement of the collective achievement. No wonder the old rally cry, "The show must go on!" carries such an electric charge.

COMMERCIALS AS MINI-DRAMAS

We can see, too, that where the rubber hits the road, drama emerges as the controlling impulse. Much of the economy is based on television commercials, which must, in thirty seconds or a minute tell a compelling story. Far from being boring interruptions in the main programs, commercials have developed so much art and imagination that they often out-perform the shows they are interrupting. There even are channels which offer nothing but commercials.

It's fun to watch the evolution of the commercial from week to week as new creative ideas about how to communicate a message are born, developed and tossed around among the various advertising agencies. Most of the techniques developed by Hollywood for feature films have now been collapsed into short dramatic experiences which, when your sales resistance is down, can look quite wonderful.

If drama is so powerful as a means of communication of what a company has to offer the public, it ought to be equally successful as a tool for internal communication as well.

THE SHOW BUSINESS IN BUSINESS

There are some additional suggestive analogies between the success of a show and that of a Learning Organization. Whether a play succeeds or fails has almost nothing to do with its competition — only with its unique contribution to the pleasure of the audience. A play that pleases its audience enough may run virtually forever. Shakespeare's plays are as alive today as when they were first performed over four hundred years ago. The film version of *The Wizard of Oz* will probably never get stale. Good theater, whether it appears on the stage, on film, or between the pages of a novel, is endlessly appealing to the human mind and has always been heavily in demand.

Similarly, some organizations seem to have been with us forever and seem as if they always will be. The Red Cross and the New York Yankees spring to mind. Generations have used Kodak film and have drunk Coca-Cola. These companies have become institutions. They have been around much longer than the average organizational lifetime of forty years because they have known how to capture and keep the imagination of the public. We'll never stop enjoying those baby pictures of us taken during a Kodak Moment, nor will we ever want to give up The Pause that Refreshes.

So the creation of an organization, seen in this light, has an artistic aspect. There's no possible limit on what art can accomplish, and also no limit to what is possible in business. We can put aside notions of winning and losing and instead attend to the excitement of continuously renewed and improved success. For it is in the gathering of energy around an idea and the bringing of that idea to life in the public arena that the organizational superstars succeed.

When we think of Federal Express, we think of a modern success story that is so deeply imbued in everyone who works with or deals with this company, that it has come to seem as much a part of our national scene as Campbell's Soup or McDonald's. Yet compared to them Federal Express has been around a much shorter time. Like most successful companies, it has a character of its own, a way of thinking about and projecting itself to customers that makes it unique and irreplaceable. The drama the company projects consists of the continual delivery of the promises implied in its advertising, its performance record and its way of dealing with the public. When we think of Federal Express we think not only of absolute reliability of on-time delivery, but also of the capacity to know exactly where each piece of mail is, and where and when it was delivered.

IMAGERY FROM THE INFORMATION AGE

Meanwhile, perhaps the great Odyssey of our time is provided by Bill Gates, a legendary figure who not only controls the way computers communicate with us and thus how we communicate with each other, but has all sorts of ideas about the future he's planning to provide for the world. In the beginning the success of Microsoft was a matter of technological expertise. Now, it is increasingly that it is finding its place in the folklore of the United States and the entire world beyond.

The uniform images projected by such organizations, furthered by every employee, would not be possible if the employees were not rehearsed in their performance so that as they go before their audience — the public stage on which their customers see them — they are perfectly rehearsed in their characters and their actions. A better way of saying this would be that they have *discovered* their parts, for drama is convincing when the players live and believe their roles.

THE DRAMA IS ON BOTH SIDES OF THE CURTAIN

In drama the preparation for opening night and all subsequent performances is to deliver a known quantity. The play that is to be performed has a script, and the actors, the director, the set designer and set builders, and all the other people involved with the production, have dedicated themselves to projecting as faithfully as possible not only the ideas of the play, but its exact design and structure. In some cases the script represents the work of a single individual. In many cases it's a collaborative product involving a great deal of improvisation, experimentation and rewriting along the way.

Just so, the successful organization has a script, its business plan, which may have emerged from the collaboration of the actors who collectively make up the Learning Organization. And it has a director — the CEO — to bring that script to life. Every director has a different method and a different style, but if the director is successful, the play will capture an audience and run for a long time. And it is not the director who will be there every night, but the actors, the technicians, the ushers and the stage crew — all of whom must keep things running as much like opening night as possible — except that continuous improvement may occur throughout the run.

If you have trouble seeing the operation of an organization as a dramatic event, it might help to consider some well-known fictional examples of business as drama. Novelist Arthur Hailey has made this the subject of several popular books, like *Hotel* and *Airport*. In the Cecil B. De Mille film, *The Greatest Show on Earth*, a large part of the excitement is not so much in the melodramatic events perpetrated by the characters as in the business of running a circus. In this film you see a great deal about what it takes to put a circus together — how the many different activities are carefully coordinated from long before the Big Top goes up in each town, until it's time to take it down again in preparation for moving on. You'll meet the director of the circus, who must deal with all kinds of problems — from people problems to logistics problems, to problems of dealing with the public — just as any manager must.

BUSINESS AS THEATER

Whether you are running a circus, a live-action amusement park or a manufacturing plant, a hospital or a hotel, you have the business of making things work to serve your customers, and you also have all your interactions with the people that carry out that business. The drama is in the combination of the two.

Just as in a good performance of a good play you want to see competent people doing their jobs well — actors playing their parts convincingly, stage crew raising the curtain on time, and make-up artists who know their craft — so when patronizing a restaurant or buying a new car you want to see the evidence of what good, competent people have done well.

All those who work for the organizations we've mentioned here, and many other excellent ones of similar reputation, have been carefully rehearsed to project all aspects of the idea and structure of the company of which they are a part.

So the analogy between the production of a play and the building of an excellent company is instructive. As the play runs for a week, a year, or a decade, the quality of each performance must be maintained, no matter how many times the actors have done it before.

HOW ACTORS KEEP THEIR EDGE

Let's go behind the scenes and observe what happens in theater that makes it possible for a group of actors to move an audience every single time. One of the comments we most often hear from actors who play in long runs is that "it's a different show every night." What exactly do they mean by that?

A good actor, making an entrance, has in a certain sense *become* the person he or she represents on the stage. And in the mind of that person, living through the events of the play, the joys, the sorrows, the surprises and the expectations are always new. Each time the actor opens that package on Christmas morning in the climactic scene of the play, the excitement of something new and wonderful but not yet known must be in his or her mind, as it is in the mind of the character.

To do this successfully, actors must be so committed to the play that they can feel it anew each time. And to do that they must bring their life energy to the part and put it behind everything they do. Significantly, they must always have more energy — more competence — than they actually use, for the ease of the actor comes from the sense that there's always more power than is being called upon for a particular action. Thus there's a certain amount of tension between the performer's commitment and what's actually being done at the moment. This tension lies in the desire to do more — to have more power, more dynamism, more creativity. The good performer is always champing at the bit to push the limits of performance higher and higher.

None of this could happen if there were no audience. Actors know very well that each audience is different. A line that brought down the house one night may go unnoticed the next. Actors learn to feel the audience, to psych out its peculiar character, and to adjust their performance to suit that audience. Of course they like some audiences better than others, but their professionalism requires that they give their very best in every performance.

FOCUSING ON WHAT MAKES A JOB EXCITING

The goal in an organization is for everyone who is involved in a job to do it in that same spirit. There must be excitement and a feeling of newness and originality the umpteenth time the worker pulls the newly cooled tubing out of the machine and prepares it to be shaped into its final form of manufacture. Inasmuch as all the actions that can be replicated perfectly every time will be performed by a machine, the human being comes on the scene to deal with the uniqueness of the job — the differences required by the nature of the process, as one piece of tubing differs from another and therefore must be handled differently.

At this point in the Ten Step process all the employees have not only played their part in the formation of the culture and vision of the company, but have also helped to build its systems. Their understanding of the complexity of what they do is strong. They've learned to respect each other's thinking — and their own — to build visual images of how they do what they do — to model it with their bodies, and to understand it systemically.

Step Ten is where the excitement, the commitment, the emotion, the passion come on the scene. This is where the employee, who has found some way of making the performance of this job an important part of life experience, brings that experience into an exciting reality.

As I go into McDonald's and order a Big Mac, even though I am aware that each employee is different, I seldom see much variation in the crisp and friendly way my order is filled. The lines and actions have been learned and are delivered nearly to perfection. At the same time, every employee seems to have a feeling of confidence and pride at working for such a good company.

As I go into Makeshift Hamburgers, on the other hand, I notice that things are disorganized. The clerk isn't really sure how much my order will cost. Some of the items on the menu are unavailable right now — not because they're sold out, but because no one got them ready. The people at Makeshift don't seem to know quite what they're supposed to do. They're like amateur actors who haven't yet learned their lines, and are stumbling their way through a poorly conceived performance.

So building a great company is like building a great drama. Everything has to coordinate, and no matter what the circumstances, even if understudies must step in, it is always true that the show must go on.

THE ROLE OF THE DIRECTOR

There are as many ways of getting a show ready for performance as there are producers or directors. But directing styles generally divide along the line of how much control is exerted over the elements of the play. At one extreme is the director-as-God, who lays down the law about every detail, and in whose productions any deviation by an actor is undertaken at the risk of one's future career. At the other extreme is the laid-back type who barely interferes with the actors' evolution of the production, and basically seems to be there only to start the rehearsal, keep it going, and declare it over at the end.

Either extreme can produce a good performance — of a show. However, as we've been suggesting through the whole course of this book, managers at every level of the modern organization can no longer assume the script will never change. In fact, they must assume the opposite. No organization can afford the luxury of management, however brilliant, that can only work from an unchangeable script. In today's economy and today's world, that is a sure prescription for an early curtain and a short run. Just as some theater companies actually improvise the show anew each night, so the responsive business may have to improvise much of what it does in order to meet the demands of a rapidly changing world economy and local set of market conditions.

So the director of the organizational drama must be able to help the actors prepare for a real-life performance where not only the script but the roles themselves may be expected to change. How does the analogy of putting on a show apply to these conditions — to the situation of the Learning Organization in the real world?

DIRECTING TO MEET THE CHALLENGE OF CHANGE

Let's go back to the theater for a moment to see how this challenge can be met. One of us has had a good deal of experience with the theater, and that experience has actually proved relevant and helpful in building the organizational drama. Though directing techniques vary, I'd like to share the one that I use here — because it seems to work in helping people with very little experience master the challenge of giving a compelling and reliable performance.

The way I've found that seems to have the best chance of producing good results is a genuine collaboration between the directors and all the others who put the show together — actors, designers, lighting technicians — even the stage manager. I once heard a director say that he would tell an actor, "You can do anything you like so long as I like it." I found this a wonderful single sentence characterization of how to direct.

In this style of directing, the director comes to rehearsal with a quality of performance clearly in mind — and then does everything possible to stimulate the actors to do something even better than that. So the process of directing is one of discovering just how much the actors can do. If for some reason what they end up with is not as good as what I had thought of, I can always tell them to do it my way. But if I watch and listen and question, I can often get them to think of things I never would have thought of at all.

HELPING ACTORS THINK THROUGH THEIR PARTS

Rather than trying to nail down all the details of a show at the early rehearsals, I keep the actors in a state of ambiguity for a very long time. They don't know what they are supposed to do, or how they are supposed to do it, and because of that they start to think. Often they protest a good deal before they start to think, but once they are thinking, wonderful things can happen.

A very simple way to direct a scene, one that works every time, is to have the actors in the scene begin by reading a few lines while moving about the stage as the lines suggest, trying to be the people who would say those lines. Then, after a few lines have been read, I'll ask an actor to tell me what the line means. Often this requires some real thought, as the actor has only parroted the line without thinking about it.

My questions are designed to stimulate the actors to think, though I'm careful to avoid saying what they should think. As a result, the actors feel as if they are thinking the whole thing through themselves. So now, when they speak the line, they will speak it with the conviction of their own thoughts.

The point is that it's usually a lot easier to do something well if you have figured it out for yourself, than if someone else tells you how it is supposed to be done.

IT'S LIKE TEACHING SOMEONE TO HOLD A TENNIS RACQUET

I could use the same method to teach someone how to hold a tennis racquet. What teachers usually do is show you how to hold the racquet. Personally, I react to that experience by wondering for the next six years whether I'm doing it right or not. When I'm not doing that, I'm wondering whether the teacher is really right, and if there might not be a better way of holding the racquet.

But if you get the person who's learning to play tennis to hold the racquet in a variety of ways and talk about each of them, she'll eventually find a way of holding it that meets your criteria. Except, because she found it herself, it will feel right to her. She will have tried a number of ways and rejected them — perhaps only after you've directed her attention to something about how it feels to hold the racquet that way.

As we continue with this, we eventually arrive at a way the player is comfortable with holding the racquet, and it's just the way that I've learned from experience ought to work best. But the player has worked it out for herself and therefore has her own newly created complete understanding of why it's the best way.

WHEN ACTOR AND DIRECTOR DIFFER

Back to the theater. What I've been doing so far is eliciting from the actors what they think they should be doing, and then evaluating how well they do what they set out to do. By the time we finish doing this with a few lines, the actors are thinking much more about how to get each line across.

Now let us say that by this process we get an actor giving a thoroughly convincing performance that doesn't fit my conception at all. At this point, the issue is no longer whether he has a clear conception of the role, but whether his way of playing his part fits in with an overall view of the drama as a whole — and specifically with my view as the director.

Again, I invite the actor to think his way through this dilemma. I may need to give him a great deal of information about other aspects of the play — other characters, other scenes, and how they affect the character he is playing. All this is to explain what I think and what I want, but I'm still maintaining minimum critical specification for what exactly he'll do with the scene. That will come from his own thinking and his own reactions to what we've said.

When I take this approach I find it possible to lead completely inexperienced actors through an intense scene from Shakespeare in a way that gets them to a chilling performance of a few lines in no more than a half hour. In other words, this approach gets extremely good results very quickly, even though it may appear to be indecisive and to take a long time.

APPLICATIONS ON THE JOB

Now in working with people on the job you can also get very good results in a very short time if you fully engage their thinking in what they are doing. The same kind of approach that serves to enhance a performance in a play can be used to explore the actions on the job. What we suggest here is a dialogue of discovery to get your employee tuned into his or her role in the ongoing drama of your organization.

This kind of dialogue is actually a rather one-sided, Socratic approach. Unlike a debate, the dialogue is not meant to provoke a sharp contrast between the beliefs or perceptions of two individuals. Instead, it is one way a person can lead another to sharpen his or her perceptions without interjecting a contrary view. It is really two people thinking together in order to achieve a clear sense of what dramatic action is appropriate.

Here's an example:

Manager: "What do you think are the most important traits of a good telephone salesperson?"

Worker: "To get the person on the other end of the line really interested as quickly as possible."

Manager: "What ideas do you already have about how to do that effectively?"

Worker: "I haven't really thought of any yet. I've just started on this job."

Manager: "Can you think of a time when you met a salesperson who interested you?"

Worker: (Tells a story about an experience of buying something from someone.)

Manager: "That's a good example. What are some of the things that salesperson did to capture your attention and make you want to buy the product?"

The virtue of such an approach is that workers learn how to evolve a method they can have confidence in. The answers to these questions have to come from the worker's own frame of reference about what is convincing, what succeeds. As the discussion continues, worker and manager together shape the role the worker will be playing, so the worker's imagination begins to take fire with the possibilities offered by the role to be played here. The process will work all the better if many of the manager's questions help the workers to explore relationships between the particular job to be done and the functioning of the organization as a whole.

When you've explored the subject together, there may still be some possibilities that haven't been touched on. At that point it's appropriate to provide other options for the employee to weigh, such as techniques suggested in a sales manual, that might stimulating his or her thinking. After that it's just a matter of getting started with the performance of making the calls.

SHARPENING PERFORMANCE IN A LEARNING ORGANIZATION

A Learning Organization needs people who are excited about thinking through every aspect of their jobs. Since all of us tend to gloss over at least some of our actions without thinking about them, this process of defining our roles gives us a chance to focus on aspects of the job we may never have thought about before. Anyone, no matter how experienced, is likely to be able to arrive at an improved performance by thinking things through in this way.

You will also find that answering these questions in a non-threatening atmosphere is fun and likely to lead to improved self-esteem. We all like to discuss and explore what we do well, and to make new discoveries about how we might do even better. If you ask me a question about my performance and I come up with a brilliant new insight about how I can improve, the insight is mine, not yours, so I don't feel you're preaching or lecturing me. I feel I am discovering something of great value. And I'll look forward to our next conversation with positive anticipation.

In a Learning Organization, such questions are constantly asked and answered. But the point of the questions is never the philosophical exploration of ideas — it is always action-oriented. When used here, after the other nine Steps have already been established, it's a way of bringing out all the subtleties that haven't previously jelled, of fine-tuning the action. For as the drama of the Learning Organization must be performed in the real world, the learning that characterizes it can only come through action, not through abstract philosophizing. Every idea that is explored is valuable only to the extent that it works when put to the test.

INVITING EVERYONE TO BE THE DIRECTOR

Let's go one step further. We're at the rehearsal, and three actors are on the stage playing a scene while a couple of others sit watching, waiting to make their entrance. You're going through the process described above, gradually evolving an understanding of the characters and actions, except now more people are involved.

One of those watching suddenly speaks out, suggesting to one of the actors on stage that a certain gesture might achieve a particularly timely effect. The actor who's playing the part listens to this and gives it a try. Then the other watching actor says, "That's a good idea, but I think if you did this it would work even better."

And again the attempt is made. At this point one of the actors now playing in the scene says, "I notice when you come at me like that I feel an emotion that makes it difficult for me to say this next line. But if you were to kind of circle around me, it would make it make more sense to me." By this time, everyone present in the room has entered the collaborative process of directing the play.

Using this method I've been able to have as many as forty teenagers with no previous acting experience working on a Shakespeare play, with virtually every one of them putting in a suggestion here and there and getting the full attention and respect of everyone else. The process is orderly, efficient, creative, exciting and empowering. It's also highly chaordic.

With so many creative minds at work on a project the quality of what can be produced is amazing. Bear in mind that I came into the project as the director with standards I had set for the production. It had to be at least as good as what I had in mind, and often this led me to seek specific line readings, specific actions, and specific tonalities in playing a scene.

But I was unwilling to let my creative imagination set the top limits of what could be done. As long as the actors did something at least as good as what I wanted, I was satisfied. Of course, if it was much better, as it often was, I was elated. For there's no way that a group of creative people all working together will not produce something a great deal better than any one of them could have imagined alone.

THE BEST RESULTS COME FROM THE WORK OF MANY MINDS

If you approach your employees this way, they may achieve only as much as you thought they would. On the other hand, they may achieve a great deal more. Whichever way it goes, you'll get the credit for leadership, and your people will appreciate you enormously because you've stimulated their thinking, which helps them feel empowered. In the end, if you handle the process effectively, you'll find that there's no way a group of creative people all working together will not produce something a great deal better than any one of them could have imagined alone.

In this situation the good leader is totally in control while at the same time fading into the background. It's an extremely satisfying way to work with people in any situation. It's an example of how you can increase your power by giving it away. As we've trained people in hundreds of seminars we've found this approach has produced better results than we could have gotten by any other means. And as we've trained others to work in this same way, they've gotten results just as good as those we have produced. Thus this method of stimulating people to think and create together is not only effective, but can easily be transferred to others.

And in every group we've worked with, the result has been the emergence of a dynamic creativity unlike what the people involved had experienced in other situations.

We think this is one of the main reasons why the Learning Leaders at Kodak produced such exceptional results. Not only did we work with them in the general way we've just described, but they also worked with their classes in the same way. People come out of such classes feeling that their thinking has been respected and appreciated, and that they can therefore do it better.

But the point is never merely to help people gain self-esteem or respect their own thinking. It's to prompt them to play a role in the company — a role only they can play. They have to find out what this role is and leave the stamp of their personality upon it. By helping them to create the role out of their own thinking we lead them gradually towards their own inner wisdom and their ability to use that wisdom to shape uniquely the role they will play in the workplace.

WHY THIS WORKS WITH A LEARNING ORGANIZATION

In the evolution of a Learning Organization, when the organization has been developing along the lines of the previous nine Steps, the personnel will all have a good understanding of how they can best work together. Teamwork, creativity and problem solving will be at a high level, and thinking will occur everywhere as part of the daily process of getting the job done. Employees will enjoy their jobs and each other's company. They will be clear about the vision of the company and will understand its interacting systems.

Over time this knowledge will become so deeply instilled that they will move through their roles with the same assurance and flair that professional actors acquire during the rehearsal period. They will understand what is expected of them, and why, and how it contributes to the effectiveness of the entire enterprise. They will also understand how their roles interrelate with those of other personnel.

As the flow of work becomes second nature to them, they'll go about their jobs with an easy assurance that comes not from simply repeating the same thing over and over, but from a grounded and broad understanding of why continuous improvement is necessary and what brings it about.

THE NEED FOR IMPROVISATION

In this Step we've moved to the realm of drama. We have shown how it can provide a metaphor and a model for managers who wish to structure their organizations as more than merely a mechanism for getting things done. With this approach, business can become an opportunity to express the kinds of creative impulses which we all would like to fulfill.

However, as we said earlier, the real life, real time organizational drama of today no longer allows the luxury of working from an unchanging script. The old way of managing the corporate drama, as if one had puppets on strings and needed only to guide them through predetermined paces, has proven inadequate to a production in which the characters, moving too quickly even for instant replay, are forever changing, the settings are constantly redesigned, and the plot is frequently transformed. The drama today is a drama that necessitates improvisation.

But this too is a skill that can be learned, an art that can be practiced. A number of years ago one of us hired a local comedy theater company to perform at a conference. Attending one of their rehearsals was an eye-opening revelation: paradoxical as it at first may seem, there is significant planning and structure embedded inside what the audience sees as improvisational theater. It takes a tremendous amount of practice to sense the cues and clues to how a fellow actor is going to respond. It is a form of chaordic structure, demanding and inspiring a great deal of trust among the players.

What is required in today's marketplace, in factories, team-building, meetings, and all other aspects of organizational activity, is a similar improvisational capacity.

At one level, particularly in organizations that manufacture a product, this improvisational capacity is reflected in the hardware. Many manufacturing corporations have already made the transition to flexible manufacturing capabilities, and some organizations are in the process of figuring out how to make this happen. The charter of the new manufacturing arena is one of structured improvisation, the ability to produce multiple versions of a product within the same factory or product line.

Some businesses have been doing this for years. The auto industry, for example, is able to produce variations on the same car during normal production. Coming off the end of the production line might be a DX, then an LS, then a GT, and so on. Other products, from cakes to pre-fabricated houses can be customized in the course of production. And companies like computer and electronics manufacturers have learned to adapt their production capabilities to ever shorter product cycles.

CULTIVATING THE CAPACITY FOR IMPROVISATION

Of course flexibility and the capacity for improvisation begin not in the hardware but in the human beings within the organization. These result from their organizational environment, their training and their minds. The cultivation of these capacities is one of the hallmarks of a Learning Organization.

The Kinesthetic Modeling techniques introduced in Step Eight, which in turn incorporate so many other practices and perceptions, are particularly useful for exploring the organizational drama. After experiencing exercises like Kinesthetic Modeling and the counting skit a few times, the people involved will so internalize this type of improvisation that when change is needed in the workplace, they will take the necessary steps almost instinctively.

Tony Steblay, of Minneapolis, conducts a workshop for organizations that provides "training for the corporate stage." Called Interplay, it teaches basic acting techniques to managers to help them express ideas, plans, and beliefs to their staffs. Using numerous improvisational techniques, participants learn to trust their natural rhythms, and learn how to make instantaneous decisions about what to do next. They also learn how to increase their ability to anticipate, a significant skill in improvisation that is crucial in today's society.

Through practicing these skills, workshop participants begin to realize the power they have to adjust to unpredictable events. As the day's sessions progress, people's levels of confidence increase as they are asked to do activities that are progressively more challenging.

THE ARTISTIC DIMENSION

The analogy of a jazz ensemble illuminates the improvisational requirements of today's organizations. All the players have their individual job descriptions (roles and responsibilities), and share a set of standards and rules, without which there would be uncontrollable chaos. But even within the structure each player, and the group as a whole, has a great deal of flexibility. They become, in organizational parlance, a self-managed work team. When all the players are playing by the "rules" of the music, and they build a relationship of mutual trust and purpose, the outcome is magical.

Think about the process like playing in a sandbox. The leadership of the organization has provided the framework or boundaries in which people can operate. Once inside the sandbox people can do pretty much what they want. There might be some subtle conditions for playing inside the sand box, but overall, as long as everyone stays within the established ground rules of the organization, they have the freedom to create and build in a manner that fit their functions and job expectations.

In *The Power Point*, Michael E. Gerber lists five essential skills that modern business must inculcate into all of its people.[1] These are the skills that underlie artistic mastery, and also are exemplified by management that knows how to draw on the very best that people have to offer, and give back to the world a monument to the human spirit.

These skills are: concentration, discrimination, organization, innovation and communication.

The artist must be able to concentrate on the creation of a work of art, must discriminate from all those ideas and materials that may be useful the ones that will contribute the most, must then organize those materials into some meaningful form, and must at this point introduce something innovative into the mix that makes the work of art unique and valuable in its meaning. The meaning must then be expressed so that the value is communicated to others. So whether you're composing a symphony, painting a picture, writing a poem, creating a dance — or managing a group of people, or running a Fortune 100 company — you must do all five of these things.

In one of our trainings we listened to composer-conductor Leonard Bernstein's recorded analysis of Beethoven's *Fifth Symphony*. When we had finished, we listed about eighteen different qualities of expression and communication the symphony contained. We then posed the question: which of these qualities had no relationship to the problems of management? After some discussion it became clear that the list we had made was as effective a guide to managing a team as it was to writing a symphony.

The five skills Gerber has named apply equally to the artist and the manager, and you'll need them if you're creating a Learning Organization. These days, if you have a job, you're doing one of two things, according to Gerber. You're either playing the game called *business*, or you're playing the game called *saying good-bye*.

CHOOSE TO REMAIN CREATIVE

As we grow increasingly conscious of our own aging, we lose touch with what our work is all about and begin to say good-bye; but when we turn inward to the youngest part of us, to the child, we can truly play the game of business. The game must be played creatively by people who care about each other and enjoy playing together. It must be spontaneous and fun. And the game must be played out in a great process which brings it to life for everyone.

The child in us will be the surest guide in this process. Spend some time with a child and note how much imagination goes into three basic mental processes: creating stories, exploring how things work, and developing symbolism. Sometimes these three can be combined into a single narrative, and most of the best children's stories do just that.

The guiding drama of the Learning Organization may do the same: may combine a notion of how the organization gets its work done with the central guiding symbols that inform that work, all woven into the story that expresses the corporate mission. This is an artistic process. No matter how sophisticated and complex the activities of an organization may be, it is not until all the participants are engaged in this underlying drama that the show will truly be on the road to success.

BRINGING THE SHOW UP TO DATE

Today's world, and the foreseeable future, promise no shortage of challenging problems. The average CEO must juggle an ever-changing array of situations requiring that people be moved around frequently, old divisions closed down and new ones created, middle managers eliminated and self-managed teams established — in short, that all players think on their feet all the time. Like the veteran actor in the classic actor's nightmare, she may occasionally feel as if she were standing naked in front of a large audience performing a play for which she has not yet been given the script.

Any CEOs or managers who feel underused, under challenged, and unfulfilled, need to address the dramatic new realities of the twenty-first century. To put it another way, consider the possibility that you are cast in a show which closed long ago, and that, even though you rehearsed carefully for your role in it, all those rehearsals are of no use to you now. You are going to have to prepare for the new drama, where the style of acting is different, and the lines are improvised.

SEIZE THE DRAMATIC MOMENT

Indeed we live in dramatic times, at a dramatic moment in history for our own country and the world at large. Economically, politically and socially this is an unusual window of opportunity — as are all periods of crisis, change, and renewal. Those who clearly recognize and seize this opportunity, and can inspire those around them with a sense of the excitement in their endeavor, are the true leaders of today and tomorrow.

Management expert Barry Sheehy believes the awareness that we are at a turning point in history is actually a powerful key to organizational leadership, because it provides a way of exciting people about their jobs and the opportunities a demand for change makes possible. "When you look at a corporation," he recently told us,

> whether it be large or small, there is an enormous inherent drama associated with the enterprise. Sometimes we tend to see corporations as soulless machines when they're anything but that, at least while they're growing and living. When I'm dealing with executives, particularly at a time when they're under duress or have difficult decisions, I try as much as possible to get them to view the act they're involved in as a drama, as opposed to a great drudgery, an exciting drama, in which in

large measure they are the players . . . .

If you can infuse people with the sense of the drama of the exercise they're involved in, it makes decisions easier and the load lighter. And frankly I think it's true: you can either see it as drudgery or drama. When I come in and see an organization grappling with the issues, wrestling with the global marketplace, trying to improve the quality of products and services, meet the needs of shareholders and employees, trying to add value to the community, there is enormous drama in that![2]

REHEARSING FOR THE NEW CHALLENGES

The rise of the Learning Organization, which is itself a great drama, is occurring at a dramatic moment. It will require boldness, courage, imagination. Managers, directors, and leaders who can tap into this sense of the drama and opportunity of their time can use it as a powerful source of energy, inspiration and purpose for the whole organization.

This means you have to be willing to practice whatever you find is of value. You must rehearse it until you bring it alive, until it becomes so much a part of you that you cannot imagine not knowing it. Thus you must become part of a new drama in which all the roles are played to the fullest, everyone knows and agrees to the ongoing movement of the action and the play is clearly a smash hit.

In this new drama you're creating, you must play to the world stage. You must learn to take our entire civilization into account as you consider the implications of everything you do. Because of the enormous resources you can create for yourselves by using the full intelligence of all members of the organizational team, beautifully coordinated in systems that work together to meet everyone's needs, you now have the opportunity to make organizational activity not only many times more effective than ever before, but also vastly more rewarding from a non-material point of view.

A NEW KIND OF FULFILLMENT

The organization of the future, if you have done your job well, will attract people to it as the most satisfying workplace imaginable. With this great goal in view, you can envision an economy and a society where the work to which people devote their lives will be the best kind of fulfillment they could hope to find.

In the world that we are in the process of creating, rising profits will reflect individuals' growing commitment and organizations' corresponding enlightenment. Such organizations, dedicated to the highest quality of service and production, will be respected by all, and a source of pride for those who participate in them. In that world the tensions between management and labor and between the public and private sectors will give way to a sense of harmony and community that satisfies the deepest needs of the whole commonwealth, and indeed for the first time fully defines the true meaning of that term.

NOTES

INTRODUCTION

1 Jim Collins, "What Comes Next?" *Inc. Magazine*, Oct. 1997, pp. 41-48.

2 Mary Jane Gill and David Meier, "Accelerated Learning Takes Off," *Training and Development Journal*, January, 1989, pp. 63-65.

3 Peter Senge, *The Fifth Discipline* (New York: Doubleday, 1990).

4 John Naisbitt, *Megatrends* (New York: Warner Books, 1982).

5 Peter Kline's, *The Everyday Genius: Restoring Your Children's Natural Joy of Learning — And Yours Too* (Arlington, VA: Great Ocean Publishers, 1988) is a book about the theory and practice of Integrative Learning written for the layman, which includes many illustrative activities that work in family or school settings. *School Success: The Inside Story* by Peter Kline and Laurence Martel (Arlington, VA: Great Ocean Publishers, 1992) presents many of these ideas in a self-teaching, workbook format.

6 Chuck Laughlin and Karen Sage, with Marc Bockmon *Samurai Selling: The Ancient Art of Modern Service* (New York: St. Martin's, 1993).

7 Alfie Kohn, *No Contest: The Case Against Competition* (Boston: Houghton Mifflin, 1986).

HOW DO ORGANIZATIONS LEARN?

1 Hans Selye, *The Stress of Life* (New York: McGraw Hill, 1978).

2 Marion Diamond, *Enriching Heredity* (New York: Free Press, 1988).

3 Howard Gardner, *Frames of Mind: The Theory of Multiple Intelligences* (New York: Basic Books, 1993). Developed by neurologist Howard Gardner, these are the logical/mathematical, the linguistic, the spatial/visual, the bodily/kinesthetic, the musical, the interpersonal and the intrapersonal. Recently he has added two more, but these seven have proved extremely useful in designing education curricula strong enough to wipe out the bell curve of student response, so that everyone in a class can learn the material with complete success..

4 Jack Stack's book, *The Great Game of Business* (New York: Doubleday/Currency, 1994), which remains the most essential text available on the general topic of open book management.

5 Lisa Marshall and Lucy Freeman, *Smart Work: The Syntax Guide for Mutual Understanding in the Workplace* (Dubuque, IA: Kendall Hunt, 1995).

6 Thomas Stewart, *Intellectual Capital: The New Wealth of Organizatioins* (New York: Doubleday, 1997).

STEP ONE: ASSESS YOUR LEARNING CULTURE

[1] See the study by Sorenson and Weber that was cited in *Training & Development Journal,* April 1994, p. 71. The study is distributed by the Center for Applied Research at Human Synergistics, 216 Campus Dr., Suite 102, Arlington Heights, IL 60004

[2] Jack Stack, *The Great Game of Business* (New York: Doubleday/Currency, 1994).

[3] Robert N. Kharasch, *The Institutional Imperative* (New York: Charterhouse Books, 1973).

[4] Philip B. Crosby, *Quality is Free* (New York: McGraw Hill, 1979), p. 52.

[5] *Quality is Free*, p. 50.

[6] Nancy M. Dixon, "Organizational Learning: A Review of the Literature with Implications for HRD Professionals," *Human Resource Development Quarterly*, Vol. 3, No.1, Spring 1992, pp. 31-32.

[7] Therese Welter, "A Winning Team Begins with You," *Industry Week*, May 6, 1991, pp. 35-38.

[8] James Kouzes, *Credibility: How Leaders Gain and Lose It* (San Francisco: Jossey-Bass, 1995).

[9] We also developed a *Facilitator's Guide* for use with the Assessment. Information about them may be obtained from Great Ocean Publishers.

[10] The stand-alone *Learning Organization Assessment* which we have created incorporates the *Matrix* into the questionnaire and simplifies the scoring process. There are various other assessment tools and group response technologies available. A number of consultants also provide assessment technology for larger organizations.

STEP TWO: PROMOTE THE POSITIVE

[1] John Hillkirk and Gary Jacobson, *Grits, Guts, and Genius* (Boston: Houghton Mifflin, 1990), pp. 101-103

[2] In his book *Care for the Soul* (New York: Harper Collins, 1992), psychotherapist Thomas Moore argues eloquently that we must treat ourselves with enough respect so we attend to our inner promptings in order to learn what our experience is really teaching us. Daily diligence in observing the most creative impulses in ourselves can keep us from losing sight of what's important as we race along the fast track to success.

[3] Patricia M. Carrigan, "Up From the Ashes," *O.D. Practitioner*, Vol. 18, No. 1, March, 1986, pp. 2-3.

STEP THREE: MAKE THE WORKPLACE SAFE FOR THINKING

[1] Linda Honold, "Manager As Coach" (Presentation), Sheboygan, WI: Empowerment Systems, Oct. 1991.

[2] Tracy Kidder, *The Soul of a New Machine* (Boston: Little Brown, 1981).

[3] Peter Senge, *The Fifth Discipline* (New York: Doubleday/Currency, 1990), p. 247.

STEP FOUR: REWARD RISK-TAKING

[1] Peter Vail, *Learning As A Way of Being,* (San Francisco: Jossey-Bass, 1996

[2] Quoted in *Scientific American*, November, 1992, p. 138.

[3] Robert Kanigel, *Apprentice to Genius: The Making of A Scientific Dynasty* (New York: Macmillan, 1986; Baltimore: The Johns Hopkins University Press, 1993), p. 234.

[4] *Apprentice to Genius*, p. 234.

[5] *Apprentice to Genius*, p. 235.

[6] *Apprentice to Genius*, p. 60.

[7] The theme of trusting in your own capacity and potential is explored at greater length in *The Everyday Genius* by Peter Kline, which expounds a view of expanded human potential.

[8] David C. McClelland and David G. Winter, *Motivating Economic Achievement* (New York: Free Press, 1969).

STEP FIVE: HELP PEOPLE BECOME RESOURCES FOR EACH OTHER

[1] Fred Rogers quoted in the *South Bend Tribune*, Jan. 23, 1993.

[2] Tom Peters, syndicated column "On Excellence," *Minneapolis Star Tribune*, Marketplace, October 27, 1992, p. 2.

[3] Tom Peters, *Liberation Management*, (New York: Knopf, 1992), p. 601.

[4] M. Mitchell Waldrop, *Complexity*, (New York: Simon and Schuster, 1992), p. 312.

[5] Multiple Intelligences Checklist by Bernard Saunders and Kaia Svien, adapted from the works of Howard Gardner (*Frames of Mind: The Theory of Multiple Intelligences*, New York: Basic Books, 1993) and Thomas Armstrong (*In Their Own Way*, Los Angeles: Tarcher, 1987).

STEP SIX: PUT LEARNING POWER TO WORK

[1] Paul Zane Pilzer, *Unlimited Wealth*, (New York: Crown, 1991).

[2] See, for example, John Horgan, "Eugenics Revisited," *Scientific American*, June, 1993.

[3] Calhoun W. Wick and Lu Stanton Leon, *The Learning Edge*, (New York: McGraw-Hill, 1992), pp. 158-159.

[4] Quoted in *The New York Times*, February 8, 1989, by Edward B. Fiske.

[5] "How Much Good Will Training Do?" *Business Week*, February 22, 1993, pp. 76-77.

[6] *The Learning Edge*, pp. 29-31.

[7] David Kearns interviewed in *Training and Development Journal*, May, 1990, p. 42.

[8] Peter Kline, *The Everyday Genius: Restoring Your Children's Natural Joy of Learning — And Yours Too* gives a complete picture of the theory and practice of Integrative Learning.

[9] Avice Saint, *Continuous Learning Within Japanese Organizations*, Continuous Learning Center, Far West Laboratory, San Francisco, CA, 1982, p. 174.

[10] Quoted by Janet Stites in "Running the Numbers: The Ruminations of John Allen Paulos," *Omni Magazine*, April, 1993, pp. 35-36.

[11] For additional information on training in Integrative Learning, contact the publisher, or call 800-634-0055 (Internet: integraLRN@aol.com).

[12] Mary Jane Gill and David Meier, "Accelerated Learning Takes Off," *Training and Development Journal*, January, 1989, pp. 63-65.

STEP SEVEN: MAP OUT THE VISION

[1] Allan Cox, "Scrap Consensus, Try Diversity," *The New York Times*, April 7, 1991, Section 3, p. 11.

[2] Jerry Harvey, *The Abilene Paradox* (Lexington, MA: Lexington Books, 1988).

[3] George T. L. Land, *Grow or Die*, (New York: Dell, 1973) p. 135.

[4] Leslie Hart, *Human Brain and Human Learning* (New York: Longman, 1983).

[5] Ralph N. Haber, "How We Remember What We See," *Scientific American*, May 1970, p. 105.

[6] Peter Russell, *The Brain Book* (New York: E.P. Dutton, 1979). He cites Alan Baddeley, *The Psychology of Memory* (New York: Harper and Row, 1976, p. 225); and Gordon Bower, "Mental Imagery and Associative Learning" in *Cognition, Learning and Memory*, ed. L.W. Gregg (New York: John Wiley, 1972), p. 76.

[7] Information provided by Harry Hoff, Principal, Susan Lindgren School, St. Louis Park, MN.

STEP EIGHT: BRING THE VISION TO LIFE

[1] Ken and Rita Dunn can be contacted at The Learning Styles Network. St. John's University. Grand Central Parkway. Jamaica, New York, 11439

[2] James Gleick, *Genius: The Life and Science of Richard Feynman* (New York, Pantheon, 1992), p. 244.

STEP NINE: CONNECT THE SYSTEMS

[1] Karen Bemowski, "Quality, American Style," *Quality Progress*, February 1993, pp. 65-68.

STEP TEN: GET THE SHOW ON THE ROAD

[1] Michael E. Gerber, *The Power Point* (New York: Harper Business, 1991), pp. 17-23.

[2] Barry Sheehy, personal communication.

About the Authors

Peter Kline's earlier, widely praised *The Everyday Genius* and *School Success* have been introducing the dynamics of learning to an ever-growing audience. An exponent of innovative, highly successful educational and organizational practices, Kline has pioneered methods that accelerate learning and bring involvement and excitement to the classroom and the workplace. A consultant to government agencies, corporations and school systems worldwide, his books have been translated into six languages. He has appeared on numerous TV and radio programs, and has been the subject of a variety of profiles and studies. His latest book, *The Butterfly Dreams,* is a novel written with Syril Kline. He resides with his family in South Bend, Indiana.

Bernard Saunders is a learning consultant specializing in the application of advanced learning concepts and the creation of learning organizations. During the past 27 years he has been involved in organizational training and development, working with Fortune 500 companies in the areas of organizational change, systems thinking, total quality, self-managed work teams, and communication. He resides with his family in Minneapolis, Minnesota.